Surrey
Within Living Memory

Compiled by the Surrey
Federation of Women's Institutes from notes
sent by Institutes in the County

Published jointly by
Countryside Books, Newbury
and the SFWI, Guildford.

COUNTRYSIDE BOOKS
3, Catherine Road
Newbury, Berkshire

ISBN 1 85306 206 5

Designed by Mon Mohan
Produced through MRM Associates Ltd, Reading.
Phototypeset by The Midlands Book Typesetting Company, Loughborough.
Printed in England by J.W. Arrowsmith Ltd, Bristol

Contents

Acknowledgements

Surrey Federation of Women's Institutes would like to thank all W.I. members who supplied material for this project through their local Institutes. A list of contributing W.I.s appears below.

Unfortunately we were not able to include extracts from every submission; to do so would have meant some duplication of content, and of course we had to take into account the total amount of space available in the book.

But all the contributions, without exception, were of value in deciding the shape and content of the book. We are grateful for them all.

Finally, we would like to thank the following in particular: Janet Blight and Pat Hunt, who drew the delightful sketches; Sally Dampney who supplied the County map; and the Surrey Local Studies Library in Guildford for the cover picture of Gomshall Mill.

Muriel Gibson
Co-ordinator

List of Contributing WIs

ABINGER COMMON and WOTTON
ABINGER HAMMER
ALFOLD Evening
ASH Afternoon
BADSHOT LEA
BAGSHOT
BANSTEAD
BANSTEAD Evening
BETCHWORTH
BISHOPSGATE
BISLEY
BLETCHINGLEY
BLINDLEY HEATH
THE BOOKHAMS Afternoon
THE BOOKHAMS Evening
THE BOURNE
BOX HILL
BRAMLEY
BROCKHAM GREEN
BURGH HEATH
BURPHAM
BUSBRIDGE Evening
CANADA HALL

CAPEL
CAMBERLEY
CHARLWOOD
CHIDDINGFOLD
CHIPSTEAD Evening
CHOBHAM Evening
CHURT
CLAPHAM
COBHAM Evening
COBHAM Village
COPTHORNE
COPTHORNE Evening
CRANLEIGH Morning
CRANLEIGH Afternoon
CRANLEIGH Evening
DORMANS Evening
DRIFT BRIDGE
THE DOWNS
EAST HORSLEY
EFFINGHAM Evening
EGHAM Morning
ELSTEAD Afternoon
ELSTEAD Evening

EPSOM
EWELL VILLAGE
EWHURST
EWHURST Evening
FAIRLANDS
FETCHAM VILLAGE
FORESTDALE
FOREST GREEN
FRIMLEY and FRIMLEY GREEN
GODSTONE
GOLDSWORTH PARK
GRAFHAM and SMITHBROOK
GRAYSHOTT
GRAYSWOOD Evening
HALE
HAMSEY GREEN
HASCOMBE
HEADLEY
HEATHERSIDE
HERSHAM Afternoon
HERSHAM Evening
HOOK HEATH Morning
HORLEY
HOLMWOOD
HOLMBURY ST. MARY
JACOBS WELL Evening
KENLEY
KENLEY VALLEY
KINGSWOOD
KINGSWOOD VILLAGE
KINGSWOOD WARREN
LEATHERHEAD
LIGHTWATER
LIMPSFIELD VILLAGE
LINGFIELD
LINGFIELD Evening
LITTLE BOOKHAM
LYNE
MAYFORD
MAYFORD Evening
MEADVALE
MERROW Afternoon
MERROW Evening
MERSTHAM
MILFORD
MILLBRIDGE
MOLE VALLEY
MORDEN
MYTCHETT
NEWDIGATE
NEW HAW and WOODHAM
NEW MALDEN
NORTH HOLMWOOD
NUTFIELD

OCKHAM
OCKLEY
OLD COULSDON
OLD WOKING Evening
OUTWOOD
OXSHOTT
OXSHOTT Evening
OXSHOTT VILLAGE
OXTED Morning
PEBBLECOMBE
PIRBRIGHT
POLLARDS OAK
PURLEY
PYRFORD
RANMORE
RYDES HILL Evening
ST. CATHERINE'S
SALFORDS
SANDERSTEAD
SANDERSTEAD VILLAGE
SEND
SHALFORD
SHERE and GOMSHALL
SHOTTERMILL
SIDLOW BRIDGE
SOUTH PARK
STAFFHURST WOOD
STOKE d'ABERNON
SURBITON
TADWORTH
TANDRIDGE and CROWHURST
TILFORD
TRUMPS GREEN
WALTON-ON-THE-HILL
WARLINGHAM
WARLINGHAM Evening
WEST BYFLEET
WEST CLANDON
WESTCOTT
WEST END ESHER
WEST END WOKING Evening
WESTFIELD and KINGFIELD
WEST HORSLEY Evening
WEYBRIDGE
WOLDINGHAM
WONERSH
WOODCOTE
WOODHATCH
WOODMANSTERNE Evening
WOOD STREET VILLAGE
WORCESTER PARK
WORPLESDON
WRAY COMMON
WRECCLESHAM

Foreword

In all walks of life – urban and rural – the pace of change in daily living in the 20th century has been breathtaking.

Surrey, though not a large county, is one of great contrast, stretching as it does from London and its encroaching suburbs to the gently sweeping hills of the North Downs – where idyllic villages are still to be found down leafy lanes under a canopy of green. The richness of Surrey's woodland is also strongly contrasted with the starker but equally beautiful extensive heath and commonland, ablaze with gold when the gorse is in bloom.

From this landscape of great variety has sprung a flood of reminiscences of almost vanished lifestyles. Surrey WI members have embraced the idea of this book with overwhelming enthusiasm, providing a goldmine of first-hand information for the social historian in years to come, and for our own archives.

Clearly the changes have not come about overnight, but the pace has been gently relentless and at times unnerving and disconcerting. The picture is painted on the canvas not only with the broad brush strokes of major events, but with the carefully coloured vignettes of everyday life.

Memory touches on aspects of life both serious and comic, humdrum or alarming, showing what ordinary people did, observed and thought about. Imagination sets the scene, and if the reminiscences coincide with the lifetime of the reader, then memory joins imagination as a compelling recaller of immediate times past. This oral tradition is precious and worthy of being preserved.

I think Jane Austen should have the last word. Fanny in *Mansfield Park* puts it so well when she talks about memory to Mary Crawford:

> 'How wonderful, how very wonderful the operations of time and the changes of the human mind . . . If any one faculty of our nature may be called more wonderful than the rest . . . I do think it is memory.'

Muriel Gibson
Co-ordinator
Surrey Federation Vice-Chairman

TOWN & COUNTRY LIFE

LIFE IN THE VILLAGES AND TOWNS

So much of Surrey has changed almost out of recognition since the Second World War, as has the way of life. Here is just a taste of Surrey towns and villages as they were, within living memory.

MITCHAM

'Some of my childhood years were spent in Mitcham, which was then a part of Surrey. Since Victorian times Mitcham had been famous for its lavender and I can just remember the last of the lavender fields. The purple fields, once renowned for their fragrance, had to give way to encroaching suburbia in the 1920s, though the name of Mitcham Lavender as a perfume persisted for a long time after that.

Another crop grown in the area was peppermint and on the rising ground between Mitcham and Sutton the strong smell of peppermint would annually waft on the summer air. The production of Mitcham Mints also became quite famous. The peppermint fields were later to become home to the very large St Helier housing estate and Mitcham and Sutton now form part of Greater London.'

'My family moved from Streatham to a new estate on the outskirts of Mitcham in 1922, when I was five years old. At that time, the road had not been made up and although the house was wired for electricity, it was not laid on in the road until later and we used oil lamps at first. The gas was laid on at the start.

It was a friendly community – we soon knew most of the people in our road and many in the surrounding roads. Just round the corner was a little church or chapel which had, I believe, been converted from some stables, where I attended Sunday school. On the social side, there was a converted barn where, once a month, a whist drive was held, followed by refreshments and a dance. A local family with a very large garden containing tennis courts, started a tennis club which my parents joined – they had social evenings as well which sometimes I was allowed to attend. I remember learning the Charleston at one of them!

A Mr Kiddell with a horse-drawn van delivered groceries and

gossip! Boys on bicycles delivered meat and fresh cream pastries, the latter for my mother's bridge afternoons.'

KINGSTON

'I was born in Kingston upon Thames. As a child I well remember the town for its two very distinctive smells. One was from the tannery which lay close to the river, and the other from Hodgson's brewery. Adjacent to the brewery was a ford known as the Watersplash. The horses would come out of the brewery pulling their drays which were loaded with barrels of beer and charge through the ford to get to the main road.

As Kingston was the County Town of Surrey, the Assizes were held at the County Hall. First the Judge would go to a service at the parish church, and then proceed with all the court dignitaries on foot to the courts, preceded by two heralds on horseback blowing their trumpets to warn people they were coming.'

GATWICK

'In the 1920s we lived in the country near Lowfield Heath – then in Surrey. It boasted little except a tiny church and a windmill in the middle of a field by the old A23. Gatwick, nearby, was a racecourse with its own station on the main London-Brighton line; open only on race days. Also next to it was an aero club which consisted of a small hut in a field and a windsock. Little bi-planes buzzed around, at weekends mainly, "disturbing the peace of the countryside" as my father complained!

In the middle of the 1930s a small round air terminal was built on the site, and the racecourse became a runway. A posh new station "Gatwick Airport" was built and a London to Paris service started. The schedule was Victoria to Le Bourget in an hour. We got an excellent train service out of it!

All is now gone, except you can see the little round terminal and Lowfield Heath church among the trappings of the vast airport. The windmill was rescued and has been re-erected and lovingly restored at Charlwood Zoo.'

WIMBLEDON

'I was born in Wimbledon, near Wimbledon Common in 1909. We often went for picnics towards the windmill. My mother took a teapot and tea and asked the lady who lived in the windmill for a jug of hot water, for which she paid two pence.'

11

'I was born and spent the first 36 years of my life in Melrose Avenue, Wimbledon Park, which – although the address was Wimbledon Park, London SW19 was on the Surrey side of the boundary, only three or four minutes walk from our house. We saw – and heard when the wind was in the right direction – the building of the All-England tennis courts and stadium, only about a mile as the crow flies, and as small children on walks with our parents saw it gradually rising. I didn't manage to see a match until in my twenties, but I remember how excited our young neighbour was to be able to get in during the first tournament held there. I also remember as young teenagers going home to lunch from school, how distinguished the ladies and gentlemen attending the match appeared to us.

I often cycled to Banstead to visit a family who lived in a cottage on a farm. Opposite the cottage was a lovely golden cornfield, above which could be seen the two towers of the Crystal Palace (very much closer than from Wimbledon). On our way we used to pass through Morden, then a small village, and saw the Underground station being built. Further on we had to cross the Sutton by-pass, then in the making, and a sea of mud. At that time there was a pathway across it for cyclists and pedestrians which took us into Sutton – just a country town then (but the hill was just as steep!).'

REIGATE AND REDHILL

'Some of my earliest memories are of being taken by my grandmother to the town of Redhill on a Saturday. The two main streets, which formed a crossroads in the middle of the town, were lined with busy little family-run shops where you could buy everything you needed, but my biggest treat was to visit the stalls in the Marketfield. I loved to see all their flickering paraffin lamps which they lit up at dusk, and an extra treat would be to have a "poke" of sweets from one of the stalls. The happy scenes from my childhood are now long gone; the crossroads disappeared many years ago, and the site of the old market is now a car park.'

'On Saturday mornings in the early 1920s my best friend and I used to walk to Reigate town via Bell Street where there was a blacksmith forge. I can still smell the burning hooves of the horses as they were being shod. We always arrived home late after spending time at the forge when we should have been shopping!'

The last flight from Croydon Airport in 1959 marked the end of an era. Many pioneering aviators, including Amy Johnson, flew from here.

CROYDON

'I was born in 1921 in Croydon, then a market town with some lovely old buildings, of which very few are still standing today.

One of my greatest memories was being taken to Surrey Street market, started in the 1800s. It was mostly vegetable and fruit stalls. Everything looked so beautiful in the evening, the naptha flares wavering in the breeze cast a warm glow on a winter's evening. A charcoal stove glowed red where one could buy a baked potato or chestnuts. There was also a sarsaparilla tank for when we were thirsty, proclaimed to be a health giving drink. Sometimes the street entertainers came with flute and bones and barrel organ complete with monkey. The boiled sweet stall emitted a delightful smell and children watched fascinated as the owner rolled out toffee and twisted barley sugar in long spirals. Small shops on the pavement sold pease pudding and faggots, saveloys and mushy peas. There was also a bacon and cheese shop and a pork-only butcher's. One could purchase one penny's worth of "pot herbs", onion, carrot, turnip and parsnip, which was the basis of a stew with some steak and kidney which cost sixpence from the meat stall. The market still trades today, but of course very differently. There was also a cattle market at South Croydon to which I was taken and enjoyed immensely; that closed down in 1935.

We used to stroll to the then famous Croydon Airport on Sundays fascinated by the different planes. It was the scene of many remarkable firsts in aviation, but finally closed in 1959. I saw the famous Amy Johnson fly from there.'

WOLDINGHAM

'Woldingham in the 1920s was a residential village, many men commuting to London. There was only one shop by the village green selling a variety of foodstuffs, hardware, boots, brooms and wellies. A baker brought fresh bread in a horse-drawn van from Tatsfield and fish and meat were delivered from Caterham, Warlingham and Whyteleafe. When it snowed heavily and roads were blocked by drifts, goods got as far as Woldingham station where residents had to collect by toboggan. Some houses had gardeners' cottages and the men turned out to dig pathways through the snow drifts. There was no salting of roads and only light snow could be moved by snow plough. No buses came to Woldingham then.'

MERSTHAM

'In 1938 Merstham was quite a village, with its row of useful shops along the High Street – a post office, sweet shop, butcher's, a large shop called Uridge's selling groceries and vegetables and fresh fish, and also a small shop run by Gordon Ball and his wife, which stocked all manner of things such as groceries, fruit and vegetables, which they would deliver to your house. There was also a Baptist chapel, a delightful cafe called the Golden Wheel, the Feathers pub, the Old Barn selling antiques, a dressmaker, a Co-op, Mr Smith the cobbler and a pub called the Cottage of Content.

Quality Street, which used to be the main road, down which the mail coach from London used to drive before stopping at The Feathers, had big iron gates at the far end, leading to Merstham House. These gates were removed during the Second World War.'

'At the end of the war London County Council decided to build some new estates on the outskirts of London, to house the thousands of people who had been bombed out during the air raids, and Merstham was one of the sites chosen. In the early 1950s they built 1,500 dwellings, to house 6,000 people, thereby doubling the population at a stroke.

The merging of the two communities was not easy and there

Life in Surrey's towns in the early years of the 20th century was conducted at a more leisurely pace, as here at Carshalton in 1913.

were faults on both sides. Many Merstham residents had lived in the village for several generations and resented the arrival of so many strangers. Priority in allocating houses to the Londoners was given to young couples with children; the husbands often kept their jobs in London, so that they had to catch a very early train and did not return home until late, leaving their wives and children in an alien environment without the support of families and friends, on whom they had relied in London. Sadly a "them" and "us" situation arose.

Gradually relations improved, as old and new Merstham residents got to know each other and began doing things together. Some people still call the area the New Estate, but soon there will be few people left who will be able to explain the significance of the name.'

CLAPHAM PARK

'Clapham Park, in the County of Surrey'. Thus ran the wording on the deeds of my father's house in Clapham, which he bought in 1920 after his return from service in the First World War. The house had been built in 1890 on what our milkman remembered as being orchards from which he had "scrumped" apples as a boy. In their place was an estate of late Victorian houses.

By the time I was born in November 1928, London County Council boundaries had long since enclosed Clapham Park, and the last vestiges of a previously semi-rural environment had all but vanished, save for the farm in nearby Clarence Avenue. This farm had six Jersey cows, and from it my mother still bought her potatoes by the sack until the mid 1930s. On Sunday afternoons we would take our dogs for a walk to watch the cows going in to be milked.

The area surrounding the farm still retained the very large "country" houses which City merchants had built during the previous hundred years or so. Their grounds contained tennis courts and wooded areas where snowdrops grew in spring; while the outbuildings which had originally housed coachmen and carriages had largely been transformed into chauffeurs' flats and garages as the motor car replaced the horse as a means of transport for the wealthy.

Up to the 1920s a "Gentlemen's Bus" (horse-drawn) ran at 8.15am along Abbeville Road to take the local gentlemen to their City offices, but this service had ceased by the General Strike in 1926, and my father used the omnibus to reach his office in Whitehall. Always a late riser, he was usually alerted to the urgency of departure by the second school bell which rang at 8.55am (the first rang at 8.50am!) to summon pupils to the LCC school in Bonneville Road. This was the next road to ours, and the playgrounds lay behind our rear gardens. The roads and avenues of our estate had been named after French towns to mark the settlement of followers of Empress Eugenie in Clapham after 1848. The freehold of our house was held by the Compte de la Bedoyaire.'

TADWORTH

'Before the First World War Lord Russell of Killowen was lord of the manor of Tadworth and lived at Tadworth Court. The Court dominated the village and the people worked either there or at the few other large houses or on the farms of the district. Tadworth Street was the main thoroughfare. It was a pretty country lane with grass verges. It connected Tadworth with Walton on the Hill which in those days was the more important of the two.

Sir Cosmo Bonsor (who later lived at the Warren) whose kindness and thought for the villagers was greater than I can tell you, kept soup ready in their kitchens for all who cared to fetch it during the winter, and at Christmas no one was forgotten. There were presents for all – boots for the boys and red cloaks for the women and girls.

Our nearest doctor was at Epsom or Sutton. I remember when my father-in-law was ill my husband went on horseback to Epsom to fetch the doctor and then had to go back again for supplies of medicine. When in need, the villagers turned to Mrs Lindsey who was an excellent midwife and cured many with her old-fashioned remedies.

Many cottages were still thatched, quite often with heather. The windmills were working – on Tadworth Green there was a kiln where clay pipes were made. A hurdler lived at Withybed Corner and there was a wide ditch where watercress grew.

Water was a problem – villagers used the dew ponds and the village well was on the village green. The roads were metalled with flints brought from the corner near Russet House. The children liked to watch the stone-breaker who sat all day by the side of the road opposite Tadworth Cottage breaking flints to repair the road.

How quiet Tadworth was in those days. As I stood in the garden on a summer's evening all would be hushed, except perhaps for the sound of a horse on the road in the distance, until at nine o'clock from Kingswood church the ringing of the curfew would come to me across the common.'

MORDEN

'What was Morden like just after the First World War? Picture a very quiet, sleepy, peaceful village. The tiny cottage where I was born in Lower Morden Lane, built in 1907, was rented by my parents for the sum of five shillings a week. Our large garden overlooked open fields, front and back, and I spent many happy hours there with my sister and brothers. The dawn chorus of the birds heralded each new day, the ducks on the ponds had a language of their own, the cows padded their way twice daily past our little house to the fields from the three farms, providing milk for the local inhabitants. The only traffic was an occasional funeral cortège, which in those days was solemnly drawn by two, and sometimes four, beautiful black horses down the lane which led to what was then Battersea Cemetery.'

FETCHAM

'It does not seem possible that when we arrived in Fetcham there was a thriving watercress business (the watercress beds being where the fire service station vehicles enter their drive). That the mill pond was a glorious stretch of water with numerous deep, gorgeous blue springs – and so many wild fowl. That there was a big barn at the begining of the mill pond between what we called the "muddy path" and the water mill, where on Sunday mornings we used to watch the local men set their ferrets to catch vermin!

There was a lovely stream, fields and woods where Cannon Way is built, with fields and woods down to the splash from Nutcroft Grove. Fields and woods spread from Cobham Road, opposite the post office, and only a few shops were in the parade, ending at the ironmongery with a farm, where old "Bags" the farmer used to bring his horse and cart with round baskets full of vegetables, hanging down the back, to sell to the local housewives.

The Reading Room was occupied by a very old couple, Mr and Mrs Wright, who used to serve us tea or cocoa, with shortbread, on the evenings we met as a Cycling Club. Opposite, in the road, the war memorial stood at the junction of River Lane and Cobham Road. An orchard ran most of the way down River Lane, and scrumping was great – until the local bobby caught you!'

FARNCOMBE

'My grandparents moved to Farncombe in 1915. Although quite a small village, it had many pubs; it must have been quite a beer-drinking community. For shops, it was quite self contained. The draper's shop was owned by Mr Phillips and I believe he had the Phillips Memorial built in Godalming in memory of his son who was killed in the First World War. You could buy such a large variety of things in his shop – anything from a warm winter vest to a packet of pins. In fact, a "paper" of pins was offered in lieu of a farthing change. The village grocer was blind, but Mr Tugwell, with his sighted brother, ran the village post office as well. When my father took my brother and myself for a walk and we happened to pass a farmhouse, he would always stop and buy us both a glass of milk, topped up with cream. It tasted wonderfully rich as it was, of course, unpasteurised.'

EWELL

'West Ewell, the hamlet in which I was born, lies about one and a half miles from Ewell village, and on very old maps we are told it was named "The Marshes". The fields around were mostly pasture but some wheat and oats were grown. The steam train ran from

Dorking North to Waterloo, stopping at Ewell West which boasted a stationmaster's house.

Just out of Ewell village at the foot of Beggars Hill was the forge. A Mr Ralph was the blacksmith and opposite, standing on the banks of the small stream, was the baker's. Coming back towards the village crossroads, there was the mill, a white clapboard building opposite The Jolly Waggoners. The large Trojan steam vehicle delivered the flour and took in water at the horse pond; the pond had a ducking stool. Mr Cracknell was the butcher and behind his shop was the slaughterhouse.

Five mental hospitals stood in the areas of Epsom and West Ewell, and as children we saw the patients being taken for walks along the lanes and to our local shops. They sometimes aroused our curiosity, but never our fear. The hospitals were self contained and to the local population they were a major source of employment.'

SIGHTS AND SOUNDS
OF DAILY LIFE

Sights that were once commonplace to older generations have passed forever from the streets of today's towns and villages – the lamplighter at dawn and dusk, the blacksmith working at his forge, the dairy bottling its own milk, the village policeman. So, too, have gone the street traders with their distinctive cries and sales patter – who could resist 'Hokey Pokey a penny a lump, the more you eat the more you jump'!

THE BLACKSMITH

'I was born and brought up in the tiny village of Merle Common, near Oxted. My father was the village blacksmith, and he and my mother were very involved with the local community. He served on the Board of Managers for the local school, the first in Surrey to introduce school meals. He was for a time on Oxted Parish Council and did much to help raise money to build the village hall. He listened with sympathy to the problems of the farm labourers who

19

came to the forge with horses to be shod and farm implements to repair, giving help and advice where possible.

My father and mother were very keen on a WI being started – my mother was already a founder member of Hurst Green WI. In his capacity as a village blacksmith my father often went into people's homes to repair kitchen ranges and saw how undomesticated some women were. He felt the WI could teach them so much. Of course WIs were very different then and many of the early members were hardworking, disadvantaged country women.

Blacksmiths had a very difficult time after the First World War as they depended for most of their trade on the farmers who were also experiencing difficulties, and many went out of business. My father, always one jump ahead, on seeing the motor car about to take over from the horse, turned his old forge into a garage and installed petrol pumps and also began to deal in motor mowers and repair agricultural machinery. At the same time he built a new forge on the opposite side of the road to take advantage of the fact that the fashion among the better-off was to buy and renovate the many old houses which were falling into disrepair. He turned his smithying skills to making fire baskets, log tongs, fire screens, wrought iron gates and ornamental ironwork generally.'

'My father was the village blacksmith; he moved to the sleepy village of Frimley Green when he married my mother in 1911, both of their fathers being blacksmiths.

Our family life was happy; we were very fortunate as my Dad had a thriving business. The local gentry had horses, and he also had the Army contract. My early childhood was during the First World War; it brought hardships and afterwards a lot of poverty. My Dad returned safely from the war, had a nervous breakdown but fortunately for us recovered and was able to take over his business once again. His brothers and 'in-laws' had kept it going in shifts while keeping their own business going in Farnborough.

In the village were the gentry, tradespeople and working class. You were expected to know your *place*. The tiny working class cottages often had only bare boards and peg rugs. A poor woman would work a whole week for five shillings – and at our house a good dinner too. Dad and Mum insisted on her sitting with us, and we children had to be polite and respectful . . . a very good thing for us, taught early in life to help others and have compassion. Times for some were very hard.'

'My paternal grandfather, who died before I was born, was a blacksmith, and my first memories of visiting the smithy at

Wrecclesham date from the early 1930s where my father's elder brother, who had inherited the business, lived and worked.

The shoeing room was situated on the roadside with a stable door for the horses to enter. Beyond this was the forge. It was a dark, windowless building with the only light coming from the open door. It was littered with tools and bits of rusty iron. Suspended from the ceiling was a row of new horse shoes which my uncle would fashion during slack periods in readiness for regular customers. He also made and repaired farm implements.

My sister and I were able to watch him take a piece of cold, dark iron, which he would place in the fire until it became red hot and then hammer it into shape on the anvil. The metal cooled quite quickly and would be reheated and beaten many times before the perfectly shaped article would be finally plunged into the water trough, causing a great hiss of steam, to cool the metal and set the shape.

The fire was a heap of coal on a raised hearth. This coal was a special type. It was so fine that it was almost dust with some larger very bright and shiny chips in it. I thought it very pleasant to run through my fingers and that it smelled quite lovely. To get a really hot fire, bellows were used and we were allowed to pull on the large wooden lever to pump air through the coal.

When horses were shod we were also allowed to watch, but at a safe distance. First, the horse's old shoes were removed and the hooves trimmed. The previously made cold shoes would then be checked for fit and if minor adjustments were necessary they would be heated up and corrected. After this, one shoe would be made red hot in the fire and carried swiftly in large tongs to the patiently waiting animal. My uncle would stand with his back against the horse's flank, bend its leg up and hold it between his knees. He would then place the red-hot shoe on the hoof. There would be a strong smell of burning and a lot of smoke but to our amazement the horse appeared to be quite calm and happy. We found it most difficult to understand that it obviously could not feel the extreme heat, but worse was to come. He then took some large, flat nails with rectangular heads, and proceeded to hammer them into holes previously punched through the shoe and into the horse's hoof. Yet again the horse remained unconcerned. We later found out that horses' hooves are like very thick fingernails with no feeling and also that the shoe nails were hammered in at an angle and did not go right up into the leg as we had supposed. If the horse was having a full set of shoes, this process would be repeated and apart from an occasional stamp of a hoof or a toss of the head, the animal would remain patiently stationary throughout.

The time that a cartwheel had an iron tyre fitted was very exciting to witness. In the yard was a raised, iron, circular platform with a metal pole in the middle. The wooden wheel which had been made or perhaps repaired by the wheelwright, was placed centrally on the platform and several buckets of water were set close by. My uncle and the wheelwright would then hurry out, carrying in large tongs the red-hot iron band which had been heated in the fire. They quickly placed it over the wheel on the stand. Immediately, the buckets of water were tossed over the wheel to stop the wood from burning and to shrink the metal. This ensured that the two parts of the wheel were perfectly bonded. This event often attracted a number of spectators and as everything had to happen very swiftly there was quite a build-up of tension until the job had been safely completed.

After the Second World War, farms and businesses became mechanised and horse-driven vehicles were no longer used. Unfortunately my uncle's business dwindled away, but he stayed in the house until his death in 1965.'

VILLAGE SHOPS

'When we were of school age in the 1920s, we were allowed to run up to the little local general shop at Warlingham to spend our "Saturday penny". There was such a selection to choose from – gob stoppers, humbugs, sherbet dabs, prize packets, Sharp's creamy toffee, liquorice laces, and many other delights. This shop, small as it was, had such a variety of goods to sell – there was bacon, cheese, biscuits, soap, cigarettes, matches, as well as all the sweets and other commodities too numerous to mention.

The shops in the locality were typical village shops. There were two drapers – one also sold hats, two shoe-menders – one also sold boots and shoes, two green-grocers – one was also a florist, a bicycle shop, a barber and hairdresser, a chemist, a dairy, a baker, a fish shop, a butcher, and three public houses, a garage and also two grocers. Most of these shops were around the village green. The local forge was about three minutes' walk from school, and we loved to run along after school to watch the horses being shod. The smell of the forge, the furnace, the ring of the blacksmith's hammer on the anvil, and the sparks flying, together with the whinnying of the horses makes quite an unforgettable memory. There is still the church hall in the village where local events are held.

Sometimes word would get around that Griffith's (grocers) had broken biscuits and we would be given a penny each to run up there (a mile away) and buy a bag full each. It was such fun searching for the sugary pieces! The village shops stayed open on Saturday evenings, and in the summer after tea we would walk to the village to do the week-end shopping, and to listen to the band which would be playing on the green.'

'Best of all tradesmen was the grocer, with his long white apron and his pencil tucked behind his ear. The shopping list was written in a little red exercise book, and we then sallied forth to the shop. My mother would be given a seat on a bent-wood chair so that she could look round and add to the list. Everything was weighed and wrapped – and often tasted – while we waited, and the senses were assailed with delicious smells. Sugar, rice, dried fruit were scooped from sacks into blue bags. Biscuits were loose in tins, bacon was sliced – not by the pound but by the number of slices required, and coffee ground for you. I loved to watch him shape the butter with wooden butter pats. Almost forgotten is the joy of that first spicy whiff as the shop door opened and the bell jingled. Without fail I would be given a biscuit or a few raisins or some other small treat when no one was looking. The order would be delivered later that day or early the next.

Smells are very evocative and most shops had their own distinctive aroma. I loved the corn-merchant with the slightly musty smell of sacks of corn and chicken feed and grass seed; hay for the rabbits and bird seed. He always had a canary in a cage singing fit to burst. The ironmonger had its own peculiar but not unpleasant smell too, with all the nails and screws kept in little wooden drawers behind the counter. Another distinctive smell was the leather at the shoe repairers. He sat tapping away at his last with his mouth full of tacks, which he never removed to speak to you. I was sure that if I watched carefully for long enough he must surely swallow one occasionally.'

THE VILLAGE GREEN

'In the 1930s the village green was the absolute centre of village life at Brockham – cricket, rounders, visiting fairs and roundabouts, the local Flower Show and of course the famous Brockham Bonfire – all took place on the green. Transport was not easy so villagers stayed much more together within the confines of the village for their sport and leisure pastimes.

Farmers were allowed to tether stock on the green and any animals found straying were impounded in the Pound, which has survived as a real feature of the village.'

THE CROSSING SWEEPER

'Before the First World War at Merstham, the roads were roughly made and constantly muddy. Old men with brooms would often sweep clean a crossing for people who would drop a penny in his box for the privilege. It was particularly appreciated by women whose long voluminous dresses often trailed in the mud. Boots were worn for that reason.'

THE BAKER

'In 1923 my grandfather (Chas Doick) fulfilled an ambition when he opened his own baker's shop in Wallington. Like most small bakeries his bread had its own individual taste made possible by blending flours from different millers.

On Good Friday all shops were closed except for bakers who for that one day only sold hot cross buns. My grandfather would enlist the help of his family to bag the buns. As a small child I was only allowed to pack the small bags – six buns.

Christmas was a very busy time for all the staff. Customers would order their Christmas cakes and choose what decoration and wording they wanted, so each cake was a unique work of art. On Christmas morning customers would bring their poultry to be cooked in the huge bakehouse ovens. The one shilling they were charged was given to the delivery boy, who took the cooked birds round in the large basket on his delivery bike.

The ovens were brick built and the baking trays were made of iron so the floor of the oven got very worn with the constant friction of metal on brick. Periodically my grandfather would call in a specialist firm from Croydon to repair the oven floor. The three men would start work late on Saturday when the oven had been out for a few hours, but was still very hot. One man would enter the oven and start work; as soon as he was overcome by the heat his two workmates would pull him out and revive him with a drink of cold milk. Another man would take his place and so it would continue until all the bricks were replaced.

Early every morning the roundsmen would load their barrows or vans with bread and buns and a small selection of cakes in their boxes. Special deliveries of wedding or birthday cakes or bulk orders for parties would be made later in the day. In the afternoon when they had finished they would call over their sales for the day. These were entered in the huge sales ledger and they would cash up their day's takings. Before they went home the barrows and vans had to be swept clean of all bread crumbs. These were soon devoured by the birds who had waited patiently on the yard wall.

The people living near the bakehouse woke every work day morning to the delicious smell of freshly baked bread as the night bakers made their way home. Within an hour or so the bakehouse was again a hive of activity as the pastrycooks started work on pastry, cakes, doughnuts, etc, etc.'

'When my sister and I used to get our Mum's Saturday shopping in Chobham in the 1940s, the weekend joint for our family was five shillings and sixpence and our weekly bread bill was three shillings and threepence three farthings. We used to ask the "Bread Lady" every week how much it was, even though we knew, as we liked to hear her say "Three and three, three"! Apart from the baker's, Mr Lascelles at the grocer's shop also sold bread, and he went round in a van and delivered his bread from a huge basket over his arm, covered by a white cloth. He was a very tiny man hardly bigger than his basket. The best buns were made by Mr Welland – soft, light brown, unglazed and absolutely delicious. The small ones were a halfpenny each and the bigger ones a penny.'

THE DAIRY

'My parents ran a dairy shop and my mother poured the milk into bottles from the churns. My father used to get up very early each morning and wash and rinse the bottles by hand in order for the milk to be poured in and a cardboard cap fitted ready for sale.'

THE BUTCHER

'I was born in Brockham in 1907 in my parents' butcher's shop overlooking the green. Meat was delivered by horse and trap. The pond opposite was used to swell the wooden wheel of the carts in summer when the iron rings got loose; the pond being shallow, the carts were driven into it and left to soak. The horses used it for drinking. As children we used a punt on it that was also used for carting sides of bacon.'

'In the 1920s most of the daily needs of the villagers could be met by the shops in Meadvale. Mr Peters owned the butcher's and Mr Marchant was head butcher. On Monday mornings the cattle were driven from the fields to be slaughtered in the yard behind the shop. They were then skinned, cut up and hung in the cold room. A lorry brought huge blocks of ice for the cold room twice a week, as there was no refrigeration in those days. Children would hang around the lorry hoping to get a lump of ice to suck. At Christmas time the butcher's had a large display of meat and poultry outside the shop and the men who worked there had to stay up all night to guard it.'

'Redhill was a quiet little market town in the late 1920s. On Mondays there was a cattle market in the Marketfield and the cattle were driven along the High Street to the slaughterhouse in Cromwell Road. On Saturdays there was a market full of vegetable and meat stalls and cheap clothes. People would wait until the end of the market to buy their meat because with no refrigeration the butchers had to sell it off cheap. It was very exciting after dark when all the stalls were lit with naptha flares.'

'In early September 1939 I was evacuated with my mother and brother from London to Guildford. I was eight years old at this time and one of my earliest memories of Guildford was of walking along a busy road in a main part of the town and seeing about two dozen young heifers being driven towards the cattle market. I was quite terrified – as Londoners we had not had any close contact with farm animals and it seemed wrong to us that these animals should be allowed to run loose through a busy town. My mother dragged us into a shop doorway and proclaimed in a loud voice that she thought it quite disgusting and that they should at least be led through on a "rope"!

Now years later I still smile when I think of how amusing my mother's remarks must have been to the local inhabitants.'

THE GROCER

'In the early 1930s there were not many shops in Cheam village, but Sainsbury's had arrived and I can remember going into this huge shop where they cut the butter from large lumps and patted it into the amount you required. Bacon was cut to the thickness you required on the bacon slicer and ham was sliced off the bone. Sugar, sultanas, prunes etc were weighed up and put into bags, which were then shaken down on the counter and closed with a few deft movements of the fingers. Biscuits were not in packets, but in glass-fronted tins, so that you could choose what you wanted.'

'Mother was born and brought up on Surbiton Hill; she referred to Londoners as almost a race apart. Father was born and apprenticed to the grocery and provision trade in Buckingham, coming to Surbiton Hill in 1921 as first hand to a company shop.

When they married in 1923, they bought the remaining lease on

26

a grocer's shop five minutes walk from Surbiton station. The cost was £500 for about 40 years with £8 annual ground rent paid on the old Quarter days. It was built in the 1860s with three floors plus basement and had been prosperous at the turn of the century but had become very run down.

My father, two men and two boys worked from 8am-7pm Monday, Tuesday and Thursday, 8am-1pm on Wednesday and 8am-8pm on Friday and Saturday until the war in 1939. Before his marriage he had worked until 9pm on Friday and Saturday. My mother, working for her baker father, did not shut their shop on Saturdays until 11pm, in case someone wanted a loaf for their supper after the pubs shut. When early closing legislation first came in, it did not apply to family employers. Later it did, and she told me they shut at 8pm on Wednesday and she and her sister would dash down to the first cinema in Surbiton. This was before 1914. Her father was not grasping and always emphasised they would find something for children sent to buy two pennyworth of stale bread.

At about the beginning of December, my father would bring scales and weights upstairs to the front room table. Our job was to weigh up small cellophane packets of Christmas luxuries – muscatels and almonds, crystallised and chocolate ginger and glacé pineapple. Fresh season's supplies of raisins, sultanas, currants and halves of peel would arrive in October. When I came home from school a boy would often be cleaning the fruit on a sort of sieve on the dispatch counter at the back of the shop. They would be weighed up in blue bags but there were always some loose in a drawer so customers could inspect the quality. Dried goods like lentils and butter beans were all sold loose and were weighed up in shiny yellow bags. Soda was in thick dark grey bags.'

THE POST OFFICE

'My earliest childhood memory, in about 1928, was of riding in father's sidecar, this was quite simply a box attached to a motorbike and one rode in it with the lid propped open. It was a pillarbox red colour as it was an ex-GPO model that had been sold off, previously used by the GPO for deliveries. Dad was the local sub-postmaster in the village of Betchworth and had quite a large village office as they go because it also had its own sorting office and postmen. The mail used to arrive in from Redhill at 5 am in the morning and in those days I recall about six postmen were employed there; deliveries were made from there to several surrounding villages as well. There was also the telephone exchange on the premises which was staffed during the daytime hours but Mum and Dad took over the evening and night duty. In addition to the PO itself, there was also the village stores to run. Telegrams were delivered from Betchworth over a very wide area, it was all part of the duties. I later learned that the sum paid for delivery was threepence up to three miles and sixpence over.'

'We had three posts every day at Bisley. If we caught the first post in the morning, we could get a letter from our uncle in London by the afternoon post in reply to it.'

'Very few houses had phones in Charlwood before the Second World War. The postal service was good, but special messages could be sent by telegram via the post office. The postmistress would then ask an older schoolchild to deliver it – one could earn a few odd pence that way.'

'When I left school in the 1930s I went to work in the local post office at Betchworth. Christmas was always a very busy time. Everyone seemed to send lots of parcels and the chauffeurs from the big houses would come with carloads. All the people who lived in the big houses around employed maids, chauffeurs and gardeners. Some had a butler and footmen, and a few had a coachman as they still had horses, carriages and traps. Early January was busy too in the post office because all the dog licences were renewed then, also carriage, hackney carriage and armorial bearings licences and male servants licences. If one employed a male servant in any capacity, a licence was needed for each.'

'Just before the Second World War we bought the small sub post office and village store of Rushett Common. The first time I arrived I remember having to dismount my cycle and walk up Rooks Hill, as it was so steep. The post office looked very romantic, roses round the door and all, but we had come from a modern bungalow to a cottage with no sanitation, only a shed down the garden, no lighting upstairs, and only gas lighting downstairs. It was all very strange, especially to see every morning and afternoon the cows being driven across the road to and from the farm opposite for milking. The sheep from Tilsey Farm were shepherded down to Bramley to graze on land that is now part of Bramley Golf Course.

Despite the rationing the little store managed to survive and the villagers came weekly to collect their ten shillings a week benefit. What lovely characters they were too. Most of them worked on the Birtley estate or for Sir Raymond Denis, and they thought nothing of walking two or three miles to the post office for groceries etc. We had

28

three local postmen who did their own sorting behind the post office in Bramley before cycling on their rounds, and we had two deliveries a day. One of them was a likeable rogue who liked his tipple. On one Christmas delivery he failed to return and was subsequently found beside his cycle fast asleep in a ditch, having partaken of too many mince pies and sherries on his round. I also remember him coming back to the shop toothless and late. He had apparently sneezed hard with open mouth and out flew the dentures. He had spent a long, fruitless time searching the grass verge for them.

After the war, cars started to come back on the road and the steep hill was lowered by the council. In 1950 my mother was held up at gunpoint in the post office and it so unnerved her that she felt she could no longer continue to run the business.'

THE BUILDER

'My father was the village builder at Abinger Common, a business that included undertaker, coal merchant, and many other services. He was, for instance, the rate collector for Abinger and had to go round the village to give people a jog.

For his building business he had a dog cart which was quite high up and was a two-seater. He nearly always had a horse which was quite fast, sometimes an ex-racehorse. This meant that he could get from one job to another quickly. Sometimes his building jobs could be five miles away. He usually had two or three carthorses for fetching building materials from Gomshall station and delivering them to site. He also had a taxi business (horse and carriage) to take people to Gomshall or Dorking stations, and to take people to Dorking for shopping etc. The carriages were usually second-hand, bought from London. There was a victoria, an open four-wheeled two-seater carriage, used in fine weather, for getting to and from Dorking (though one had to alight at Coast Hill to reduce the weight for the horse); a brougham, which was a closed carriage for one or two horses; and a brake, a light waggonette with seats which was ideal for taking children on their Band of Hope or choir annual outing.'

THE POLICEMAN

'The local policeman used to pass regularly on his beat and if you slept in the front of the house you might awaken in the night to see the light of his bulls eye lantern shining round the room as he flashed it at each house to make sure all was secure.'

'My father came to Surrey by accident in 1911. He lived in a village in Cumberland and when he couldn't get a job the village policeman suggested he joined the police. There was a vacancy in the Reigate Borough Police so he applied and was appointed – without an interview so far as I know. He had looked at a map and could only find Ramsgate which he thought was the place and he looked forward to living by the sea. When he arrived it took him a few days to discover he was in a different town. He met my mother when he was on duty at a big fire at the gas works in Hooley Lane, Redhill. She was a children's nurse at a big house in Reigate and had gone with a friend to watch the excitement. My father joined the army in 1915 and went to France. He came home on leave at some point and they got engaged during a snowstorm on top of Reigate Hill. They were married in 1918 when he came out of the army and their first home was a little terraced house in Albion Road.

Our house was lit by gas downstairs but upstairs we only had candles and little paraffin lamps. I remember one evening I was in bed but still awake when my father came home. He came up with a candle and gave me a ham sandwich which he said he had brought from the Old Bailey for me. It was a great treat and I kept asking when he was going for some more but I don't think he ever did. I imagined the Old Bailey was a marvellous shop!

Just before I was born there was a big scare about a Sinn Fein plot to murder some members of the Royal Family and the government. The Prince of Wales, his brother and some of the government ministers were sent down to Reigate Priory in secret and were guarded by the local police. My father was one of these as he had been in the army and could use a gun. He was gone for some time until the scare was over. Afterwards he told my mother he had been guarding the back gate into Bell Street and was most impressed by Churchill, who left by the back gate instead of going back to London with the rest of the party through the main gate.

In 1927 my father was promoted Sergeant and we had to move to Redhill. I remember we celebrated with sardines for tea – a great treat as we rarely had any tinned food.'

THE FIREMEN

'In 1916, after a disastrous fire at Bregsells Farm near Holmwood station, the villagers decided to have their own fire station. One hundred pounds was quickly raised by public subscription and the fire tender (horse-drawn) was based at the corner of Betchets Green Road and the A24 where the modern house "Woodlands" now stands. The fire alarm was a brass horn, operated by turning a handle. My grandfather John William Hoad was the general carrier and carter. He lived in Steyning Cottage, on the main Horsham Road and kept his horse in the yard at the back. There were regular fire drills and I used to enjoy turning the handle of the alarm. It made an awful noise, but when my grandfather heard it, he would run to the stable and let the horse out and the horse would trot along Norfolk Road and around the corner to the fire station all on its own, ready for duty.'

'We had a part time fireman living in our house in Guildford Park in the 1920s. He worked for the Council in the Water Department and he was an authority on the fire hydrants. A bell at the top of the stairs rang at nine o'clock in the morning and six o'clock in the evening just to make sure that the alarm was working and every time there was a fire this bell would ring, twice for a town fire and three times for one in the country. At the first ring he would be off on his bike and down to the fire station, which in those days was at the top of North Street. He could get there in three minutes he said.'

THE COFFEE HOUSE

'I was born in 1918 in Guildford into a family business called in those days a coffee house, though it mainly served lunches to business people. Although I was only four years old when we left there, I can remember the smell of roast beef joints being cooked. This business was on the corner of North Street and Commercial Road.'

THE RAILWAY STATION

'There were two booking clerks at the station at Cobham in the 1950s, where the booking office was open all day, a stationmaster and a resident porter called Bill, a local character whom we all knew. The level crossing near my home was manned, the signalman living in the red brick railway house across the line. We used to see him crossing the line with his tray of tea. As drivers went through his crossing, he would wave. His signalbox is demolished now and the crossing is automatic. There was still one steam train on the line in 1957, which went by each afternoon at four o'clock. We used to watch for it.'

THE LAMPLIGHTER

'I don't know at what age I fell in love with the lamplighter, but it was about 1915 in New Malden.

The curtains all over the house were pulled across just before it got dark and I took to scrambling up onto the wide window seat and sitting there between window and curtain and day dreaming. Then the lamplighter came into my life; well, not literally, he was outside and I was in. The streets were lighted by gas lamps and hanging from them was a chain with a ring on the end of it. The funny, little, old man came along pushing his bicycle. He would stop at each lamp and, with a hook on the end of a pole, he would slip the hook onto the ring and pull. Ploop . . . the light would come on. Teddy lay beside me untended. When I had seen my lamplighter light all the visible street lamps and seen the night take over from the day I would grab hold of teddy by the ear and lug him off to bed.'

'A few years before the onset of the Second World War, my father lit the street lamps in the village of Cranleigh.

Every evening after school, in the autumn and winter months, I was sent down to the village to wait for my father in the porch of one of the local public houses, with his flask of tea and sandwiches. After finishing his daily job he went straight on to his extra job of lamp lighting.

He rode an upright bicycle, and as torch batteries were unheard of, his cycle lamp was powered by a soft white powder called carbide. When ignited it gave off a clear, bright light. Under his arm he held a long wooden pole with a hook at one end. Inserted into the street lamp the hook pulled down on a small chain. This released the gas and ignited a soft meshed bulb and the lamp was lit.

Most streets had two or three lamp standards, and in all sorts of weather my father cycled around the village while I returned home in the dark, our street being last to be lit, and last to be put out. About 10.30 pm he went out again to extinguish the lights, and I was woken from my warm bed to go downstairs to keep my mother company until his return home.

In 1939 lighting street lamps was understandably discontinued, and after the war electricity came to our village, and the lamps were converted. Some of the old lamp standards still remain today, a constant reminder to me of my father and part of my childhood.'

SATURDAY EVENINGS IN THE SUMMER

'I was born and grew up in Caterham Valley and when I look back to my childhood days the sun always seemed to be shining. I loved the summer time.

In the centre of our village, there stood a large water fountain and you could press the lions' heads which were on all four sides and cup your hand under the water and get a drink. We lived about half a mile from the centre of the village and we used to dance along at my mother's side each Saturday evening to make our way to the fountain.

All the shops were open and we'd wave to my father who was the Master Butcher at Knight's the butcher's shop. The Silver Band was the attraction and they looked so bright in their navy blue and red uniforms. We knew all the bandsmen. We watched Mr Smithers, the painter, blowing his trumpet and getting very red in the face.

We called the area around the fountain The Square, and the local people stood around chattering and being pleasant to each other. We always persuaded my mother to stand outside Broad's, the baker's. There was an open grating on the pavement and we loved to smell the bread baking. We could look down and see the bakers pushing loaves into the oven and it was beautifully warm standing there.

My mother would talk to her friends and my brother Bob and I would play hopscotch, or marbles. My big sister Freda stood apart from us with her teenage friends. We'd all pause to clap the band when they'd finished one item.

I can still hear the chink, chink of the collecting box. It was wooden with a handle at each end, and a very pretty lady came around with it. She had long pearls and a lovely hat and she always smiled and said thank you when you put your coin in her box.

We knew when the band played 'God save the King' that we would say farewell to our friends, and hanging on to my mother's arm, would make our way, a little more slowly to our homes.

What lovely summer Saturday evenings, so very warm and friendly.'

COUNTRY LIFE FOR THE BETTER OFF

'In the early 1920s we always had two small donkeys who pulled the two lawn mowers, which were guided by the gardeners. The donkeys wore beautifully made little leather shoes, which strapped up with little buckles like a child's shoes. Our first experience of riding was on these very amenable donkeys – "the moth-eaten mokes".

We were in the depths of the country and pumped all our own water with a big machine, and made all our electric light with yet another machine – both of which periodically ceased to function. We were a household of six children, two parents, a governess, a nurse, three maids, and an uncle – 14 in the house . . . and every drop of drinking water had to be boiled on the kitchen range.

The summer was wonderful. First the cutting of the big cornfield

– an enormous steam engine positioned at each end of the field with a small machine propelled up and down the field from one engine to the other. Then the horrible moment when the last area of standing corn was "beaten" to flush out terrified rabbits and smaller creatures who were all killed. The hay-cutting was the other great time when we could actually ride on the carts back to the rickyard, pulled by patient cart-horses.

My father used to go to the station every morning in the pony-trap – high on two wheels, pulled by "Dandy" – whom the groom drove on the way back.

By the mid 1930s tennis parties on lazy summer days were part of growing up. One had left school by now, and Oxford and Cambridge were "down" (the only Universities that appeared to exist at all) so mixed tennis parties were a great social event. In Surrey there were usually some "chinless wonders" from Sandhurst or the Guards at Pirbright too. Most courts were grass, beautifully kept by the gardeners, though I do remember one or two hard courts – the latest thing.

Tea-time was almost a ceremony – no bun-and-cuppa in a deck chair. We all processed indoors to the dining room – polished table decked with elegant china and silver; wafer-thin cucumber sandwiches and delectable home-made cakes with the hostess (the lady of the house) presiding with the silver teapot and making conversation to a set of suddenly rather tongue-tied youngsters. The bowl of flowers on the tea-table was always of sweet-peas and gypsophila it seemed. Tongues loosened again once we were outside, and maids brought out trays of drinks towards six o'clock – home-made lemonade being *the* most delicious and refreshing.'

KNOWING YOUR PLACE

'Before the Wentworth estate was sold in 1920, children used to go bird scaring on the estate. The people who lived in lodges on the estate had to curtsey to the countess when they opened the gates for her to go through in her carriage.'

'At Abinger Common at about the time of the First World War, the rector's wife Mrs Hill had a single-seat cart with bells on it drawn by a donkey. As children we had to curtsey to Mrs Hill, but if we heard the bells coming we would try to hide behind the hedge to avoid this.'

'When the summer holidays came round in Bookham, horse-drawn waggons and carts picked up the children from local schools to take them up to Mrs Greville's at Polesden Lacey for tea and entertainment. The entertainment was usually a conjuror. After the tea – sticky buns, sandwiches and lemonade, the children had to gather in single file in the drive. Mrs Greville, with her butler, gave everyone sixpence.'

CHARITIES AND CLUBS

'At Trumps Green, between the wars, the Edgell Wyatt charity provided an amount of coal at Christmas if you had a tin plate with the house name on it on the wall.'

'There was a Boot Club at Merrow school. Your parents saved up and got a coupon to spend on shoes; we always had good shoes (or boots) and our father mended them. The National Deposit Friendly Society helped to pay the doctor's bills and paid "sick money" if the breadwinner was ill. There were also coal clubs to help buy fuel.'

STREET TRADERS

'I remember before the Second World War hearing the muffin man's bell on Sunday mornings, also the sellers of cockles and winkles from their handcarts; and particularly the Hokey Pokey Man who would shout "Hokey Pokey a penny a lump, the more you eat the more you jump".'

'In the 1920s the man selling watercress would walk down the road at Badshot Lea calling "Watercress, watercress", and we had to dash out if we wanted to buy.'

'My recollections as a child are of the street sellers – the muffin man with a tray on his head and a bell which he rang; the shrimp and winkle man who came on Sunday with his handcart; the cat's meat man; the Hokey Pokey man (Italian ice cream); the hurdy gurdy man with his monkey; the lavender lady and the gipsies selling clothes pegs.'

'Each Sunday we had the Italian ice cream man with his highly coloured barrow who stood calling "Hokey Pokey ice cream" – we would get a cupful for a halfpenny. Later on the Walls ice cream man came, ringing his bell on a bicycle with a big box fridge on the front, with the famous slogan "Stop me and buy one!".'

'The cats meat man came in his governess carriage, cutting up cats meat. If you had a glass jar to give him, you had a windmill in exchange. The other cries were the "Knives to grind" men, which included repairs to pots and pans, and the lavender ladies with their cry "Won't you buy my sweet blooming lavender".'

'The knife grinder was most exciting. He had a machine on wheels. He sat on a little stool and worked the machine with his feet on the treadles; a metal wheel whirred round and the knives and scissors that he was given to sharpen were held against this wheel and sparks flew in all directions. "Chairs to mend, chairs to mend" was another cry, and if you had any broken cane chairs the mender would sit outside your house on the pavement and spend many hours patiently threading the cane in and out, fascinating for a small child to watch. "Ripe strawberries, ripe strawberries" was another cry that we loved to hear, for every summer the strawberry man came round with his horse and cart and we would rush out with a large bowl to be filled.'

'Another feature of life in the 1920s and 1930s was the rag and bone man. They were gipsies who came round with a horse and cart and would buy rags and bottles. Our Auntie Ethel was a dressmaker and had quite a lot of rags. All the little pieces were saved and put in a bag and when we heard the rag and bone man calling, we used to ask him over, and he would give us a few coppers or even a whole sixpence.'

'Halfway down Halebourne Lane in West End was a bridlepath which we called Blind Lane, leading to Rye Grove. Blind Lane was also known as "Gipsy Lane" because that was where they parked periodically in their gaily coloured Romany vans. They used to call at our doors with their baskets of lace, lavender and clothes pegs, and they worked in the nurseries – of which there were many in West End. They also used to collect rags. We also had calls from turbanned Indians with their suitcases full of silk underwear. Our local farmer delivered the post and the milk, and he also had a 'box affair' which he used if we needed any pets put down – he'd keep the door firmly closed with his foot.'

CHURCH AND SUNDAY SCHOOL

Sunday was a special day, set apart from the working week, and the church or chapel was often at the heart of community life. Most children attended Sunday school and the annual outing was a treat to be looked forward to and remembered.

SUNDAYS

'Sundays were very special to my early childhood. We wore our best clothes; they would be everyday clothes next year! We went to church, a service run for children, then in spring, summer and autumn we all went for a family walk. It does not sound very exciting, but it was. There was so much to see, so much to look for and one met other families, stopped to talk or walked on together. Home to tea which was always a bit special on Sunday.

We had Sunday toys and Sunday books, father would read us stories, mother would tell stories she made up; she was a great story teller. The games were quiet ones, puzzles, games of skill or board games; no cards on Sunday, no playing out of doors. In the winter we would be sitting round the fire, four pennies put out ready and as it got near four o'clock we would listen for the bell being rung as the muffin man came down the street. When the bell got nearer my brother or I would snatch up the four pence, open the front door and stop the muffin man, who lifted the big tray off his head for us to choose the four best muffins. Meanwhile mother would have boiled the kettle and made the tea while we got the toasting forks and toasted our muffins at the fire.'

'For as long as I can remember we went to see our grandparents on Sunday morning, and I used to go on Dad's bicycle sitting on a cushion which he tied onto the crossbar. I loved it. He also used to take me to Bisley churchyard, and I sat on his coat and played with his watch and chain while he trimmed the family graves while Mum got the Sunday dinner. We had to be home by 1 pm to be ready to walk to Sunday school in the afternoon. In the summer we were taken for a walk in the evening, which almost all families did in those days. We certainly did walk some miles.'

'After our marriage in 1956, we joined in the local Sunday evening entertainment which was to walk up to Holmwood Common and sit and watch the traffic returning from the coast. It was "bumper to bumper" on the A24 from 6pm onwards.

The cricket pitch at that time bordered the Horsham Road. At least one "six" went through a windscreen, but the best ever tale of a "lost ball" was the one that landed in the back of a passing lorry and ended up in Brighton.'

'Family gathered at Grandma's regularly for Sunday dinner around her large table, its concealed leaves extending it to full size. When in season sweetpeas and maidenhair fern filled a Victorian epergne, its lustre glass horns sitting in an elaborate silver base of twining stems and leaves. I used to think it *so* beautiful and breathed in the fragrance – vying as it did with sizzling roast aromas and garden vegetables . . . to a background conversation of politics, farming and gardening. There was always a selection of soft-fruit tarts to follow with custard or top-of-the-milk (which was creamier than our diet-conscious skimmed or silver-topped varieties now). Home-made wines and cordials replaced today's claret and hock.

I used to think the adults so *old*! As they settled into a chin-on-chest, somnolent posture, I saw them reflected in the gilt mirror surmounting the large marbled fireplace; shepherd and shepherdess on the shelf, the grate full of brass fire-irons and screen. Grandma would draw the heavy wine plush curtains a fraction to plunge the room into pools of sleep-inducing shadow.

My brother and I would then escape to the identically-proportioned room, across the wide hall where the sun glanced through the coloured glass panes of the porch. A shared delight lured us into this cold parlour of stiff-backed chairs and unused mustiness, complete with aspidistra and with a long since unplayed upright piano with brass candle-holders. It was the wind-up 'His Master's Voice' Gramophone. Here it was that a love of music was firmly rooted.

The happy hours spent there! Taking turns winding up . . . sometimes forgetting and then turning the handle feverishly as the music ground up an octave!

Beyond the bay window there stretched a lawn and borders to the thick boundary hedge. Half way down, a white-painted settle (in need of a fresh coat) stood under the monkey-puzzle tree where father and sons would sit later enjoying the late afternoon sunshine.'

CHURCH SERVICES

'Church loomed large in our family life before the First World War. Father and my brothers were in the choir and we looked forward to our Sunday school treats in the summer and at Christmas. We were fortunate as our rector's daughter produced plays. We rehearsed at the rectory and gave the performance in the church hall.'

'Attendance at church was much greater than today, but perhaps performed more as a duty – everyone dressed in their Sunday best and hats and gloves were a must! Church of England services were strictly according to the Common Prayer Book – Holy Communion, Matins and Evensong. Other denominations in the village were the Mission Hall, Wesleyan chapel and a Salem chapel. Early in the Second World War the Roman Catholic Notre Dame Convent School from Faversham in Kent was evacuated to Lingfield and this was the introduction of the Roman Catholic church to the village – this school became a part of Lingfield life taking in local pupils and remained after the end of hostilities. It became well established and still thrives today. On summer evenings after Evensong the robed choir from the parish church would process into Old Town adjoining the church and the vicar would hold a short open-air service. The Mission Hall sometimes held a service around the village pond. Estate employees were expected to attend church by their employers and the church organist would contact the estate owners at Christmas asking if the choir could visit and sing carols to their house parties – they would be given mince pies and punch and, hopefully a cheque for church funds.'

'On Good Friday at Cranleigh before the First World War we took baskets and went into the woods to gather primroses to decorate the church for Easter. The primroses and little wild daffodils were placed in small jars along the windowsills and surrounded with green moss, and they were the main decoration in our church. The nine o'clock bell was rung by the verger every Sunday morning. This had been the custom for hundreds of years and it was only stopped during the Second World War when it was forbidden to ring the bells. The passing bell was also rung by the verger when someone died, a different bell for man, woman or child.'

THE BLESSING OF THE HORSES

'There used to be a ferry across the river to Shalford Road, where you can walk up through the Chantries to St Martha's on the top of a very steep hill. Until a few years ago services were held once a year for the Blessing of the Horses, where each horse was presented with a rosette after the service.'

PAYING FOR YOUR PEW

'Seats in church at Brockham had to be paid for at three guineas a year. Your name was attached to the end of the pew and no one else ever sat in it.'

'In church at Charlwood the better off and the tradespeople had their own pews, marked with their name. We had to call the rector "Sir" and the rector's wife "Madam". No toys, no spending of money, no housework and no mending on Sundays.'

GIRLS IN THE CHOIR

'During the Second World War we had Sunday school in the village hall at Headley. The older boys were in the choir and we girls badly wanted to join but the choirmaster was having none of it! We badgered him for ages and eventually threw down the gauntlet – we challenged him and the boys to a rounders match on the cricket pitch, if we won he would let us join the choir. We thrashed them. Eight girls then spent the next few weeks sitting in the front pews to prove how right we had been. Meanwhile, several ladies of the village made us gowns out of blackout material.'

SUNDAY SCHOOL

'The four of us started at the Methodist Sunday school at Capel at a very early age, attending every Sunday afternoon – they were really very happy days, we enjoyed going so much and received such lovely Christmas gifts, etc from our teachers there was never any parental pressure necessary. We were still attending Sunday school until well into our teens. In addition we were expected to go to "Chapel" twice on a Sunday – 11 am and 6.30 pm. I must admit that some of the preachers those days seemed to read the longest chapters they could find in the Bible, while some of the sermons seemed to be never ending.

'We went to chapel at Farncombe every Sunday. I also went to Sunday school and on the Anniversary each year I had a new hat, fine straw trimmed with a wreath of daisies, poppies and cornflowers that were made of material and wire.'

'I attended the Congregational, now United Reformed, church in Beacon Hill during the Second World War. Sunday school was in the afternoon and I remember singing such choruses as "I'm H.A.P.P.Y." and "Jesus wants me for a sunbeam". We spent time making models and drawing pictures as well as listening to and reading aloud the simplified Biblical stories. Of course prizes were given for regular attendance, and I still have a "Book of poems and morning songs" presented to me in 1945. Highlights of the year were the Nativity play in church at a special service and the Christmas concert in the hall on a Saturday evening.

I can remember one Mothering Sunday particularly well. We were all given little posies to take home to mother, they were of primroses and violets except for one which was of white lily of the valley, for my friend Norma to place before a photograph of her mother who had died during the year.

As soon as it was possible after the war we went on a Sunday school outing each year to the seaside, either Littlehampton or Bognor. We had a picnic lunch, organised games on the beach and usually a tea in a café.

Rationing did not stop the members of the congregation and mothers of the children clubbing together to provide a really superb tea at Christmas.'

THE SUNDAY SCHOOL OUTING

'When I was a child at Guildford before the First World War, each year in the summer all the children in the Sunday school would have a treat. We would all be taken to a local park for an exciting ride in large carts drawn by two strong horses (each cart) lent by local farmers. We seemed to be all dressed in white cotton frocks with large straw hats, and I wore a sash made of silk around my waist. On those occasions the weather was always hot and sunny. When we reached the park we would play games, races, rounders and ball games followed by a lovely tea kindly donated by a local baker. We would all sit in a circle on the grass, with the vicar we would say grace and then start tea. Our mothers would come along after tea to walk us home, tired but very happy. At Christmas we would have another treat. All the Sunday school children and teachers would meet at the Church Hall, sing all the old carols and a conjuror would entertain us or we would have a magic lantern show and a lovely tea would follow. After tea Father Christmas would appear on the stage with a large sack on his back full of toys, one for each child, also small bags made of cotton material full of sweets tied up with ribbon. Our vicar would give out prizes for good attendance, say a prayer and then each child was given an orange at the door.'

'The highlight of the summer for most children in Farncombe when I was a child in the late 1920s was the Sunday school outing to the seaside. All the Sunday schools in the Farncombe area joined together and arranged for a day trip to the seaside, usually during June.

A train was booked from Farncombe railway station to take us either to Littlehampton or to Hayling Island. If you attended the Methodist Sunday school you were able to go free of charge but if you attended the Church of England Sunday school, you had to pay one penny for every absence from Sunday school. So you can guess which of the Sunday schools had the most support!'

'We went to Sunday school every Sunday morning for as long as I can remember, then into the eleven o'clock service with my mother. Home to dinner, then back in the afternoon at three o'clock Sunday school, home again for tea, and back for the half past six service.

One of the great events in our young lives in Knaphill was the annual Sunday school treat. A record of a treat held in the Hermitage Park show that 25 quartern loaves, 130 pounds of cake, ten pounds of butter, five pounds of tea and 20 pounds of loaf sugar were used, and each child was given an ounce of sweets. The children marched from the village to the park headed by the band of the Bisley Farm Refuge School. Later the children were taken in horse-drawn vehicles a little further afield. Eventually petrol engines took over, and one year children were taken on a coal lorry, seated on forms on the back of the lorry. The winter treat provided another form of entertainment – this time with "Dissolving Views". This proved to be magic lantern slides. A record shows that a resolution was passed at a teachers' meeting "that the popular game of Kiss in the Ring be discouraged"!'

GETTING ABOUT

At one time, if you wanted to get about you had to walk, unless, of course, you were wealthy enough to have horse-drawn transport.

The first cars were greeted with excitement and curiosity, and the first bus service in a community could draw a large crowd to watch its inaugural journey.

DOCTOR ON HORSEBACK

'Before the First World War our doctor came around on horseback, which meant someone had to hold the horse while he called on his patient. He also rode to hounds. Later he came in a smart "gig" driven by a coachman. Our postman came in a red PO van. He sat on top above the horse. He collected the mail from the post office and emptied the letter boxes. I remember too the fire engine dashing through the village, drawn by two handsome horses.'

HANSOM CABS

'When you arrived by train there would be a row of hansom cabs waiting with their horses. A rug was always put over your knees, and this always smelled of horses. There were bags of hay hanging up, so if a horse wasn't working he could nibble the hay.'

PONY AND TRAP TO SCHOOL

'In 1925 I was old enough to start at a little morning-only school in York Road, Woking. In those days we kept a pony and trap which my mother drove, and she took me and fetched me home each morning.

We travelled along the Egley Road (now the A320), then a quiet road by today's standards. Topsy, the pony, was well trained to normal traffic, but she heartily disliked Foden's steam lorries, and we seemed to meet these fairly regularly. On seeing one in the distance Mother had to dismount and turn the pony's head away from the terrible sight.'

SHOPPING BY PONY AND TRAP

'During the First World War my aunt had a pony and trap which was a blessing for shopping in Guildford. Broad Street had no shops except for one little sweet shop where I can remember buying sherbet dabs and strips of liquorice for a halfpenny each. The pony, called Joe, was a lively and sturdy Welsh animal, but he had not been properly broken in – this meant that when trotting along a road he would suddenly decide to turn off down a side street. I shall never know how we survived! He did not like standing still, so my

Before the advent of the motor car, country people either walked or used a pony and trap to go to town for the market or to do their shopping.

job was to walk him up and down the High Street in Guildford while the shopping was done – I was under seven years of age! Getting into the trap was quite an art too; I had to get my foot on the step while the trap was moving, and heave myself up as best I could.'

THE TRACE HORSE

'In the 1920s Jack, the big trace horse, stood at the bottom of Wimbledon Hill with his owner, waiting to be harnessed to lighter horses with heavily laden carts to help them up the hill, which was very steep in those days.'

WATCHING THE CARS GO BY

'I remember when young coming home from visits to Sussex to see my grandparents, and driving through Purley on a Sunday evening where there were always people standing just to watch the cars go by. We as children waved to the people with "royal waves".'

THE FIRST CAR IN THE VILLAGE

'The main A322 road through Bisley was a narrow lane at the beginning of the 1920s. When we were young we used to play on the main road, spinning our tops. The first man in Bisley to have a car was old Mr Jardine, who had a Trojan, with a chain that ran round the side of the vehicle. It made a terrible noise – we could hear it a mile off, and all the children used to run to the road to see it go by – or perhaps break down!'

'The first car in Bletchingley was owned by Dr Pratt. The driver would sit down low in front with the doctor behind him under a canopy.'

OWNING OUR FIRST CAR

'My father had a car before the First World War, so we were quite posh! It was a huge Daimler and Gerald and I could sit, and the twins could lie on the floor and still leave plenty of room for the grown-ups to sit comfortably on the back seat. It was an open car of course, with a very large hood which had to be put up in rain, otherwise we could enjoy the sky and I well remember loving to watch the stars as I lay cuddled up in a fur rug.'

'Motoring was very different from today. Journeys took much longer, and if you drove above 40 miles an hour that was considered quite something! My father had a car (a Scripps "Booth") and would take the family out. The car had no top and when it rained he had to stop and pull the hood over, which had perspex windows in the sides which always seemed to have holes in them. The spare wheel was on the side as well as the petrol can. There were very few garages, so it was wise to always carry petrol. The car often had a puncture. I remember helping my father to mend the puncture and change the wheel. Sometimes an AA man would appear on his bicycle and stop and help you – if you were a member. Going up the hills was always an adventure, and there are plenty of hills in Surrey. The car would easily stall and you had to get out and put stones behind the wheels, and hope you were able to do a hill start without slipping back.'

'In 1920 my father bought his first car – an Austin 20 Tourer. It was obvious that we should have an Austin, because both my parents came from Birmingham, where Austins were made. An uncle bought the car for us and drove it down one Saturday. He took father "round the block" several times on Saturday and again on Sunday morning, but then he had to return home by train and father was on his own! There was no driving test, but of course there were not many cars. After a few weeks we set out for a holiday in Pembrokeshire. It took us two days and several punctures.

45

The car being a tourer was an open one, but it rained then just as often as it does today. The car was therefore fitted with a hood, which the manufacturers claimed would unfold from behind the back seats at the touch of a button and shoot out over the passengers so that it could be fixed to the windscreen and no one got wet. This was the theory, but in practice we often got drenched.'

THE CAR THAT RAN ON GAS

'I remember rationing after the Second World War, and in particular petrol rationing since my father was running his MG car on gas – ordinary, household gas! He had a large gas bag fitted to the roof of the car, a gas supply installed in the garage with a gas tap, and after some adjustment to the petrol engine, he had a supply of fuel to take the car from Sanderstead where we lived to, perhaps, Chelsham and back (an outing into the countryside of Surrey). It was, of course, essential to ensure that there was enough gas to get home since he could only fill up in his own garage. This ingenious arrangement allowed him to continue using his car throughout the war and afterwards, to travel to Addiscombe where he was running his builders merchant's and coal delivery business, and to Kenley where he was helping to run the ATC (Air Training Corps).'

THE FIRST BUS SERVICE

'1912 saw the arrival of the first motor bus in Bletchingley, to run from the Whyte Harte to Redhill. The fare was threepence and on the early Saturday morning workman's bus the fare was only a penny. When there was snow and ice everyone would have to get out of the bus at the bottom of Redstone Hill and walk up so the bus could make it empty. The passengers all got in at the top, to continue the journey.'

'In the 1920s, in the wake of various housing developments in the Chipstead Valley, a bus service was inaugurated and the neighbourhood stood in their front gardens to watch the first No 58 bus make its journey to the terminus just before the bridge at the junction with Howe Lane. Many of the buses had "Thomas Tilling" written on the side, the upper decks were open to all weathers but a rainproof covering was attached to each wooden seat and gave some measure of protection to the passengers. There was an outside wooden staircase, a conductor who dispensed gaily coloured tickets and a driver who would stop at any convenient spot to pick up passengers. This new bus service was a means of easy access to the countryside and at weekends, which for most people did not begin until work finished at mid-day on Saturday, crowds of people would spill out from the bus terminus to spread out across the fields, lanes and woods of Chipstead, Woodmansterne and Banstead. A relative who lived in a small cottage in this area, in response to the growing demand for Sunday afternoon teas, decided to use her front sitting room and large garden for this purpose and I remember the hustle and bustle of those Sunday afternoons with the grown-ups providing pots of tea, sandwiches, scones and jam, and fruit salad and cream whilst I endeavoured to look after my three small cousins.'

ON THE TOP DECK

'It was a treat to go to Redhill to shop. It cost twopence on the bus so we did not go often. It was an open-topped bus and we loved to go upstairs. When the bus was approaching the low railway bridge, the conductor would come halfway up the stairs and shout "Duck your heads", which we would all do until we were safely through to the other side.'

'In 1932 I went to Reigate County School, and I had to go by bus which seemed quite exciting. The buses then were open-topped double deckers and it was a point of honour to travel on the top whatever the weather. The seats had canvas aprons like pram covers across them and on wet days they had pools of water on them so we crawled underneath. No grown-ups came upstairs in bad weather so we had the top deck to ourselves. When it snowed we made snowballs and threw them at pedestrians below.'

TRAMS AND TROLLEY BUSES

'Having been born on Poet's estate at Carshalton, I remember the trams on the route from Sutton to West Croydon which were operated by an arm extended from the roof of the vehicle to an electric cable above, and ran on lines rather like trains do now. The trams were replaced by trolley buses before the Second World War, and these were operated in a similar way, except that they had two arms. Otherwise they were driven in the same way as buses are today. These were much more comfortable to use and were quieter than the trams. The route covered was extended from Sutton to the Crystal Palace via West Croydon.'

OUR FIRST CYCLES

'With our savings after the Second World War my sister and I bought our first cycles – £7.50 each, black Raleighs, sit up and beg with rat trap pedals.'

THE AA MAN

'My father spent his First World War gratuity on a motor cycle and side car, a Matchless RK 47. This was during the General Strike to get himself to work. The AA man wore a brown suit with riding breeches and long leather boots, and he stood at crossroads and saluted you as you drove by. Since the engine seized up frequently he was much in demand. Shell petrol was tenpence a gallon.'

GRANDAD'S TRICYCLE

'My grandparents rode an unusual tricycle. Grandad sat at the back with crossbar and handlebars, while grandmother was in front between the two wheels, her handlebars coming round her back and sides – nothing in front of her at all. I sometimes had a ride on a seat on the crossbar.'

PEOPLE THOUGHT NOTHING OF WALKING

'Before the Second World War people thought nothing of walking long distances for work or pleasure. We lived in Fetcham and regularly used to walk into Dorking on a Saturday evening when there was a dance at the Dorking Halls, and after the dance we would walk back home again. Many people, including the little children, would walk from Holmwood to Dorking for a major shopping expedition, returning home with the pram laden with food and weary children.'

OR OF CYCLING

'In the late 1940s I was nursing at Epsom, and on my nights off would cycle 17 miles to Guildford where my folks had a furnished house – there was little traffic on the roads then.'

THE STEAM TRAIN

'We lived in West London, and after the death of my great-grand-mother we continued to visit my great-aunt and her family in

Fernhurst. It was always exciting for me, but there was one part of the journey I hated. I was fine on the Underground, and riding in the "big train", but to get on to that train I first had to pass the engine. The beginning of the platform at Waterloo held for me all the terrors of the most fearsome of today's monsters. It stood there, belching steam and heat, and the light of the fiery furnace flickered over the driver's cab. I prepared myself for the ordeal by creeping between my parents, or, if possible, getting on the side farthest from the thing. I took a deep breath and held it as we went past, my steps quickening to get by as fast as I could, and I counted myself lucky if the monster didn't let out a great steaming snort just as we were level with it.'

THE BRIGHTON ROAD

REMINDER OF A PAST AGE

'When I first moved to Reigate Hill with my parents in 1926, every Tuesday a stage coach drawn by four horses and carrying passengers in period dress, travelled from London to Brighton and returned every Thursday. Living near a bend in the road, the coachman always sounded the horn when passing our house. The horses were changed at the White Hart Hotel which was then situated in Bell Street, Reigate. This ceased after a few months. I understand that the American, Mr Vanderbilt started the stage coach journeys before the First World War. He went down in the *Lusitania*.'

AUGUST BANK HOLIDAY MONDAY

'One year in the 1930s my holiday included the Bank Holiday weekend, then at the beginning of August, and it was decided to spend the Monday in Brighton. Cars were scarce in those days so most people went by train but the family owned a van used for its business, and it was decided to use that. There was room for the driver and one adult in front but, after much sweeping and tidying, wooden chairs were placed in the back for the younger members of the party which included me. Surrounded by picnic baskets and other seaside paraphernalia we set off, but as soon as we reached the Brighton Road we realised that the rest of South London also was making for Brighton – busy roads were not just a prerogative of today. I had never seen so much traffic on a road before. There were bicycles, motorcycles, vans, cars, small charabancs and even horses and carts. It was a very noisy, good humoured journey but steadily moving towards the coast. Once there, it did not prove difficult to park the van as, of course, no parking restrictions existed.'

BILLBOARDS

'We had a car and quite frequently visited the South Coast in the 1930s, traversing the beautiful Surrey countryside. For me the journey really began as we left the built-up areas and joined the Croydon by-pass at Thornton Heath. There was an enormous billboard advertising Odol toothpaste, showing a pretty girl with a wide smile and in large letters "Odol – The Pearly Way to Brighten". I need hardly add the play on words (The Purley Way to Brighton) appealed to a child.'

RIDING TANDEM

'During some holidays between the two world wars my mother rented a house at Reigate. We often went for walks near the river at Sidlow Bridge, where the purple loosestrife grew in abundance. When we reached the main road near the church (it was the main Brighton Road then) there were dozens of couples on tandems coming back from the coast or a day out.'

CHANGING TIMES

'My first memories of Surrey are trips in the family saloon as a change from our more suburban surroundings and an excuse for my parents to practise their driving out on the open road. This was before the days of driving tests. I remember the view from Newlands Corner, the Punchbowl at Hindhead, the pond at Friday Street and even visiting the caves at Reigate! We also had the excitement of a roadside puncture, running out of petrol and stalling halfway up Pebble Hill! On Sunday afternoons, by the late 1930s, the main roads through Surrey – the Brighton Road, the Worthing Road and the Portsmouth Road – could be quite busy and one started to find the quieter lanes. This meant getting stuck behind the cows going for milking or an odd farm cart at hay-making time. With the war and the restriction of petrol for private motoring, cycling came into its own and this was our main means of getting around locally, as buses were very infrequent – once in two hours or even once a day in outlying areas. We also did a lot of walking and a visit to the cinema could mean two or three miles walk in the blackout, with the possibility of an air raid warning and having to take cover in a road-side ditch!

After the war car ownership grew, almost imperceptibly, until the streets were strewn with parked cars, one, two or three to a house. This has changed the lives for the good for so many people, but like all changes it has brought difficult problems to village life. During the 1960s several motorways were constructed through the county, to cope with the massive increase in traffic, and the years when this work was going on were very traumatic for those of us who lived nearby and some villages have been permanently changed by new bridges and access roads.'

CHARACTERS AND ILL-DOERS

When everyone knew everyone else, local eccentrics and characters tended to be regarded with affection and good humour. Cruelty, however, could lead to the village expressing its feelings with 'rough music', a very effective way of letting a wrong-doer know that his neighbours would not tolerate such behaviour.

POACHERS AND SMUGGLERS

'There was a lot of poaching before the First World War and after a keeper was shot on West Park the poachers used to warn the keepers of estate owners Locker Lampson and Palmer's the biscuit manufacturers that they were coming through that night. Copthorne was the local gang headquarters for goods heading for Reigate and convoys from Chichester harbour were often carried through Petersfield and Hindhead. There were rumoured to be caves under Akehurst Farm. However, tons of food were shifted up from Groombridge to London.'

'On summer days in the 1930s we would walk from Fetcham up the Ridgeway, an unmade road of lumpy chalk, crossing the country road, past the little house with its chickens and straight onto Fetcham Downs. Sometimes we would turn right and pass Roaring House Farm, where we would hang over the wall watching the ducks and goats, and marvel at the tall hollyhocks and the rich colour of marigolds. We learned how the smugglers hid at the farm out of the way of Customs men – though few Customs men were prepared to tackle them in any case. They would bring barrels of brandy up over the Downs and when the cry went out that the Customs men were near, they dug a hole, known as a "swallow", and buried the barrels until they could retrieve them.'

ROUGH MUSIC

'At about the time of the First World War, a man who lived at Smugglers Cottage was known to have sworn at a Copthorne woman, so for three nights rough music was dished out. Rubbish was tipped there and trays and pans banged. Opposite Harbers Cottage near the Cherry Tree was a grocer's cart and the owner had tethered a pony in a field with nothing to eat and so rough music was dished out to him also.'

GIMLET JIM

'There was a period in Kenley in the 1920s when a burglar known as "Gimlet Jim" eluded police capture time after time. All windows had wooden frames then, so the man used a gimlet to enable him to open the catch on the window. One morning there was great excitement – Gimlet Jim had burgled the house next to ours. The people who lived there had two dogs which slept in the kitchen but they had not woken up. After a time the burglar was caught, and I was rather disappointed that the excitement was over.'

'PIGGY' MOON

'Grandfather Percy Moon was the local butcher and slaughterer between the two wars. He was a man rather larger than life, and his crude trade would not be tolerated in these animal orientated days, but was then very necessary. He was a kindly man and would not cause more distress than needed. Certainly, animals did not have to travel in terror before leaving this life, and most local farmers used his expertise. He plied his trade in Reigate, and was locally well known even to being given the nickname "Piggy" Moon (he was a large florid-complexioned man and despatched many pigs). His great joy each year, recounted whilst propping up many a bar, was

52

riding the leading elephant in the yearly Circus Parade. This travelled from Dorking to Reigate each spring and Grandpa always had this honour. He looked very grand evidently, and enjoyed it very much. We children certainly enjoyed listening to the tale sitting round the fire after Sunday tea.'

THE GRAVEDIGGER AND THE MIDNIGHT BAKER

'In the late 1940s Pedler Barnes was the Holmwood gravedigger. He worked as a labourer by day and dug graves by night, aided by the light of a lantern. Late one evening, a young lad from the neighbouring village of Beare Green was walking past the church on his way home when he noticed a dim glow in the churchyard. It was an eerie scene and at that moment Pedler chose to step out of the grave he was digging, covered from head to foot in grey clay. The lad truly thought he had seen a ghost and it is believed that he holds the sprint record from Holmwood to Beare Green!

In the house where Holmwood Tyre Service now conducts business, lived Mr Crofts, the baker and his sister, "Pudgy" Crofts, the village schoolmistress. Mr Crofts' bread was renowned in the area – beautiful crusty loaves which he would deliver as far afield as Coldharbour; but Mr Crofts refused to start work at the crack of dawn so the bread was never ready before late afternoon. The smell of the freshly baked bread as we came out of school was irresistible. Mr Crofts baked the bread in his back yard, where he also kept chickens and pigeons, and occasionally we found the odd "unusual currant" on the buns, but that bread was far too good to waste, we just picked the dirty bit off and ate the rest. Mr Crofts used to start delivering his bread at about 5pm and finished late at night, hence his nickname. One day the bread was later than usual. Miss Crofts explained that her brother had not been feeling too well but that customers would get their orders. Mr Crofts finished his round in the early hours of the morning. Next day, he was dead.'

ECCENTRICS

'Cranleigh, like other places, had its eccentrics in the early years of the century. Miss Beck used to walk up Mead Road balancing her umbrella on the tip of her finger, and one of the farmers would turn cartwheels along the meadow path. It was said that our fox-hunting doctor wore his huntsman's jacket under his coat when visiting patients, and it was remembered that in the middle of the 19th century the schoolmaster used to ride up the village on an ox.'

'A Bisley eccentric in the 1920s was its rector, John Gwyon. His odd behaviour was such that the congregation dwindled to about three or four, and the church was in a sorry state. He always paid his paper bill in farthings. When he died (sadly by his own hand – he committed suicide on Boxing Day 1928) he left a strange will, leaving a Trust to provide knickers for the poor boys – not of Bisley but of Farnham! Each garment was to be marked "Gwyon's present". The will was contested and over-ruled. The builder's report on the church the following year stated that the heating had not been used in twelve years.'

GIPSIES

'At the beginning of the century Knaphill was a small hamlet of a few houses and farms clustered at the foot of Anchor Hill. On top of the hill stood the Anchor Hotel with its stables and a small thatched farmhouse. Apart from a few houses there was nothing except common land between there and Brookwood station. Various paths and tracks led across the common. In summer the tracks were very sandy, but in winter they became a sea of mud. It was the practice then to cut gorse, heather and shrubbery from the common and lay this upon the muddy tracks to make them suitable for horse traffic. Squatters, usually gipsies, would pitch little wooden shacks on part of the commonland. If they remained there without attracting the attention of the authorities they could legally claim the land.'

'We had our share of gipsies on the common at Holmbury St Mary. One in particular, "Dark Liza", sold pegs, laces and in their season the small daffodils known as Lent Lilies. Baskets of primroses followed on. Dark Liza had two daughters, Mary and Alice. Alice was sent by the Chapel people to Canada to improve her "lot". We never heard of poor Alice again.
    As children we walked miles picking the "hurts" (whortleberries). One shilling a pint was the rate, and four quarts was a full day's picking. One did not pick any leaves – this was taboo. The gipsies, to our disgust, used a wide comb and picked leaves and all.'

'From about 1915 there was an encampment of true Romanies in Ockham. They were in caravans, all horse-drawn. Their chief, whose name was Morella, came to our house for my mother to write to her son called Mark, somewhere in Kent, and tell him they would "come for the horse". When she died, in true Romany style, the rest of the gipsies burned her caravan and moved on.'

HOUSE & HOME

THE HOUSES WE LIVED IN

The houses we lived in are often remembered with affection, even though they could be cold and inconvenient. The heart of the house was the kitchen, the only room sure to be warm and where family life went on, from cooking to relaxing after a day's work. After both World Wars, new estates were built and for each generation, the new houses seemed to be the height of modernity.

OUR HOUSE

'I was born in 1912, the youngest child of a farm worker at Box Hill Farm. I had four brothers and five sisters. Our cottage had three bedrooms, and I shared one with my mother and sisters. My father and brothers shared another bedroom, and a lodger used the third. We had a kitchen that was used as a family room as well as a scullery, and of course an outside loo. There was a large garden for my father to grow vegetables in.

No tradesmen called at the house, and we had to go to Dorking for everything we needed. I remember having lots of stews, mainly rabbit stew and on Sundays we had steak and kidney pudding for lunch. Other days we had bread and cheese. As a special treat we were given Camp coffee and seedy cake, but I didn't like either!

I went to school in Dorking until I was ten, when we moved to Brockham. After school we had to collect wood from Box Hill for the fire. We worked on the farm picking up stones to repair the roads with, or pulling up mangels and swedes etc. We also sold buttonholes to the visitors to Box Hill. There were no toys so our work was our entertainment.

Mother also worked in the fields. We often wondered what she did whilst we were at school, and I later realised how difficult it must have been for her looking after all of us and working as well.

At Christmas our stockings were filled with one orange, nuts and a handkerchief from the lodger. We had no presents at all on our birthdays.

My brothers went to work at the farm or the stables, and all of my sisters went into service. I left school at 4.30 pm when I was 14, and at 5 pm the same day I was in service at Box Hill.'

'I came to Shellwood, in the parish of Leigh, with my large family in 1915. After living with all mod-cons in Fulham it was a shock to have no piped water. We had a spring water well in the garden with a pump and a rain water well nearer the house which was pumped through into an outhouse over a stone sink. If we had a dry summer the rain water well dried up and the spring well would be so low that it had to be drawn up by bucket on a rope as the pump did not work. We had a filter for our drinking water and my mother had milk pails which were filled every morning for the rest of the household needs. At one time water was so scarce that the Water Company put a stand-pipe about one mile down the road and my father went there to collect water in a tub in a pony-cart.

The lavatory was another problem, it was situated at the bottom of the garden – two seats, one for grown ups and one for the children. In the dark evenings it meant putting your coat on and having an older brother or sister with a hurricane lamp to take you there.

There were three or four children of school age in the family and we had a mile and a half to go to Leigh school. My mother would be at the door at 8.15 am sharp to see us go and to make sure all was in order, including lunch bags, there being no school dinners in those days. She was particular about time. We had no other children living near us so we had to keep together and get home by four o'clock or woe betide us!

We had our baths in the out-house, in front of the copper fire and this was constantly going for one thing or another. We had piped water and a bathroom in the house early in 1930.'

'Unless you happen to have lived in the village of Chobham, it is quite possible that you have never heard of Pennypot Lane, so named, it is believed, because beer was at some time sold for a penny a pot in a house at the other end of the lane. It was called Penny Pot Cottage. It is still in the same spot today. This is where I was born in 1920.

There were no amenities in the lane in those days. I grew up with a paraffin lamp to read by and a candle to light my way to bed. Water came from a well in the garden and was pulled up by a bucket on a long pole with a clip on the end. I can so well remember, when summers were hot and dry, my father putting the old tin bath on the barrow and going to a small stream (called the Bourne) and filling the bath with water, covering it with a sack; but by the time he had pushed it back home a lot of the water had been lost. This was done on washing days and bath nights – what a chore this must have been. I was in my teens before water and electricity were laid on in the lane.

What a hard life my mother must have had. We only had a small kitchen range for cooking, an open grate with a small oven at the side. How my mother managed to dish up our meals I shall never know. The chimney was a very wide one and we could see the sky if we looked up, but it did have a bread oven at the back and hooks where the bacon could be smoked. Sweeping the chimney was quite a performance. My father would find a large holly bough and this he would pull through from the top. Just imagine the cleaning up there must have been.'

'We loved our house at Bisley Green although it had only two bedrooms and two living rooms downstairs. The front room was only used on Sundays during the winter, when a fire was lit and we played ludo or snakes and ladders in the evening with Mum and Dad. The room we really lived in at the back was not very large, but we had an open fire, at first about a yard off the floor, and an oven at the side, and on this all the cooking was done. The flames went all round the kettles and pans and they got very sooty. After this we had a range, which we thought was wonderful as all the fire was shut in, so nothing got sooty any longer and Mum could keep her saucepans clean outside as well as in. I had left school before we had an open fire like the ones we have today, and cooking was then done in the scullery on a three burner oil stove. The lighting was oil lamps and candles for a great number of years after I was married. There was a stone sink, and a pail of fresh water was always kept on a small table. This had to be drawn from the well with a pole – one well for two houses. When the weather was very hot a clean pail with buttermilk was lowered on a rope down the well a short distance and then the rope fixed through a ring on the well lid, and this was better than any fridge.'

'In 1920 home was on the edge of Camberley and Bagshot Heath where father was a head gardener. It was a very cold tied cottage, frost patterns in wondrous pictures over the bedroom windows in winter. Downstairs in the kitchen parlour was a blackleaded range, heavy pots and kettles. A big dresser contained the best china and jugs, on hooks. The scullery was down a step adjoining the coal house. In the back yard was a bucket toilet closet, typical of many, with a scrubbed bench seat, Jeyes fluid and newspaper squares threaded on a string for toilet paper.'

'In the 1930s we moved to a house in Croydon with a bathroom, smart tiled fireplaces in all rooms, a gas cooker and a geyser in the kitchen – all mod cons. The rent was £1 a week. Before the war home owners were in the minority, even the middle class rented.'

'I was born in 1933 in Dorking. My parents lived in rooms until I was ten months old, and we moved to the house I lived in until I was married. It was a terraced house, two up, two down and cellar. All water was outside. We had a washhouse across a yard with a flush toilet, and a cold tap. An old brick copper stood in the corner where the water was heated by fish boxes or any wood obtainable for washing and baths. In the summer we would have our bath in a galvanised bath in the washhouse. My mother used to carry all the hot water into the kitchen when the draught under the door became too much, and we had the bath in front of the fire. I clearly remember the day we went "posh" and my father took out the old blacklead range and put in a tiled surround fire. I was so proud!

I married in 1953 and we started, like my parents, "in rooms", but 18 months later we bought our first home – a semi-detached house, newly built, with three bedrooms, a bathroom, separate toilet and central heating. It was like heaven to me after what I grew up with . . . or without.'

'The house I lived in for the first twelve years of my life is approximately 500 years old and reputed to be Redhill's oldest house. In my days there it was condemned but is now a listed property. Apparently it was usual to fell the wood as near as possible to where a house was to be built; timber was not allowed to season but was used "green" so over the years, as the wood dried out, it would acquire curves.

The windows were small (in my day they were of the sliding variety but have since been replaced by small paned ones) and upstairs in the summer it became unbearably hot. Because it was built into a bank there were no windows at the back and none at the side either. The floors were stone-flagged and in the days before central heating, would "sweat" if there was a change of weather. Because of this we had two layers of coconut matting on the floor with the carpet on top. In our only living room, which was an irregular shaped room, the floor was not flat but curved down towards the fireplace which was situated in one corner. The dining room table had to be placed at the top end of the room before the sloping floor began.

We had no bathroom, of course. The lavatory was "out the back". In other words right around the house at the bankside. Expeditions to the lavatory were not undertaken lightly on dark winter evenings! I never went alone but would persuade my brother, Alan, to go with me, armed with a hurricane lamp, which was placed on the floor of the lavatory. It had a wooden seat which extended the whole width of the lavatory and when we had finished we would stand on it holding the chain down, open the door, pick up the lamp, let the chain go and run as fast as possible before the noise of the flushing drowned the sound of any bogeymen who might be lurking.

For bathing we used a tin bath. We had two – a long one for my father and mother used in the kitchen, and a smaller one for us children. In the winter the small bath would be brought in front of the fire so we had our bath in comfort – the water got colder but the heat from the fire made the bath hot to the touch.

The house had only two bedrooms. At the top of the stairs was the room – just an open area really including the stairwell – I shared with my brother. He had the larger end with the window, I the end at the back of the house under the eaves. My bed was pushed end-on towards the eaves and I couldn't sit up in bed because of this. I had a small table with a reading lamp, book case and a cupboard for my clothes and that was all there was room for. A "modesty" curtain went across the middle dividing my brother's half from mine but it was never drawn. At night we could play all sorts of guessing games from our respective beds, until my mother would call up the stairs "go to sleep".

In the winter the butterflies found the oak beams over our staircase a wonderful place to hibernate, the dark underside of their wings hardly showing up against the wood. My mother was forbidden to use the cornice brush at this time of year for fear of disturbing them.'

UP THE STAIRS AND DOWN THE GARDEN

'Some of the cottages in Bisley (which have now either disappeared or been "gentrified") had no staircase. You had to climb a ladder to go to bed! Our Uncle Alf lived in a cottage like this – and he had a wooden leg. Having climbed the ladder, with difficulty, he used to prop his leg up in the corner of the bedroom. Old Tom Pocock lived in Charity Cottage, and used to keep a pig indoors. He also used to take it for a walk.

Oil lamps were used for lighting. Most cottages had lavatories tucked away down the garden. It was necessary to take a candle with you after dark. I was afraid of the dark, and used to persuade my Dad to go with me. He would stand outside and say "Do be quick – I'm getting frozen out here". My sister was not afraid of the dark, and she used to clear off to the lavatory when there was any washing up to be done!'

'Some people in Hurst Green had two-seater toilets. One girl was not allowed to go on Wednesdays as they came to empty the bucket!

There was the danger of fireworks being thrown under the door around Bonfire Night. The *Christian Herald* was torn into sheets and hung on a nail for toilet paper. At school if you wanted to go, you had to ask for paper and sometimes were given only two sheets. A rose often grew around the outside loo and was known as the "closet rose". Youngsters often threw stones onto the corrugated roof.'

'In a house in Sanderstead visited in 1911 there were two seats in the privy side by side and two people used them at the same time. Another privy had one adult size seat and one child size.'

THE HEART OF THE HOUSE

'The kitchen was the hub of life. It had a huge dresser across the far end of it, with cupboards and drawers at the bottom. Above were shelves for the dinner and tea service with cups hooked all along the lower shelf and jugs on the next one. The very top shelf was reserved for the huge meat dishes only used at Christmas, and in front of them candlesticks. On the righthand wall by the dresser stood the old black iron gas stove (very modern then!) and next to that the cooking range. This was kept beautifully black and shiny and was used most of the winter. Hot water kettles were kept going all day, as there was only cold water laid on and that in the scullery! A brass fender kept folk from brushing too close and getting burnt. The fire had a metal door, which when lowered revealed the glowing coals behind clay bars. Just right for toasting bread or crumpets, on a three pronged metal toasting fork with extending handle. To the left of the fire was the oven and some very tasty dishes came out of there. The top was used to boil the veg and of course the kettles.

On Friday nights the wooden clothes airers were brought in and large towels hung on them, these were arranged round the fire with enough space for the big tin bath in front of them and we had our weekly "tub" there. "Tinies" first and a topping up from the kettle before the next child got in! On the right of the range was Father's large wooden armchair with cushioned back and seat. Beside it was a cupboard with his "bits" in and on top of it his pride and joy – the wireless set complete with two sets of ear phones! He would sit and twiddle the "cats whiskers" until he got the London station and then we were allowed to listen on the earphones.

Opposite the cooking range was a well scrubbed wooden table and chairs. The table was covered during the afternoon and evening with a chenille cloth, but in the morning was used as ironing board, cookery board etc. We had most of our meals on it, unless we had company, when we were allowed in the dining room. In the corner by the door from the passage was another door into the cupboard under the stairs and the coal was kept there. You can imagine the dust when the coalman came! He tramped down the passage from the front door to kitchen with a hundredweight sack of coal and then tipped it into the cupboard under the stairs. We children were made to sit and count the sacks and make sure we got the ten or 20 ordered!'

LIFE ON THE FARM

'I was christened Primrose because I was born on Primrose Day, 19th April 1917. My father always worked on a farm as a cowman. My earliest childhood memory was when I was about three years old and Mother was expecting my next sister. I can see her now in the black-iron bedstead with shiny brass knobs which could be unscrewed and the snow-white fringed bedspread. The bedroom floor was bare boards, stained with varnish, on which lay some pretty rag rugs. These rugs were made from sacks from the farm and one used a rag needle to pull through short strips of material, mostly woollen, old coats and other wool clothing, very close together so it formed a solid rug which never seemed to wear out. On the shelf in the bedroom was a little china pot where Mother saved the money to pay for the nurse and the doctor. I was allowed to count this, or rather, play with it. When the new baby arrived it was placed in the large drawer from the bottom of the chest of drawers, which had been prepared with soft bedding, then put on a long wooden bench next to the bed by Mother's side.

It was a hard life on the farm. All water had to be drawn up from the well and heated in large black iron kettles on a coal burning stove called a Kitchener. We bathed once a week in a long galvanised bath in front of the fire, taking it in turns, children first, followed by our parents.

The lavatory was in a wooden shed several yards down the garden. It consisted of a wooden box-like seat with two holes, one for the adults and a smaller one for children. It was quite a frightening place for a child, as underneath the seat was a deep pit. A sack of quick-lime and a shovel were kept in the shed and Father would shovel some of this lime into the pit from time to time in order to cleanse it. If one needed to go to the lavatory after dark one used a lighted candle in a jam jar.

As a child I recall I didn't have many clothes but Mother was a good seamstress and could make most things out of something else. Mother always mended our shoes too, she really was a "Jack of all

Trades". We grew our own vegetables and kept a few chickens and there was plenty of rabbit stew.

Musical Evenings were a joyful time, when Father's brothers came to visit. Uncle Reg would play his melodeon, Uncle Alfred would drum on a tin tray and Father would play the spoons. Together they would all sing with the help of Mother's home-made wine!

Mother could sing too, as before her marriage she had worked in London for a "titled" family and being able to visit the music-halls could memorise the popular songs from the shows. A happy scene I like to remember is Mother sitting in her high backed chair on one side of the kitchen stove with her work basket and a pile of mending, the oil lamp on the shelf just above her shoulder enabling her to get the best light and Father sitting on the opposite side. One or other would start a song and one song would lead to another, their never-ending repertoire causing lots of laughter. I used to really enjoy it and still remember many of the old songs.

We moved house several times as seemed the practice then, the man always trying to improve on his job and his wages. Every move we made was with waggon and horses, not that we had a lot of goods and certainly not surplus. The furniture was loaded first then the bedding, each lot wrapped in a sheet. Right at the back of the waggon (so it was taken off first) was a galvanised washing bath lined with a table-cloth and inside was all the food and crockery for our first meal in our new home. The very last things to be put on the waggon were the broom, the bucket with scrubbing brush and floor cloth. Mother always left the house clean.'

LIVING IN THE PRE-FABS

'In the east end of London we loved living in the pre-fab houses, constructed as temporary accommodation on a bomb site after the Second World War. The luxury of having an inside toilet and bathroom! There was a rhyme: "Down in the jungle living in a tent, Better than a pre-fab, no rent." The tallyman would call to collect the money each week and to collect money for selling us clothes and shoes.'

BUYING BY AUCTION

'My father bought our house in Woldingham at an auction in June 1944 at the Greyhound Hotel, Croydon. During the bidding the air raid sirens sounded and my father and the auctioneer were the only people who didn't dive for cover – my father got the house for a song.'

THE NEW ESTATES

'In the early 1920s estate roads were not put in before the building was begun, and when we moved in to Thornton Heath there was no made up road or footpath, just trodden earth or a quagmire according to the elements. In these conditions no wonder that the lady in the house opposite used to carry her schoolboy son over the threshold and made her husband sit on the front doorstep and pull old woollen socks over his boots before she would let him in. After a year or two the road was made up and they began by laying kerbstones roughly in the position they would be laid but upside down, which meant a long line of rough granite. To walk down the road on top of these, of course, became the only accepted way of going to school and many were the grazes and bruises sustained.

When it was all made up and our front garden path had been crazy paved, it became one of my Saturday jobs to "shake out" the hall mats and rugs, sweep through the hall, sweep the front doorstep,

City dwellers came in search of country life within easy reach of their work in London and new housing was built for their needs. This house in Knaphill was built for £450 in 1905, including stocking the garden.

64

right down the path to the front gate and then the whole of the footpath that fronted the house, the dust and dirt going out into the gutter. Nearly every household performed this chore, consequently the roads were always clean and tidy. There were road sweepers and in the summer water carts came round to sprinkle the roads and lay the dust. Also, if someone was very ill, straw would be laid all over the road to deaden the sound of the traffic so that they were not disturbed.'

'When I was four, my mother, a war widow with a pension of ten shillings per week plus five shillings for me, had the opportunity to move from the Isle of Wight to a council house in Guildford Park. We were thrilled – it had all mod cons; a bathroom adjoined the kitchen, the bath water had to be carried in a bucket from the large galvanised copper in the kitchen, firelit of course, and a flush toilet was only a step away from the back door. By today's standards its mod cons fell short but it was better than where we had come from! Nevertheless its storage space was capacious. Two bedrooms had fireplaces so this made room for cupboards in the recesses on each side. The small bedroom had a large recess also for clothes which could be curtained off and the hall had room for a dresser and a recess under the stairs big enough for a large pram to be stored.'

'I married in 1954 and two years later we bought our new house in Wonersh for less than £2,000, but when you consider it was my husband's ambition to earn £1,000 a year, it puts the price in perspective. There were about three cars owned on the whole estate of over 50 houses. I carried on working as a secretary to buy essential items such as a fridge and washing machine, which was electric with a mangle on top.'

'In 1957 our bungalow at Littleheath was new, part of the extensive post-war development of the commuter belt. There was an important brickworks here dating from Victorian times which closed down only in 1958. It was known as the Oxshott Brickworks, and there were "Oxshott Fireplaces" at one of the Ideal Home Exhibitions in the mid 1950s. A farm stood here too, with a dairy herd. The cows used to be brought up for milking from the fields towards Stoke. They held up the traffic and my husband called them "an anachronism", but he said it with regret. Both brickworks and farm have long been replaced by dwellings.

The houses on our estate were built with garages or car ports for one car, and with one bathroom and quite extensive gardens. Nowadays houses such as these are being built with garages for two or three cars, with two or more bathrooms and with smaller gardens. In the late 1950s the fashion was for "landscape gardening" on the small scale, with flowering shrubs predominating. There were a number of flower nurseries. Not everyone had or could drive a car. Young housewives had bicycles and their husbands used to take them to the shops at the weekend in the car. Shops would still deliver, and we had deliveries of groceries, greengroceries, meat and bread.'

THE DAILY ROUTINE

Every housewife had her daily routine, even those who were able to have help in the cooking or cleaning. While many tasks have remained much the same over the years, refrigeration has made the daily shop unnecessary and the need to draw every drop of water from a well or a pump has thankfully gone. Bathtime on Saturday night was a family affair, youngsters first, in front of the fire. The day electricity came to the house was indeed a red letter day for the whole family – despite being rationed at first to 25 watt bulbs!

A REGULAR ROUTINE

'Washday was *always* Monday. Ironing was mostly done on a wooden kitchen table covered with a blanket and sheet. Flat irons heated by the fire were gradually replaced by electric irons. Before irons had thermostatic controls the temperature was judged by the judicious and swift application of a wet fingertip – the sharper the hissing noise, the hotter the iron. If the fingerprint showed, and no hissing sound, use for wool. An alternative method was to hold the iron about an inch from one's face, and an experienced laundress could tell exactly whether it was suitably heated for the fabric.

Darning was a regular Tuesday chore. Most socks were hand knitted in the 1920s and very vulnerable. There was daily dusting of every room and a regular weekly routine for thorough cleaning of every room. Vacuum cleaners gradually replaced Ewbank carpet sweepers and stiff brushes for the cleaning of carpets. Blacklead was used to polish grates and "Ideal" boilers, and the back step was scrubbed twice a week.

Baking also had its regular day, often Friday. Meals were usually very predictable, the only variation being due to seasonal changes. Pre-war school children had a fairly long dinner "hour" (no school meal) allowing them time to get home for their main meal of the day.

A typical week's dinner menus for middle class might have been:

Sunday	Roast
Monday	Cold meat, bubble and squeak
Tuesday	Shepherd's Pie
Wednesday	Sausages
Thursday	Stew
Friday	Fish
Saturday	Ham.'

'The daily life of the family as I grew up in Croydon in the 1920s was very humdrum by today's standards. A weekly wash took place on Monday. On Tuesday it was ironed. The downstairs housework was done on Wednesday and Thursday, and baking, shopping and bedroom cleaning took place on Friday and Saturday. Meat and perishables were fetched daily, there being no refrigerators in the home, just a cool, walk-in pantry. Milk often curdled in hot weather, and to prevent this the milk was boiled. The diet was equally monotonous. Roast on Sunday – beef or lamb (chicken was for Christmas or when you were ill). Cold joint on Monday with bubble and squeak. For the rest of the week the joint was minced and made into cottage pie, or there was mutton stew, always with pearl barley and sometimes dumplings. Sometimes a steak and kidney pudding. Sausages were suspect and rarely eaten. Desserts, then called puddings, consisted mainly of milk puddings, jam roly poly or stewed fruit and custard.'

'My mother had been trained by her German step-mother in all the finer details of what a housewife should know and she was determined that, although I was at boarding school in the 1920s, I should not miss out on such valuable knowledge. Every room in our house at New Malden was turned out once a week, fire grates blackened, every bit of brass or silver polished, damp cloth taken over every glass surface, including pictures. All upholstery was brushed.

The regular daily chores were the worst; knives were not stainless and so blackened with every use; the front doorstep had to be whitened daily, and the kitchen was even worse! Food was cooked with much more fat than nowadays and this made washing up a real penance because there were no detergents, only soap, which left a horrid rim of thick grease round the sink or washing up bowl. There were also no rubber gloves in use so hands became revoltingly greasy and smelly and no wonder the teacloths needed boiling in a copper in the wash-house. There were no taps to the copper so all the water had to be carried there and the fire stoked with wood and coal. In those days it was considered wise for the housewife to know first hand how all these details should be dealt with because staff quickly get to know how much you know and their standards are regulated by it.'

HELP IN THE HOUSE

'My father was the village builder at Abinger Common until about the 1930s. With a family of seven children we had a 15 year old girl to come and do the washing up and lay the table and general running about jobs. We had a woman to do the bedrooms, a woman to do the washing once a week, and a woman to do the mending. A man came once a day to pump the water – rain water from the roof went through a sand filter to an underground tank and had to be pumped up into a tank in the roof.'

'Although my parents were what is known as "of moderate means", a special helper came in on Mondays to help with the washing, and we also had a "daily" and a resident cook and house parlourmaid. They wore black or brown dresses in the morning with white aprons and caps, and green, or once, daringly different, burgundy, with ecru aprons and caps in the afternoon. How I loved joining them in the kitchen for lunch when mother went to town (which meant Oxford Street) for a day's shopping.'

LEECHES IN THE WATER

'Our cottage at Bookham just after the First World War was an old wooden place, with just a well with a pump in the garden. It was not unusual to find leeches and frogs in the water. All water had to be boiled and there was a bucket toilet at the bottom of the garden.'

BATH AND BEDTIME

'I was born in Lyons Cottages, just off the Dorking High Street, in a row of little brick houses with a tiny front garden where the mangle with the wooden rollers stood. The tin bath, which hung on the back wall, was brought in every Saturday night for everyone to bath before the fire, the water having been heated in a copper which stood in a corner of the kitchen with a fire underneath fuelled by cardboard boxes from Mann's shop a short distance away. A gas mantle hung from a high shelf above the range, which was polished every week with black Zebra Polish. It was very cosy sitting there on a Saturday night after a bath, eating beans on toast and listening to my mother reading a story. Then it was off to bed with a candle and a flat iron, heated on the stove and wrapped in an old sheet.'

'Being the youngest and only girl, I went in first and then more hot water was added for the boys. Hair was shampooed only occasionally and then rain water was brought in from the butt outside. Hair was regularly brushed every night before bed.'

'In summer crickets would chirp in the hearth of our cottage at Ash in the 1940s.

Baths were taken in a zinc bath tub by the range. The water was heated in large saucepans on the cooker. This meant the stove had to be really roaring so one bathed with care as the side of the metal bath became very hot in front of the fire. We all undressed downstairs as there was no heating upstairs. One became expert at discreet removal of clothes. Nighties were supplemented by bedsocks and shawls. A candle lit our way to bed. My sister and I shared a room at the top of the stairs. This had a sloping floor made of wide planks that sagged between the heavy beams of the downstairs ceiling. At night mice slid about. One heard the delicate scatching of their feet, then the noise of them slipping on the uneven floor.

Opposite our two beds was the smoking ham cupboard, connected to the chimney of the range below. The door to the cupboard was made from four or five wide planks of wood. These had worn away at top and bottom over the 500 or so years of the cottage's life. It was very draughty. The candle flickered and we snuggled down wrapped in shawls, our feet on the hot wrapped bricks that we'd heated in the oven. One never put on clothes from the bedrooms without airing them first. They had to be re-ironed in any case as the damp made them full of crinkly creases. The ironing was done by flat irons heated on the stove and rubbed on the large block of washing soap, this made the garments smooth and shining.'

GOING ELECTRIC

'Although our house in Merstham was built in 1924, all the others in the road were late Victorian and lit by gas. No electricity cable had been laid so we were lit by gas too. This is a bit of an exaggeration, as only the downstairs rooms had gas and in the two bedrooms and the bathroom we had to use candles or a little paraffin lamp.

In 1932 all the householders were notified that a main electricity cable would be laid in the road and anyone who wished could be connected. Each house would be allowed six ceiling fittings and one wall socket – any more would overload the cable. Payment would be made through the meter for the next six years; this was included in the shillings which were put in the slot every week. We decided to have the six ceiling lights in the kitchen, the living room, the sitting room, both bedrooms and the stairs. We would still have to make do with candles in the bathroom – anyhow, it was dangerous to have electricity where there was a lot of water! The one wall socket, a little two pin affair, was to go in the sitting room as eventually we might have an electric fire.

One day a gang of workmen arrived with pickaxes and dug a trench the whole length of the road, then each house had its own little trench sprouting from the main trench. From the air this must have looked like a giant fish's backbone. The cable had to enter each house at the nearest point to the main so everyone's front room had a board about a yard square fixed to the wall and screwed to this were two large metal boxes, one black and one green. The black one was the meter and I know the green one was important because it was sealed with little lead discs. It didn't enhance the decor in any way, nor did the conduits which enclosed the actual wires. They were black metal pipes which were secured by brackets to the walls, across the ceilings and up the staircase, and in no circumstances were they to be covered or painted. After all, they would technically be the property of the electricity company for the next six years.

About a month later the final connection was to be made. I remember running home from school that afternoon to see if it had really happened. Electric light was still a novelty, even the school and the shops were lit by gas and so were the street lamps. Dangling from the kitchen ceiling was a flex, a flat white shade like a coolie's hat and 25 watt bulb. This was the standard for all fittings, but later we daringly replaced the living room bulb with a 40 watt one. I pushed down the little brown switch and the room was flooded with light. It was like magic. No more matches, no more little chains to pull up and down to adjust the brightness and no more delicate gas mantles which would crumble if they were inadvertently touched. Everyone became interested in the sixpenny coloured shades in Woolworths and most people changed their white sitting room shade for one which gave a more cosy appearance.

I can never understand why there weren't more accidents. My mother acquired a Trojan electric iron and a Goblin cylinder vacuum cleaner, but to use either of these she had to remove the light bulb from its socket and plug the iron or cleaner in instead. The tiny two pin wall socket had no earth wire but fortunately it never caused any problems.

The six repayment years were completed just before the war so the conduits could be painted to match the wallpaper and a little cupboard was built round the meter board. It was not until the 1950s however that the conduits were finally removed and the wires chased into the walls.

Today in the same little house there are at least two lights in every room, even the larder and the cupboard under the stairs have their lights. There are about 20 wall sockets and two dozen electrical appliances to keep me warm, freeze my food, clean my carpets, wash my clothes, dry my hair, entertain me and so on. I am grateful for all of them, but none can give me the same thrill as when an excited seven year old ran all the way home, pushed down a switch and filled a room with light for the first time.'

'We had our first TV in 1958, rented. In 1955 I used to hire a Hoover washing machine for an hour a week at the cost of two shillings and sixpence. We purchased our first washing machine, a small Hoover Mark 1, in 1958. I had my first Hoover vacuum cleaner in 1957.'

'Our house was one of the first to be electrified in Addlestone and my father then had a frigidaire for his meat. Until then great blocks of ice were delivered by the ice man each week.'

THE RENT MONEY

'When I was old enough to walk the three miles into the town, in the 1930s, I would take our rent money to the landlord. Our house belonged to the Wey Navigation. I can see now the musty office that one stepped down into, with its tall desks and thick ledgers. I never saw the writing in the ledgers but I am sure it would have been copperplate, as the rent book was beautifully receipted.'

WASHDAY

Washday remains in the memory for the sheer drudgery which women faced every week, as they fetched the water, boiled the

copper, washed the clothes, rinsed them and starched them, put them through the mangle, and dried them – hopefully it was a sunny day. Then the whole lot had to be ironed with a flat iron, or later a gas iron, and the next week the toil began all over again.

SUNDAY/MONDAY

'When I was a child, in the mid 1920s, any contrast between the "gracious living" of Sunday and the "hard labour" of washday Monday was not apparent to me.

Sundays brought best clothes from the wardrobes for the morning church service and the leisurely day ahead but these were rarely seen again until the following Sunday. For women and girls hats were the order of the day, bare heads in any church being forbidden. A photograph of my mother and me sitting on a grassy bank during a Sunday afternoon walk, submerged beneath cloche type hats, shows that this sartorial formality was continued throughout the day.

There were no shops or cinemas open, with the exception of a few newsagents, and certainly in my home no serious gardening or DIY activities took place on the Sabbath.

The day of rest concluded with an evening usually spent in conversation or around the piano with friends and extended family, a day passed in gentle activity but punctuated by a series of meals which by today's standards would be considered gross.

However, a busy day was ahead for the "washer women" of tomorrow who must put away their Sunday best hats and put on colourful bandanas to protect their Marcel waves from the inevitable steam ahead.

The laundry equipment at my mother's disposal comprised the kitchen sink (literally) and a modern gas copper which had recently replaced a built-in brick one heated by a coal fire beneath it. A galvanised iron bath was brought in for the mixing of her "dolly blue" used in the final rinsing of her whites and last, but certainly not least, a huge wooden mangle stood in the garage. Since all the bed linen and towels were home laundered, also blankets and curtains at spring cleaning time, this was indeed an essential item.

The final drying operation was not only time consuming but frustrating on wet days when indoor lines had to be improvised or the clothes stored away in baskets to await a dry day. One tends to remember the good things in life more readily and my memories are of the sweet smelling dried washing as it came in from the sunshine to be folded and put away.

A simple evening meal sufficed on Mondays after which my mother hastily tidied herself prior to singing madrigals with the local town choir – no relaxing with TV for her!'

POSS-TUB AND POSS-STICK

'Washday in about 1918 started on Sunday night when the copper in the corner of the scullery was filled from the one and only cold tap in the house. On Monday morning before going to his work, about 7 am, my father had lit the fire under the copper and pulled out into the yard the heavy wood "poss-tub". By breakfast time the water in the copper was bubbling hot. The hot water was then ladled into the tub and bar soap was shredded into it. Meanwhile the copper was refilled and the fire stoked up. Clothes had been carefully sorted, white cotton ones to be washed first, which was done with a "poss-stick". The cottons were put back into the copper and boiled, then put through a blue rinse, this in the large stone sink in the scullery, then starched. I can still remember the smell of boiling clothes when we came home from school at twelve o'clock for our dinners.

The washing process must have been repeated several times, involving the tipping out into an outside drain of the wood tub, and putting of all the clothes through the large wooden rollered mangle.

When we arrived home from school at four o'clock the washing lines were full and the scullery floor, of stone, was being scrubbed.

Next day when we came home from school there were all the starched, sparkling white, pinafores and petticoats ironed and draped over a huge clothes horse to air in front of the big black shining range in the kitchen.'

SORTING THE CLOTHES

'I was born in the year 1910. One of my earliest memories was of washing day, which was usually on a Monday. In those days there was no electricity and some houses had no gas, so all water was heated over a kitchen range and a copper, which was in the scullery. The fire had to be lit, by wood and coal, the copper filled with water from the tap. Clothes to be washed were sorted in piles, sheets and all white linen and cotton articles in one pile, then woollens, handkerchiefs, socks and stockings, and dusters in separate piles. When the water was hot, it was ladled out by a copper dipper. Hudson's soap powder and Sunlight soap were used, articles placed on a scrubbing board and scrubbed, then rinsed in warm water and then in nearly cold. Table-cloths, pillow slips, tray cloths, napkins and handkerchiefs were then rinsed in blue water and after that, with the exception of hankies, were then starched. The woollens were rinsed in fresh water and socks etc followed. Then they were put through a wringing machine to expel the waste water and at last

73

hung out to dry. Then the boiler was cleaned and everything in the scullery scrubbed and washed. Big tin baths were used to wash the washing, in those days the sinks were very narrow. The filling of the boiler for fresh water and emptying of same, as you can imagine, was very tiring. When the clothes were dry they were all folded neatly, ready for ironing the next day.'

'The most abiding memories revolve around the specific chores allocated to particular days of the week; notably Mondays. Mondays were set aside for an entire gamut of necessary chores, and chief among these was the washing. It is perhaps impossible for those born into our present high-tech society to appreciate the complex and lengthy operation this entailed. Firstly, the copper in the kitchen (or scullery) was lit, then sheets and pillowcases were washed and scrubbed prior to boiling in the copper. In those days bed linen was universally white. Next came the towels and table cloths, followed by the coloureds, which were washed, rinsed, and run through the mangle before being hung out to dry. In their turn came any woollens, a veritable mountain of socks, and my father's long johns, vests and so forth. The whites, having benefited from a thorough boil, were rinsed, blued, the table linen starched, and the entire kit and caboodle run through the omni-present mangle.

Needless to recount, the aforementioned procedure occupied the entire morning and a large slice of the afternoon, mother's work interrupted by us children arriving home for a midday meal of cold meat and bubble and squeak – standard Monday fare for most families in those days. And the domestic working day did not finish with the washing, for the water in the copper was further utilised for cleaning the cooker and scrubbing floors; evidence of the "nowt wasted" maxim we practised.

Tuesday was a day for ironing, and I clearly recall my mother being immensely proud when the family budget stretched to the acquisition of a gas iron, a massive appliance with the gas audibly popping away inside, but a vast improvement, I dare say, on the cumbersome and basic flat iron.'

FOOD AND DRINK

Most people living in the Surrey countryside grew their own vegetables and fruit, made their own wine, bought dairy products direct from the farm, and many kept chickens and a pig. The killing of the pig provided a welcome addition to the diet, the bounty often being shared in the village before the days of refrigeration.

KILLING THE PIG

'We always had a pig in a sty at our homes in Badshot Lea in the 1920s, and we also had chickens. When we had a pig killed, Mother used to make lard out of what she called the "flay". It was cut up in pieces and rendered down into lard. This used to be put into basins and the skin that was round the flay was put into boiling water. This would soften it so that it could be stretched over the basins to keep the air out. The remains after the lard had been strained off, she called scraps. With them she made a kind of mincemeat with sultanas and fruit. We children used to enjoy the scrap pie she made with it. When we lived in the house with running water, we used to make our own chitterlings . . . *not* our favourite job! The insides of the pig were held under the cold water tap to drain all the muck out of them. Then the next day Mother turned them inside out and gave them another good wash. After a thorough cleansing they would be cut into lengths and plaited, then boiled. When cold they were fried. My father was the only one who ate them. . . . I guess he was at work when they were being made!

When we moved into the farmhouse, we made our own bacon. My father made a wooden tray, big enough to take a side of bacon. This had a drain hole in it. Block salt was mixed with a couple of ounces of salt-petre. This was rubbed into the flesh of the side, and was allowed to drain away. It got rid of the blood. Then it was rubbed with just plain salt for about ten days. It was then dried off and rubbed with pea flour. Meanwhile the oak sawdust would be got ready, and the fire all ready to start. My father rigged some gear up the chimney to hang the side on. In about ten days or a fortnight it would be ready. My mother also cooked the pig's tongue and pressed it. The old saying was "one could use all of a pig except his squeak!"

When the harvest had been gathered in at the farm opposite, we were allowed to pick up any ears of corn that had been dropped. Sometimes we had enough to feed the hens for almost a year – until harvest time came round again. When my mother did the chickens to sell, the birds would be starved for a day before killing. Then mother would prepare them in the usual way, but she always used the feet as well. She would pour boiling water over them and after a few minutes we could scrape off the outer skin. It wasn't until a couple of customers had given the feet back that she stopped doing them for sale.'

'Before the First World War most people in Brockham kept pigs and chickens and folk went from door to door collecting peelings and food rubbish from people who hadn't got a pig. When the pig was big enough, they brought it to my father, the butcher, to be slaughtered, for which he charged one shilling and sixpence. Chitterlings, the pig's intestines, were cleaned, cooked, and hawked around the village in a barrow.'

'When a pig was killed we used to have the huge white body hung on a hook in the ceiling beams of our scullery, and it could be a very nasty experience to dash out there in the dark and run into it. This was of course before electric light was brought to our part of the countryside. I cannot remember how they got the bristles off or whether they had help to joint the animal but I do remember the smoke hole. This seemed then to be a very tall building and was about eight ft square. The hams and other joints to be smoked were hung around the sides, while oak sawdust smouldered on the floor in the middle. Parts of the pig not suitable for this treatment were distributed around the village. There were only nine houses at Merle Common at that time. Everyone kept chickens and several families had goats which were tethered on the common.'

'At about the time of the First World War, Mr Abrehart of Peaslake had a day of pig killing and was a little the worse for wear at the end of the day from drinking the home-made wines. The pigs were kept behind the cottages at Holmbury on common land, and provided us with pork, lard, bacon and brawn, the bacon being cured in the old chimneys.'

HOME MADE WINES AND BEER

'My mother always made her own wine before the Second World War. Rationing put a stop to this, as the large quantities of sugar necessary were not available.

Wine was for high days and holidays only, so it was not surprising that it quickly went to the head or legs, and that it had the reputation of having "a kick like a mule". There were no short cuts in those days (no wine-making kits) and the ingredients had to be gathered the hard way, from the fields, hedgerows and gardens. Cowslips, dandelions, elderflower and elderberry, parsnips, and gooseberries for wine; nettle beer and sloe gin, and blackberry vinegar.

I remember the faintly "boozy" smell of the spare bedroom where the wine was kept in large earthenware crocks, with slices of toast with the yeast on floating on the top. When it was eventually bottled it was not unknown for there to be a loud explosion – often in the middle of the night – when a bottle "worked".

One year she decided to make rhubarb wine, and had the bright idea of taking a short cut and extracting the juice by putting the sticks of rhubarb through the mangle. Not a good idea, as it turned out, as the acid in the rhubarb rotted the wooden rollers!'

'My mother used to make parsnip beer instead of parsnip wine – it meant she added yeast and hops. My brothers-in-law could get drunk on it but mother didn't even taste it; she didn't like the smell of it even though she made it. We never knew how she got it perfect.'

'My mother brewed her own beer . . . until some blew out the bung and she had to sit with her hand over the bunghole until we children came home from school. That was the end of that!'

'We had an elderberry tree in the garden and my mother made wine. We went blackberrying to make jam and wine, and at midday when the dandelions were in full bloom we picked baskets of these for wine making. Mother would toast some bread, boil the fruit and place yeast on the top of the bread, which was then put into a stone crock to work. It was then bottled and put in the larder under the stairs. Most years there was a terrific bang from the cupboard when we were sitting quietly, as the wine exploded, blowing the corks off.'

SELF SUFFICIENCY

'We had no dustbin, neither was there a refuse collection in Worplesdon Hill in the 1920s and early 1930s.

All the ashes from the fires were saved. The large cinders made up the paths, the fine ash was reserved as a slug deterrent around vulnerable plants. Newspapers and scrap paper were kept to light the fires. Very few goods came wrapped.

My mother did not go out to shop regularly; almost everything was delivered to the door. Milk was measured straight from the milkman's churn into our jug, seven days a week; and bread, unwrapped, onto the kitchen table six days a week. The grocer delivered his goods weekly, taking the next week's order away with him. The ironmonger also came weekly; here you walked up into his van and made your selection of soap, polish, paraffin etc.

Dozens of eggs were delivered from a poultry farm in the spring. They were then placed carefully in galvanized buckets full of isinglass to preserve them.

My father was a clever gardener, and our large garden made us quite independent of the greengrocers. We had the fruit and vegetables in their seasons. Clamps were made to store the root crops, runner beans were salted down into large crock jars, and soft fruit to spare was made into jams and bottled in Kilner jars. We also had a large store for apples and pears. All the peelings and garden waste was put on the compost heap. We had no mains drainage so the crops in the dry weather were irrigated with the pumped out cesspit water.

When my mother did go into either Woking or Guildford she would buy fruit such as bananas, oranges and lemons. I remember wooden boxes of wrapped tangerines, but these only at Christmas time. Grapes were a great luxury, and usually reserved for the sick.

Occasionally we opened a tin of food – Canadian pink salmon (very cheap then) or a tin of tomatoes. Golden syrup also came in tins – these tins have changed hardly at all. They made, when empty, good containers for nails etc. The other tins were mostly hammered flat and used to block a hole in one of the sheds; a piece of flat metal could be put to many uses. Almost everything was recycled.'

'On our farm near Lingfield in the 1920s, I can remember my mother "dry cleaning" my three older sisters' school skirts, box pleated navy serge, by dipping them in a bowl of petrol. This was done in the garden and the skirts then hung up to dry.

My father reared geese for the Christmas market, and mother made all the down into pillows – some we still have. The down was put into old ticks and baked for hours in a cool oven to sterilise it, then made into cushions and pillows. The geese were sold oven-ready for about ten shillings each.'

FISH AND CHIPS

'Friday night was fish and chip night. Before the First World War my friend's mother drove to Gomshall station from Holmbury in her horse and trap, fetched a box of wet fish, took it to the stream by the Compasses, gutted and washed it, and the village had its fish and chips. My sister remembered it as excellent.'

MILK, BUTTER AND CHEESE

'Our house was in an ideal spot, within easy walking distance of Guildford town but surrounded by fields and farmlands. Our milk was delivered each morning in a large milk urn with its gill and pint measure clipped to the side, and we had our own jugs ready to receive the rich creamy milk fresh from the farm at the end of the lane. It was safeguarded from flies and dust by being covered with beaded muslin covers and placed in the roomy cool larder where all the food was stored, meat going into a wire mesh safe.'

'We moved to Gaterounds Farm, Newdigate in 1924. My job was to make the butter. I had to turn the heavy churn around, sometimes for an hour before the the butter came, and then pat it into half pound blocks and deliver round the village for two shillings a pound. Everyone in those days was so friendly, I would walk around the lanes and the old men in their gardens would stop and have a chat.'

'In the 1930s cheese was relatively cheaper than today and was eaten quite a lot. You had bread and cheese, or bread and butter, but not butter and cheese together!'

GLEANING

'In 1947 Shepperton was still a village with lots of farms. On Friday evenings in late summer, my dad would take my sister and me in our home-made barrow (an old wooden box on two old pram wheels) to a local farm in Charlton village to go gleaning. Gleaning was going into the fields after harvest and collecting all the straw and corn that was left. Nowadays they burn it! What a waste. We loved these outings, first the ride in the barrow (we had to take turns), then the time spent supposedly filling the sack with straw and picking up the ears of corn, rubbing them between our palms then blowing off the chaff. Given the chance we would pop the corn into our mouths instead of into the bag. Dad never got cross, just let us enjoy ourselves with the other children there.

After about two hours it was along to The Harrow, a little very old thatched pub with seats outside. Here we had ginger beer in stone bottles and sometimes a giant arrowroot biscuit. Then the walk home as the barrow was full with a sack of straw and bag of corn. Our chickens did appreciate all our hard work.'

SUNDAY DINNER

'Before the First World War my father would purchase sixpenny-worth of bones from the butcher in Redhill, add butter beans and simmer on the open fire overnight. This was our Sunday dinner – and delicious.'

'Sunday dinner at my grandparents' home at Burpham was always roast and a suet pudding was made – a slice for the meat course and one or two with treacle for the dessert.'

DOING THE SHOPPING

It was once possible to do all your shopping without carrying home a single thing. Local shops took your order and delivered to your door every week, while 'shopping on approval' allowed you to try clothes on at home and have the ones you didn't want returned to the shop.

THE BUTCHER, THE BAKER . . .

'Shopping seems to be a dominant feature of the 1930s. I can well remember a young man coming to our house once a week, sitting in the kitchen while mother dictated her grocery requirements for the following week. Queueing and trolleys were not known then. The butcher called every day, as did the baker with a never to be forgotten smell of freshly baked bread under a cloth, with an array of loaves for mother's choice. If we as children were around the cry went up for a "Coburg" – then we all got a crust! The milkman called twice a day with his can and one pint measure, or half pint as required, and the greengrocer came twice a week. All the tradesmen were paid once a month.'

'When my parents moved into their first home, traders made it their business to inform them where their various shops were, hoping they could recruit a customer at the same time. The baker called with a covered, hand pushed cart at first, though this later became a horse-drawn cart. The milkman delivered milk from an open cart. The local corner shop was a branch of a shop in Richmond. Initially, a young man would come round and ask for an order at the door and mother would hand it to him. It would then be delivered by bicycle. After the Second World War they used a little van for deliveries after having received an order over the telephone. One settled the bill in person at the shop next time.'

'In the 1920s tradesmen called at your door. At Thornton Heath the milkman called twice a day, once early morning so that you had fresh milk for breakfast (no fridges then!) and again later in the day when you could also buy butter, eggs, cream etc from him. He drove a horse and cart. The baker called every day, pulling a two wheeled covered cart, bringing a large two compartment basket to your door, one side full of assorted loaves, the other all kinds of cakes and pastries. The butcher called for your order and then delivered, the grocer called to collect his money and your fresh order which was delivered next day, the greengrocer came round with his horse and cart two or three times a week, the oil and hardware man came once a week also with a horse and cart. The fishman came round with a kind of 'stop me and buy one' tricycle. If you wanted him to call you put an 'F' up in your window. Shopping seemed a lot easier then.

There was the other side of the coin. Unemployed and ex-servicemen used to come round in ones or groups, singing in the streets for the odd coppers which would be thrown to them. Then there were the hawkers who knocked on the door to sell you things and young men trying to sell vacuum cleaners. Most front gates had a plate fixed to them which read 'No Hawkers, No Circulars, No Canvassers.'

WINKLES AND WHELKS

'Sunday afternoons the muffin man would come round Wallington carrying a large wooden tray on his head. He would be followed by the winkle man. He sold winkles by the pint, for which my dad placed a standing order, and my young sister and I would "winkle" them out from their shells using a pin, making sure to remove their little black caps. They would then be liberally sprinkled with pepper, salt and vinegar and, with thin slices of bread and butter, Dad would have them for tea.'

'Edna's father was a Kingston fishmonger who delivered with a horse and cart, but used a trap in summer. Edna used to be picked up at school in the spring to be taken to Claygate to pick primroses, the horse walking through the Hogsmill stream at the watersplash on the way. Her father was well-known for his shell-fish and Edna had to hurry home from school to prepare the whelks and mussels and take the orders out before school – her father having described which house to go to by the colour of its curtains and painted front door.'

THE COALMAN

'Coal at two shillings and sixpence a hundredweight was delivered weekly in Wallington by a man with a horse and cart. Although he called for a number of years I never knew his real name, he was always referred to as "Sugar" by everyone.'

'I can remember my mother exclaiming in horror one day when the coal cart came through the road. "Good Heavens, the coal has gone up again. Just look at that. It is two shillings and sixpence a hundredweight!".'

SHOPPING ON APPROVAL

'Before the Second World War we used to drive to Guildford to shop. Mother would park the Austin Seven outside White's or Harvey's.
    Inside one of the shops she would choose coats and dresses for me, or for herself. A small selection of suitable ones would be wrapped in tissue paper and boxed up to be taken home. Once there she and father together could make a final choice.
    Next morning Mr Wicks, the local carrier, would call at our door for those not wanted and return them to the shop, packed as before. The cost of those kept would be added to father's account. This was "shopping on approval".'

A BONUS TO FETCH IT YOURSELF

'At Bramley we had the baker coming round and from Guildford the bigger stores like International would deliver once a week. If they didn't deliver there was a local fellow who called himself a carrier who had a cart and he would collect your goods from the shops. We had a fishman, who would push a cart round the village. My mother always walked into Guildford and during the Second World War she would bring the goods home in a pushchair once a week.

82

In those days the International Stores would allow her a ten shilling bonus on her goods because she fetched them herself.'

MARKET DAY

'In the 1920s some areas were too isolated for bus transport and a van used to take the residents to market on the weekly market day. It was tarpaulin-covered, with solid tyres, so by no means luxurious. Some of the passengers would be taking their own produce, so they sat on wooden benches or planks, facing each other, putting their goods – eggs, vegetables or fruit according to the season – underneath their seats. Sometimes the van was so heavily laden that it was necessary for the people to get out and help push when they got to a particularly steep hill. The road surfaces were very rough and stony with very little tar to stabilise the surface. On reaching the market town they would dispose of their wares and then proceed to get their weekly purchases, either at the market stalls or in the shops in town.'

'On a Saturday afternoon (in those days men worked on Saturday mornings) it was my grandfather's invariable custom to take his attache case and go "down the town" on the tram. On the occasions when we children were taken into Croydon for Saturday shopping we might meet him in the market. Croydon's market is now a dull place of fruit and vegetable stalls, but before the war it was magical, especially in the winter, when the stalls were lit by hissing naptha flares. Although we never patronised it, I can still smell the stall which sold tiny saucers of shellfish and jellied eels, with the customers standing round sucking their fingers. There was a lovely home-made sweet stall, where you could buy all sorts of boiled sweets which would stick together in the bag in a great gorgeous tasty mass before you had time to eat them. How insipid and boring today's hygienically wrapped and boxed apologies seem by comparison. The other great delight of the market was the sarsaparilla man. How could you describe him to a modern child, used to slurping "coke" out of a can? My recollection is of a huge machine, all dark red and gold, with burnished taps, from which the brown liquid was drawn frothing into a glass tumbler which was afterwards rinsed for re-use. Was it rinsed in a bucket, or had the wonder machine got a special washing-up sink as an integral part of it? I rather think it had, but childhood memory plays strange tricks. But there can be no mistake about the joy if Grandpa bought us a glass of sarsaparilla.'

THE FLOWER LADY

'Weekly in the 1930s we had a short, but exceedingly round, lady, brown faced and rosy cheeked with a gorgeous smile, who carried a circular basket, nearly as big as herself, full of wonderful cut flowers. Somehow she held the weight of the basket on one arm or shoulder. She travelled on a red double decker bus from Richmond to Petersham, two miles. She eventually gave up this travelling but could still be found in Richmond itself selling in one or two places.'

PRICES

'During the First World War my mother-in-law had 16 shillings a week to keep two adults and four children, out of which she had to pay four shillings rent. My housekeeping for the first year of married life was £2 a week, ten shillings for rent and two shillings and sixpence for electricity and gas.

In the 1920s we could buy reels of Sylko for a penny each, or two for a penny ha'penny. In 1935 I used to buy Morley's silk stockings, fully fashioned seconds, at a small haberdashery shop in Guildford for two shillings and elevenpence ha'penny.

In 1936 when I moved from Burpham to Guildford the Blue Saloon Buses ran a half hourly service, the General Buses from Kingston and the Green Line from London to Guildford. The fare was twopence and the services could be relied on.

My grandmother's house was sold in the 1950s for £220. Recently it was sold for £80,000.'

WHAT WE WORE

In the days before central heating layers of clothes were a necessary part of life and comfort was not high on the list of essentials – though hats were. Once no one would have dreamed of leaving the house without a hat, man or woman. Mother made most of the family's clothes, out of necessity, unless she was lucky or wealthy enough to have a "little dressmaker" to undertake the chore for her.

LAYERS OF CLOTHES

'When I was young at the beginning of the century in Thornton Heath, houses were cold and we wore layers of clothes. I remember stays and several petticoats – a flannel one and one trimmed with lace. Knickers too had lace frills. Little girls wore pinafores. Out of doors we always wore hats and gloves, and mufflers in winter. For special occasions I had a sealskin muff hung on a cord around my neck. We wore button boots which had to be done up with a buttonhook. When I went to work I wore a long skirt to the ground. This had a braided fringe which collected the mud from the road and had to be regularly brushed with a stiff brush. All our clothes were made at home by my mother or a "little dressmaker" – there were no shops to buy readymades. I put my hair up when I was about 17, but had it "bobbed" when the fashion came in. For many years I kept my cut-off hair in a crash bag.'

'I started school in Whyteleafe in the 1930s, and my main memory is of having to wear combinations and discovering how hazardous it was trying to spend a penny. It took me hours to get out of them – and there wasn't always that much time to spare! What with that, and the flannel on my chest, and a large mohair scarf crossed over my chest and fastened at the back with a safety pin, life was quite difficult.'

'The older generation were not as liberated as the young "Flappers" in the 1920s. The ladies wore bloomers and combinations with buttons, liberty bodices and corsets with suspenders, garters and woollen stockings, button boots, gloves and veils, and always an overall for work. The men wore long-johns and vests, day and night, breeches and leather knee-high gaiters. Flat caps and bowler hats for special occasions, also trilbys and panamas, gloves and spats. Farm workers wore "whirlers" tied under their knees to stop rats running up their trousers. Walking sticks and parasols were popular.

Babies were tightly wrapped in binders to stop their navels protruding. Their gowns were very long.

Elderly men in flat caps sat on the seat by the forge in Chiddingfold, chatting and passing the time away.'

HATS

'When I was small, everyone wore a hat when going out. Girl children started by wearing bonnets, then hats with an elastic under the chin, straw or panama in summer and velour or felt in the winter.

Boys wore felt hats and often sailor caps. School children wore a hat with a band, or a cap of their school colours. Unluckily, people then knew which school you went to if you misbehaved.

At the beginning of the century ladies wore very large hats with wide brims, decorated with flowers, fruit or feathers and even life size birds. The hats were secured by hatpins into their hair which, being long, was piled on the top of their heads. About 1920 when the shingle hairstyle came this was no longer possible so the fitting cloche hat was worn.

In each town would be milliners, to whom ladies would go to choose a hat or have a hat made to match their outfits, or even have an old hat remodelled and retrimmed. They now seem almost extinct. Men for informal occasions wore soft felt hats with a dent in the crown, called a trilby, or tweed caps. If they worked in a town or up in London a bowler hat was required.

Then there was the top hat, now only seen at weddings or Ascot. My father, who was a hatter in Bond Street, went up to town wearing a top hat until he died in 1939. He was a familiar sight at East Croydon station. My sister and I felt very proud when we walked to the station with him on our way to school. Mostly he wore a black top hat, but if the weather was very settled in the summer he would sport a grey topper.

I think the car must take a lot of responsibility for the decline of the hat; they made getting in and out of a saloon car more difficult and during the war clothing coupons could not be spared for a hat.'

WELL DRESSED

'My sister and I as youngsters in Oxshott in the 1930s were dressed in hand-made dresses and knitted jumpers and cardigans. Mother used to buy material from Harrods and John Lewis. For a time she bought our winter coats there as well. They had little velvet collars. "Chilprufe" was another type of coat she bought for us. We also wore leggings, fabric or knitted ones, when it was cold. When I reached 14 I had a broderie anglaise white cotton blouse to go with a full three-tiered bright red skirt my mother had made me, which I wore over a three-tiered white skirt slip decorated with broderie anglaise. I made a black and white checked cotton full circular skirt as an alternative and used a firm wide red fabric belt to pull me in round the waist for maximum effect!'

'The fashion I remember my mother wearing in the summer in the 1930s was an edge to edge coat and large cartwheel straw hat. She had her hair henna-ed with a Marcel Wave. My mother made most

86

of her clothes and mine. She used to tell me the story of how she saved for her sewing machine by missing the odd lunch and putting away the shilling until she had enough money – £5 at that time.'

GRANDMOTHER'S CLOTHES

'My grandmother wore a black skirt and a flannel petticoat, and a cotton petticoat with a tape around her waist with a drawstring bag that had the odd sweet or penny in for the children. She also had corsets that supported the bust, and these were heavily boned. Her morning blouse was navy blue and white and her apron the same, and she had a black sateen apron for afternoon. When she was older and had rheumatoid arthritis, we used to take her out in a wickerwork bath chair with three wheels, two at the back and one at the front with a rod and a handle for the occupant to guide it.'

'My granny never wore anything but black, with a little bit of white lace around the neck, and fastened with a heavy silver circular brooch. Her long full skirt reached to the ground and just inside the hem was tacked a kind of braid, with a fluffy edge, to sweep the floor and protect the hem from wear.'

IN SICKNESS AND IN HEALTH

In the days when the doctor was called only in dire emergency, most everyday ills were treated with home-made remedies or patent medicines, often remembered with disgust today. Perhaps the cure was so awful it was better to soldier on through minor illness! Sometimes, though, serious illnesses struck, and memories of scarlet fever and smallpox are particularly common. The treatment suffered by small children sounds almost inhuman today. 'When I fell in the playground I cut my head on the wall. It needed six stitches – "children don't feel pain" they said, so there were no painkillers,' remembered one woman.

'Thick woollen vests were often put on, with brown paper over the chest in very cold weather, and these stayed on all winter, often accompanied by the smell of goose grease or camphorated oil.

Treatments were preventive medicines to a large extent – castor oil, cod liver oil and malt, Virol, brimstone and treacle and syrup of figs. Parents had a fiendish delight in seeing that our bowels were kept open. This meant constant visits to outside lavatories, cold, dark, complete with spiders, mice, daddy long legs, plants, and the cut up newspaper hanging by string on a hook or nail. There were also socks filled with salt and heated till warm and placed around sore throats, and boiled onions placed in ears to cure a bad earache.'

'I once put my finger in the cogs of the mangle and nearly lost the tip. My aunt put on lily leaves that had been soaked in a special mixture, and it was tied up and left for several days. It healed but it has never been quite straight at the top.'

'I suffered from travel sickness as a child in the 1940s and there didn't seem to be any cure, other than sucking barley sugar which I didn't like. My mother was told to wrap me up in brown paper and sit me on brown paper as well, then I would feel alright. The brown paper had to be next to my skin and I did itch and prickle! This was done faithfully each time we went for a journey on the bus, and I was very embarrassed as the paper crackled every time I moved.'

'We knew we were really quite "poorly" if we were kept in bed *and* a coal fire was lit in the little cast-iron grate in the bedroom. The ultimate in luxury and cosseting. Bowls of beef tea, hot milk – and if you were really unwell, jars of Calves Foot Jelly (port wine flavour was best) and Brands essence of chicken from the chemist were the delicacies to tempt the invalid palate.

My mother told dire tales of chesty children in her youth being larded with goose grease, and then sewn into their undergarments. Another faithful friend was a piece of red flannel warmed on the fireguard to soothe aches and pains. It had to be red, evidently – white wasn't the same! Poultices – both kaolin and bread poultices – were liberally applied, hot, to "draw out" infections. Brown paper soaked in vinegar really was used in the old days for both headaches and black eyes. A large cold key down the back stopped a nose bleed.

Warts and their cure were one of life's little mysteries. Folk magic came to the fore and the remedies were many, and often bizarre. It was alleged that if a piece of raw meat was buried in the garden, by the time the meat rotted the wart would drop off! Children would be taken to the gas works to take deep breaths to cure whooping cough. Dock leaves, then as now, were the antidote to nettle stings, and wild comfrey – known as "knitbone" – was wrapped round the affected joint as a cure for sprains; witch hazel was used for bruises, and oil of cloves to soothe an aching tooth.

Coughs and colds brought out a variety of remedies, many including the use of honey. My mother made blackberry vinegar to relieve coughs and sore throats. Her recipe was: pour one pint cider vinegar onto one quart blackberries. Store in an earthenware jar for a week, stirring each day. Strain off the juice and bring to the boil with half a pound of honey and a pound of granulated sugar. Stir until the honey is dissolved. Bottle when cool. Sip slowly, a teaspoonful at a time, to relieve coughs.'

'Among many patent medicines were Iodine Lockets, which were suspended by a tape around the neck and were supposed to ward off all ills. They were sold by Boots. After a bath in front of the fire we were rubbed with three oils, two of which were camphor and cloves. I also had a square of camphor inserted in a little cotton pocket in my woollen vest. Liquorice powder or syrup of figs was administered on Friday nights.'

THE TOOTH PULLER

'My grandfather, Frederick Brooker, was born in 1876 in Merstham. He lived in a pretty cottage in School Hill with his six sisters and one brother and went to the "old" school in Quality Street which is a now a private house. His father was a gardener and every week my grandfather and his brother and sisters would load a cart with garden produce and push it to Redhill to sell. He had many memories of his childhood, but the one which always fascinated me was his story of "The Tooth Puller".

Every year a Fair was held in Quality Street (as it is to this present day) and he would, in company of his friends, go to it although it is doubtful that he had any money to spend.

Among the many stalls and booths was a cart belonging to Mr Farquahar, the Tooth Puller who had a board which offered "painless extractions"! The luckless patient would sit in a chair on the cart, and watched by the crowds would have his tooth extracted. This involved a little help from his assistant who was equipped with a trumpet, who at the critical moment as the tooth was drawn, would blow very loudly on his trumpet to drown the cries of the patient.

The tooth would be held up for inspection and then tossed into the crowd. A truly painless extraction!'

SCARLET FEVER

'In 1928 I went down with "tonsillitis", had a week off school and then went back. Then mother had the same thing, two days later so did my father. The next week my brother had the same sore throat – but he had a fever too. Scarlet fever was diagnosed and he was isolated in his bedroom, with a sheet across the doorway. A few days later I started to peel. When the doctor saw this he went into the hall and shouted up the stairs, "Graham, you can come down, the whole family's got it." So started six weeks of total isolation. Our doctor stayed an hour, writing letters for us – to my father's firm, to Graham's firm, to my school, to mother's sister to let all the family know.

The tradesmen continued to deliver what we ordered, although we had to run up bills for the six weeks. No one else called on us except the vicar, who put on a white coat as he crossed the threshold. He brought us strawberries and raspberries and cream! Another visitor was a lady Christian Scientist friend. Each time the doctor called he would say, "Has that d. . . woman caught it yet?" But, of course, she didn't. Many neighbours crossed the street rather than pass our front gate, and the next door folk went indoors every time we appeared in the garden.

On the last day we all went out for twelve hours – my father and Graham went straight to the hairdresser's! Every window and door was sealed with sticky paper and the house was fumigated, and all our clothes, bedding, books, games etc were taken away for fumigation. When we came back in the evening we opened the door to be met by a terrible smell. The one bonus was that we had no flies, wasps or other insects for at least two years.'

'In December 1927 I, a six year old, was sent home from school on my own feeling very ill. Within two hours I was in Cuddington isolation hospital with scarlet fever. I had to stay for six weeks not knowing where I was or what for. I was allowed one rag doll from home and it was taken away at night. Parents were only allowed on Wednesdays and Sunday afternoons and then not allowed inside. I saw my mother and father through the window and thought they could not find the door. I was slapped because I was making a fuss; so had the awful experience of seeing my mother led away weeping. For Christmas I was sent a box of chocolate Father Christmases, but as all sweets were pooled I never got one. There were only a few battered toys and no one supervised the play. Indeed no one spoke to the children, only to give snappy orders. The nurses were underqualified and over worked. Unseen I rushed out into the snow in my nightie. The next day I went home and soon collapsed with severe jaundice which nearly killed me.

The same epidemic saw my future sister-in-law in the Tooting Graveney Hospital at nine years old with the same unfeeling and inadequate care. She washed her hair in cold water with no heat to dry it, so had pneumonia which kept her in hospital for three months. We have come a long way since those days. Thank God.'
'My memories go back 65 years, to when I became another victim of scarlet fever. I was the youngest of eight, and definitely the baby. Panic stations! To stay at home you had to have carbolic sheets hung everywhere; no-one had to go to school or to work. Needless to say, I ended up in an isolation hospital. Arriving there I had a carbolic bath, then along came a nurse with scissors and clippers – first with the scissors then over and back with the clippers. Saturday arrived, and visitors could only look at you through the windows. I was shouting "Mummy, Mummy!" when suddenly my mother cried "Oh! my God, my child – I didn't know her". My lovely head of blonde curls off – I looked like Convict 99.'

'In 1924 I was taken ill with scarlet fever. The nurse that came to take me to hospital wore a red cloak to warn people her patient had the fever, and I was taken to Staines isolation hospital in a horse drawn ambulance. My father and brothers were not allowed to go to work for three days, and my sister couldn't go to school. The council men came and fumigated the house.

When my parents came to visit me they were not allowed in the hospital, but had to speak to me through the window which made communication very difficult. I can remember the time of year because there were two wards, scarlet fever and diphtheria, with a quadrangle in between, and on Guy Fawkes night there was a bonfire and firework display in the quadrangle, and the patients' beds were pulled to one side of the ward so that all could see the display.'

SMALLPOX, DIPHTHERIA AND POLIO

'Smallpox was a dreaded disease in the early years of this century, most fatal to the young. My grandmother must have been nearly 70 when she had smallpox. She had to remain at home as there was no isolation hospital. No one was allowed in the house, only my mother. All the food was sent up and down by a pulley through the window. There was no doctor in Holmwood then; one had to come riding out from Dorking or Capel, and you had to pay him. I'm glad to say that my grandmother recovered.'

'In 1929 there was an outbreak of diphtheria in the Merrow area, and quite a lot of young people died. My brothers were considered carriers and were put in the isolation hospital, which was at the far end of Dennis Works. I fortunately didn't get it. We had the first ever testing at school to see whether we could catch it or were immune, and I and one other child were the only ones with immunity. After the Second World War we also had a serious outbreak of polio, which affected many children.'

HAVING TONSILS OUT

'I remember during the First World War, our kitchen table being especially prepared for the doctor to use when he removed the tonsils of two of my brothers in our home.'

'I had to go to Great Ormond Street Hospital in the 1930s to have my tonsils out, and can remember coming round and seeing lots of children laying on mattresses on the floor with blood everywhere and many children being sick . . . and being taken home in a taxi.'

THE DOCTOR

'Whilst still at school in the 1920s I had a heart complaint for 18 months, and our doctor at Caterham Hill used to call every Wednesday, which cost five shillings a visit out of the 18 shillings my mother, a widow, drew for a pension (ten shillings for her, five shillings for me and three shillings for my sister). Luckily my mother got a domestic daily job, and she used to sub-let a couple of rooms which helped to pay the 16 shillings and sixpence rent.'

'My father was a family doctor in the 1920–50 period in Wallington. In those days the surgery was at the doctor's home and there were few group practices. This of course meant patients coming to the front door for morning and evening consulting hours and through the day for bottles of medicine made up in the small dispensary. Each bottle was neatly wrapped in white paper and sealed with red wax. There were also frequent phone calls and many is the time I can remember preparing for an outing only for our plans to be rudely shattered by an urgent call – a great disappointment to a child. Even on my wedding day in 1943, the reception was held at home and in the middle of the celebrations a man with a badly cut hand came to the house to be stitched up.

Things must have been very hard during the Depression and also the war years when so many patients were evacuated. I remember helping my father write out his accounts with "an early settlement would oblige" written on the bottom but I am quite sure he never refused to visit a patient who was unable to pay.'

THE DISTRICT NURSE

'In 1925, the year of my twelfth birthday, my mother, a fully trained State Registered Nurse-Midwife, was appointed District Nurse for the parish of Worplesdon and we left London to take up life in the country.

The Worplesdon District Nursing Association was a totally voluntary body (this was before the days of the National Health Service) and was run by a committee of highly dedicated ladies, particularly the Hon Secretary Miss Evelyn Thompson of Perry. It was affiliated to the Surrey County Nurses Association and was subject to their rules and periodic inspection. The money to cover my mother's salary of £200 per annum, paid by a monthly cheque of £16 13s 4d and considered quite a good sum in those days, was raised mainly by annual subscriptions to the Association, graded from one shilling to five shillings according to one's means and/or social standing! Extra money was raised from time to time by the odd jumble sale or bazaar, when one was delighted to raise as much as £20 or £25.

Each week my mother would report to Miss Thompson, pay in any monies she had received (a few pence per call in addition to the subscription) and discuss any matters concerning the patients. Miss Thompson always showed a keen interest in all the families and was sincerely concerned that no-one lacked anything – food, fuel, clothing or medicines. A great deal of needful help was given to many in the most tactful and unobtrusive way.

My mother, for her part, was entitled to a whole four weeks holiday each year, usually taken as one fortnight in Spring and another in September, but apart from that had no official "time-off" or "rest days" but was on duty 24 hours a day to deliver babies (most of whom were delivered at home then), tend the sick, give blanket baths, dress wounds, render first aid etc and could only wangle the odd few hours break "in between babies" by asking a nurse from a neighbouring parish to cover for her in case of an emergency. Her life was considerably eased after a few years when she was given a second-hand two-seater car with dickey seat by a grateful patient and her husband, who also taught her to drive.

When that car needed replacing I remember that she paid a whole £10 for the next second-hand one, after which each replacement became a slightly newer model until in 1938 she paid £50 for a two year old Austin Ruby Saloon – luxury! But by that time her salary had risen to £400 per annum.

Nurse Hope served Worplesdon for just over 30 years and her proudest memory was of being chosen as "best probationer nurse of her year" to be one of a guard of honour to a very old lady – Florence Nightingale, when she visited Bristol Infirmary not long before she died.'

'In 1952 I was living and working as a young District Nurse Midwife in Surrey. At that time, in the infancy of the NHS after the war, life was very different from today, both in hospital and in the district.

Nearly all District Nurses were single, as they were not accepted for training in hospital otherwise – indeed several girls in my training set at the London Hospital, Whitechapel, were dismissed because they married. Everyone worked from about 7.30 am to 8.30 pm with three hours off during the day and half an hour for lunch and a quarter of an hour for tea at about four, and supper at the end of the day. In their royal blue dress and navy coat, made to measure by Gieves in Buckingham Palace Road, District Nurses, on the contrary, were on call for 24 hours, and arranged work and visits to suit their situation.

In my first few years, I moved about the county every two or three weeks, filling in for established nurses who were beginning to go on training courses, or annual leave. In my first job as a District Nurse in Shere, lodging was arranged for me by the regular nurse, with a delightful couple who lived in a very old cottage opposite the pretty willow-lined stream. They had no bathroom and my landlady would bring me hot water morning and evening and provide my meals. She had no telephone and I had to arrange my visits with the well-loved local GP by public telephone every morning and evening. Diabetic patients were always first on my list – long acting insulin was not generally available, nor oral treatment, so the patients were waiting for their breakfast.

A patient becoming pregnant at this time in the early 1950s would automatically expect to have her baby at home, unless it was her first or there were other reasons for hospital confinement, decided by the GP. In this area of Surrey, she would go to St Luke's where Sister McCarthy was in command, or the Jarvis Maternity Home, where kindly Sister Dorothy Day in army square and sandals was similarly in charge. There must be many women today who remember with varying emotions these strong, efficient women.

If a patient was to be delivered at home, she would attend both doctor and midwife antenatally – her bedroom would be prepared by patient and family, a maternity pack etc delivered and when labour started the District Nurse Midwife would advise the GP of progress and, if he wished, he would come in and deliver the baby or leave it to the midwife. The labour was usually a happy family time – patient, family and midwife knowing each other very well by this time. Domestic help was generally by courtesy of Granny – husband did the general running around. Sometimes it was necessary for the husband to dispose of the after-birth in the garden if the fire was not suitable – indoor sanitation was not by any means universal. Many of my cases were conducted in obscure places such as a bare room over a junkshop in Kingston, by oil lamp as there was no electricity, and baby started life in a drawer instead of a cot – a house boat at Chertsey, with very little headroom and no washing facilities – a double council house in Walton on the Hill on Derby Day, where I had to be escorted across the racecourse by the police because the roads were closed all day for the races. The mother-to-be was the eldest of a very large family who had a room with her husband in the family home. I've never forgotten the excitement and happiness in that house. On other occasions in Chertsey, whilst staying in the District Nurse's house, I found on the doorstep buckets of coal for my fire, and fresh caught fish – the donor remained anonymous.

It was quite rare for nurses to have to look after elderly people alone. Mother was nearly always at home to look after the young and old – as this gradually changed, and women and young people left home for paid work, so did the nature of the district nurse's work change. There were no warden controlled flats, except places provided charitably by philanthropic employers for ageing employees, such as Whitely village, and the almshouses for those who qualified. Special accommodation grew out of necessity as people lived longer in better health.'

LADY BYRON'S NURSING FUND

'When my parents settled in Ockham, among their early require-ments was a doctor as a second baby was expected. Mother asked the ladies where the doctor came from and they told her it was Dr Ritching from Cobham, about four miles from Ockham. Dr Ritching was the founder of the little cottage hospital at Cobham, which was opened by the Duchess of Albury from Claremont in the early years of the 20th century. A nursing fund was established and endowed by Lady Noel Byron (widow of the poet) mainly for the benefit of the poorer classes, so that they might call upon a professional nurse at all times. This operated until the coming of the NHS in 1948. To this day, a small Christmas gift of cash is paid to senior citizens in Ockham from the legacy of Lady Byron.'

THE CHEMIST

'The chemist shop at Woodside in the early 1930s was run by two sisters, one of whom was the dispenser. Doctors were called in only in dire emergencies and the chemist prescribed pills and ointments for the majority of ills. I remember the waxed boxes containing ointments and one in particular prescribed for a face sore. It had white ointment on top changing to pink halfway down. When consulting the chemist you were ushered into the back parlour that lay behind the shop. I can see now the thick red plush tablecloth with bobbled fringe that almost reached the floor.'

BABIES AND MIDWIVES

THE REGISTRAR

'At about the time of the First World War a Registrar came to Limpsfield from Caterham once a week. He rented a room in the village for two shillings and sixpence and that was where all births, deaths and marriages were registered. The cottage is now known as Registry Cottage.'

HAVING A BABY

'Between the wars, mothers choosing to have a home confinement subjected the rest of the family to the "Monthly Nurse". This formidable lady, normally a spinster, and the equivalent of today's midwife, lived with the family and looked after the mother and baby for a month. Mothers themselves were confined to bed for the first two weeks after the birth. If, however, the birth took place in hospital, then there was a risk that the babies would get muddled up. They were kept apart from their mothers in a large nursery, and never labelled. There were many stories of mothers nursing the wrong baby.

One-parent families, whilst rare, were regarded with a mixture of disgrace and dislike. Sadly, the babies of unmarried mothers were often left in the country and brought up by countryside families, up to the age of five, when they were placed in orphanages. These children were known as foundlings.'

'When my eldest child was born in 1937 the word "pregnant" was seldom heard outside the doctor's surgery. A visit to him once a month completed preliminary training, and we disguised the bump as much as possible.

I had a stunning outfit of a loose jacket and a skirt on a bodice with a large tuck down each side. Both were let out with a running stitch seam as often as necessary.

When my husband announced at the office that he had a daughter, one of his colleagues exclaimed "You can't have. Your wife wasn't having a baby when I saw her yesterday!"

Meanwhile I was in a small nursing home at four and a half guineas a week. The first week was spent rather boringly in bed, but after that – so long as I was back for feeding times – I could come and go as I pleased for shopping or anything else.

I was taught how to change a nappy – which was really two nappies; a large muslin square and a bulky towelling square clipped together in a triangle with a large curved safety pin. The babies were taken away at night and bathed, so on the last day I was shown how to bath the baby.

When we got her home, we put her on the sofa in her wicker carrycot and were gazing at her when our large Schnautzer dog placed his paws on the back of the sofa and gazed down at her with equal consternation. At three weeks old, we none of us knew her very well . . . yet.'

'Moaning Minnie again (the air-raid siren), and time to gather up the baby, the knitting and possibly some biscuits and hurry to the air-raid shelter – a dug-out with corrugated iron for roofing, duckboards on the earth floor, and no heating. Some months previously I had started producing my daughter in this environment – going into labour in the shelter, before progressing to the haven of a nursing home. Here all was efficiency and optimism. My daughter was born in the only raid-free night of the Battle of Britain, a beautiful blonde bundle, the only girl at this time among a clutch of beefy boys.

The morning dawned beautifully sunny, and above the blast wall outside my window the sky was dazzlingly blue . . . until about mid-day when the sun was suddenly blotted out by sinister dark German bombers. Within a few seconds bombs were raining down on the nearby airfield and works. Many workers were killed as they made their way up to their canteen for lunch, and we mothers in the home were quickly pulled into the corridors, given two blankets and a baby from the nursery. My portion was one of the aforementioned beefy boys . . . but who had my daughter? After much rushing of ambulances to the sorry scene at the aerodrome, things calmed down. Within a few days I was back in my own home with my own baby – both of us none the worse for German intervention!'

'My brother was born in Merrow just before the Second World War ended. We had filled his pillow with thistledown so that he would not suffocate. Mother lay in for three weeks and I ran the house, cooked, washed, cleaned and cared for her. The baby was not washed for a month as it was bitterly cold – he was wiped with oil. The fire in mother's room was kept alight all the time. She fed the baby herself. After the month she went to be churched, and later the baby was christened.'

'Just after the war in 1947, my daughter was born, in fact just before the National Health Service was brought into being. I had to pay to go into hospital for 14 days. I was admitted suffering from labour pains on a Thursday night, going off in an ambulance on my own. My husband could not accompany me as the ambulance could not return him home and being night time there was no other transport available.

Our daughter was born during the early hours of Sunday morning but no visitors were allowed. My husband came to visit but was sent away by the sister because no one was allowed in the labour unit. Remember food was still on ration at that time so until your baby was born the hospital office did not accept your ration book, which meant that you had no butter, jam or sugar. I remember I was still in the labour unit when my breakfast came, consisting of a boiled egg, which was black when the top was taken off, and a piece of dried bread. The sister was so disgusted she went to her own case in which she carried her own rations, and put some butter and marmalade on my bread.'

FEEDING THE BABY

'Naturally I cannot remember what food I had as an infant, but I remember my brother, who is four years younger than I, having cow's milk diluted by a special formula, and given him in a boat-shaped bottle with a teat at one end and a rubber valve at the other. When he was teething he was given a crust of bread to chew and I can still remember the slimy object that I found between the cushions of an easy chair.

When my children came, feeds had to be given with absolute regularity four hourly, at 6 am, 10 am, 2 pm, 6 pm, and 10 pm. Cow's milk was not favoured, so they had National Dried Milk – a powder made by well-known firms such as Glaxo or Cow & Gate, but heavily subsidised by the Government. Orange juice produced by the Government was undrinkable, as it was so sour.

My grandchildren have breast feeding on demand. Today from a very early age babies are taken in carrycots by their parents to the shops, on visits, to dinner parties and other social occasions, so the source of their nourishment is always available.'

ILLEGITIMACY AND ORPHANS

'Evie was illegitimate, and in the first part of the 20th century that was a slur and a scandal. She did not attend the nearest village school because of the taunts of her fellows. She lived with her grandparents who, mindful of the child's sensitivity, sent her to the school in the next village, which entailed a walk of three miles there and three miles home. Evie would call for me as we lived just over a mile from the school we both attended. My mother was slightly troubled by my friendship with her, and when she felt strongly about it forbade me to walk home from school with her. I was fond of Evie and would walk with her to the corner of the road and then hurry on alone so that my mother would not see us together.

Evie was very poorly dressed. Her grandfather was a jobbing gardener with very little pay, and her mother in service in London – Evie being the result of her seduction by the son of the household, not an uncommon occurrence in those days.

But Evie was clever at music; she played the piano very well and sat in the school hall and played the Grand March for us to proceed from the playground to our classrooms. One of the ladies in the village paid for her music lessons, and when we had our annual school concert she came to hear Evie play, and sat majestically on a special chair in the hall, "sshing" every time an interruption was heard during Evie's recital. Evie was also one of the bell ringers at her local church.'

'In the 1920s West End's vicar was the "Boxing" Rev Robbins – so called because he gave boxing lessons to the local young boys. His wife was responsible for my Dad and his brother coming to live in West End in 1924, when they were twelve and ten years old respectively. A society in London contacted Mrs Robbins to see if any local families could take in "Pension Boys" who needed a home. There were seven children in my father's family, and when his mother died in childbirth at the age of 38, and his father died as a result of war wounds, the family was split up. The eldest girl was out at work, the next two were sent by Dr Barnado's to Australia, the youngest two went to different relatives, and my father and his brother came to West End. Despite being scattered, they never lost touch. The Rev Robbins died one Christmas morning while getting ready to take the Christmas services.'

FUNERALS AND MOURNING

STRAW ON THE ROAD

'I remember straw being laid across the road when somebody was seriously ill and close to death to deaden some of the noise that the horses and carts made. It stretched from one gutter right across the road to the other.'

FUNERALS

'Holmbury had something unique, a Burial Guild. The gardeners and any available persons performed this service for villagers. They wore their best suits, bowler hats and a navy blue guild sash. They thought it a great privilege to provide their services.'

'Between the wars in Copthorne, all the schoolboys were in the choir, and got half a crown for weddings and half a crown for funerals. The parson, Stafford Young, tolled the bell immediately a person had died, and by the ringing they could tell if the deceased was male or female, and a toll for every year of age. Funerals passed Vigars Yard and all the old ladies turned up for every funeral.'

'In Chiddingfold in the 1920s and 1930s a village woman laid the body out and the coffin stayed in the house (usually open) until the funeral. A horse-drawn hearse or horse and cart, preceded by an undertaker in a top hat, walking, would take the coffin to church. Everyone stopped as it passed and the men took off their caps as a mark of respect. All curtains were drawn in the house of the deceased, and black armbands were worn by relatives for several weeks. The bell tolled as the coffin approached the church.'

MOURNING

'My mother told me that when Queen Victoria died my grandmother tied black sashes round the dresses of her and her sisters in mourning. Presumably the boys had black armbands.'

'My eldest brother died in 1932 after a motor cycle accident and there were 120 wreaths. I had the task of sending black-edged cards out. Mourning clothes have largely gone now, but I was kitted out in black for the occasion and I was only 16.'

BROOKWOOD CEMETERY

'Worplesdon Hill is a sort of suburb of Worplesdon. In the early 1900s most of the land was owned by the Necropolis Company of London, and they created Brookwood Cemetery. It is one of the largest in Europe – if not THE largest. Since 1985 it has been owned by a Turkish Muslim, all 420 acres of it!

When I was a child in the 1920s Brookwood Cemetery was like a beautiful park. Graves were carefully tended by families, helped by the 100 to 150 skilled gardeners employed by the Necropolis Company, but it is now abandoned and parts of it derelict. In the 1920s and 1930s a train ran from a special platform within Waterloo Station to a terminus inside the cemetery known as North and South Stations, carrying coffins and mourners from London to Brookwood, and the mourners alighted and the coffins were removed to a hearse prior to burial. Refreshments could be bought at the station, which included a bar if more than a cup of tea was felt to be necessary!

Very few people in those days had a car, and the way through the cemetery to Brookwood was taken as a short-cut to the station, shops, post office etc, but one had to be careful as the gates were locked at sundown! I think in the present climate very few people (let alone children) would venture a walk through the cemetery in the day time, let alone after dark. The cottages which housed the staff have been sold off or have fallen into disrepair.

On the land which became Worplesdon Hill, large houses were built and bought by wealthy people. A number of people who lived in this part of the "Stockbroker Belt" found the train service from Brookwood to Waterloo a great advantage; a brisk walk through the cemetery thoroughfare or ten minutes in the chauffeur-driven car and one was at the station.'

CHILDHOOD
&
SCHOOLDAYS

CHILDHOOD IN THE COUNTRY

'On reflection, being a child in the 1920s and 1930s was a happy accident of birth. One was just in time to catch a glimpse of a world that was to disappear for ever: a world where children could roam over the countryside in perfect safety and where old people were respected.' Surrey children were very aware of the seasons and the different delights each brought – from skating on frozen ponds to picnics in summer woods or long evenings playing in the late sunshine. Much of Surrey was still deeply rural before the Second World War. There were drawbacks, of course, and life could be very lonely for a single child in the depths of the country, but the simple things of life provided lasting delight and yesterday's child experienced a freedom which has been lost in the years between.

BREECHING A BOY

'My father was born in Kent, where his father was a blacksmith at the asylum. He remembered being sent to school, in about the 1880s, with long blond curls and wearing a velvet dress; boys and girls were dressed alike then. Later he was "breeched" – boys' first trousers were quite an event.'

A VERY LONELY LIFE

'As a very small child in 1908 I was brought to Bramley. That was a very lonely life. You have a whole community now but then the cottage was on its own entirely. You would see another one right across the field and that was all there was. Right up until the time I was five years old and started school I had to walk down Iron Lane under the bridge to the bottom of the lane to meet other children from Thorncombe Street.'

PICNICS

'As a child I lived in a bungalow on the outskirts of the small hamlet of Owlsmoor. Everyone had enormous gardens so there seemed plenty of space. Most of the roads were made up with gravel to keep them firm, and no street lighting shone anywhere. Lovely woods, with trees of all colours and types, surrounded the whole place. We had picnics there in summer and collected chestnuts in winter.

My mother enjoyed picnics and would gather together other mothers and children who would bring sandwiches, egg if they kept chickens, jam if they didn't, and bottles of home-made lemonade. Plenty of cake was provided by my mother. One lady never came without bringing a big bag of toffees. She used to hide some of them and we ran races to try to win more. Everyone had to carry something and we generally walked two or three miles into the woods before finally choosing a special place for our picnic. When the food was all eaten, and no more toffees were left and we had exhausted all the games we knew, it was time to collect fir cones and fill up every empty container (these cones were stored away for lighting fires in the winter). Then home we trudged, grubby and tired, but before bath and bed the copper had to be lit for heating the water.'

DEAR OLD BELMONT

'Belmont hasn't changed much physically over the years. It has a short, ugly High Street, but when I was a child it was full of friends – not just those fellow shoppers, but all the shopkeepers who never changed. Tom and Stan and George at the butcher's – George had lost a finger in the sausage machine, the lovely smell in Mr Last's baker's shop and the chill of Hodge's dairy, the newsagent's and tobacconist where my father was always sending me to get 20 Gold Flake, the grocer's where Mr Watson was rather severe, but his wife let my sister and me sit on the counter and choose a biscuit each from the glass-lidded tins. There was a café where my mother and her friends had coffee every morning before taking the children for a walk on the Downs, and then home to a lunch prepared by the maid.

We'd often cycle to Banstead or walk across the Downs and over the sheep bridge and up to the smithy at the war memorial end of the High Street. It seemed so rural compared to Belmont. We would stand on tip-toe at the stable door of the smithy to watch the horses being shod. At the nearby Banstead branch of Hodge's Dairy we'd be refreshed with ladles of milk from the brass-bound churns. There was a pond at the far end of the village, and a lovely old cottage tea-rooms. Sutton Lane was very narrow as it neared the village and it was always great fun to be on the upper deck of the 164 bus as it approached the village and experience the buffeting the windows received from the overhanging trees.

A good afternoon out would be a bus ride to The Woolpack, and

then cut across Chucks Meadow, down Park Lane and head for
Chipstead – right turn along Outwood Lane to take tea at Dene
Farm. Refreshed by scones and jam and cream and home-made
cakes, we'd walk on till we reached Kingswood and finally back to
the Brighton Road, and no more than a ten minute wait for a number
80 bus back to Belmont.

Our Sunday school treat every year was an outing to Colley Hill.
Chessington Zoo was a popular venue for birthday parties – also
The Sugar Bowl at Burgh Heath. The pond at Burgh Heath was an
annual "must" when we filled up jam jars with frog spawn which
slip-slopped around in our bicycle baskets as we free-wheeled most
of the way home.

Very few families had a car in Belmont. The train and bus services
were frequent and the roads were so quiet that bicycles were a child's
acceptable transport. There were times when a car would have been
helpful. Parties in the Christmas holidays often seemed to be given
by friends who lived at the back of beyond and we would trudge
through miles of snow and slush in our Wellington boots, carrying
our shoe-bags containing our bronze sandals. Most of the parties
were along the same lines – simple games, quizzes, tea with bridge
rolls filled with sardine and tomato paste or scrambled egg, followed
by iced fairy cakes and jelly. The best game of all was Murder in
the Dark.

Every third Sunday we had to visit my grandparents in Streatham.
We hated having to put on our best bibs and tuckers and travel to
noisy Streatham, especially in the summer when we could have been
romping in the field at the end of the garden with all the other
children in the road. It was just so wonderful to find ourselves
changing trains back at Sutton onto the Belmont, Banstead and
Epsom Downs platform and to watch for the fields on either side
of the line as we approached dear old Belmont. Before the footbridge
was erected the little porter – who was *always* on duty it would seem
– would help us across the lines with the push pram! Then we'd skip
back home through the village and past the church to our dear little
semi-detached house.'

SKATING ON THE POND

'Winters in the 1930s were mostly very cold. Ice formed on the
windows and the pond on the green at Forest Green froze solid,
safe enough for all the children to slide or skate. My brother and
others had skates on a board; you nailed the back to the heels of
your shoes and a strap came over the front of the shoe.

A few days before Christmas my father and brother would go and find a tree, either on Leith Hill or at Holmbury. My brother Jack climbed the tree and would saw the top off. We would decorate it and candles in the clipholders were lit.'

DOWNS FOR A PLAYGROUND

'The Downs at the top of the road in Merrow were my playground during the 1940s. With my two sisters in tow, all my spare time was spent there. We gathered fruit – blackberries, strawberries, sloes, nuts, and cones and wood for the fire; bunches of flowers for Mother, hips, acorns and conkers; foxglove seeds for medicine. The rabbits needed greens and the chickens had bracken for bedding. We went gleaning for corn and searched for mushrooms. Other children, poor things, wore Liberty bodices and long stockings, even in those very hot summers when double summer time meant going to bed when it was really six o'clock. We wore just a pair of cotton knickers for playing. Summer meant a new pair of Clark's sandals and no socks; but in wartime there were no shoes in the shops at all to fit me, so for three glorious summers I wore no shoes on holiday. My feet hardened in a few days and I could run across the Downs, not feeling the flints or thistles. We played with hoops, marbles, tops, two-ball bouncing games, skipping and five-stones, and I owned a scooter.

In the house I turned the sewing machine handle for hours while Mother made our clothes – summer dresses with matching knickers. They needed no pattern . . . just cut out half, fold over to match – all a little bigger than last year. Aprons, home-made coats with a pixie hood to be worn with a scarf crossed over the chest and pinned at the back by a large safety pin, she made them all.'

PLAYING IN THE EVENING

'A street lamp stood outside our house in Guildford Park in the 1920s, just in front of my bedroom, and in my younger days I would watch for the lamplighter to come with his long pole to ignite the gas lamp. We had gas lighting indoors too, and great care had to be exercised in lighting the fragile gas mantle as it shattered to fragments if touched by the match.

I would gaze longingly from my bedroom window as the older children played around the street lamp during the dark autumn evenings. There was something special in being allowed out to play in the dark by the light of the street lamp. There was no traffic to speak of in those days so we could play happily in the road – depending on the seasons, of course, we played hopscotch, marbles,

107

tops, rounders, cricket, conkers, and a great thrill was riding an old boneshaker of a bike, minus tyres, up and down the road.

As I grew older I too was allowed out to play in the dark under the lamplight – but soon, far too soon, we would all be called in and autumn and winter evenings would be spent round the kitchen range, a small fire alongside an oven with a large black kettle singing merrily away on top.

It was a lovely unrestricted childhood. We could wander at will for miles around the fields that surrounded us, though the field that rose up in front of my bedroom window was forbidden until haymaking was over. Then we loved to climb to the top to see what was over the other side! Now that hill is topped by Guildford Cathedral and the old farm gate is replaced by an elegant wrought iron and gilded gate with ornate steps leading up to the cathedral. I can remember as a child the grown ups saying "It'll never be built in our time".'

A CONTRAST OF SEASONS

'As I was the eldest of several children, it always fell to my lot to escort them to the lavatory way up the garden, often with a candle for light if the torch batteries were low. As there was only room for one at a time in there, star gazing was the thing to do whilst waiting outside! I remember that the Plough constellation was very prominent in the clear sky of a cold and frosty night.

Haymaking, on the other hand, always seemed to take place on sultry evenings. We would hang from our bedroom window as the rick was being built below, making the air thick with dust. We would watch with fascination until the horses were led back to the stables when it was dark.'

A 1940s CHILDHOOD

'Thinking of my childhood the most common thread running through those days is the amount of walking my family did. We didn't own a car until I was about 15 years old and every weekend we would hop on a bus from Milford to either Thursley, Hindhead, Brook or Witley and walk through the leafy lanes until we were tired and then catch a bus home. We always took a ball with us and would throw it across the lanes to each other. We rarely had to stop for cars. We cycled to the golf course and gathered blackberries and we collected sweet chestnuts to roast on the fire. We used to toast bread on a toasting fork over the fire and spread it with dripping sprinkled with salt – a tea-time favourite on winter days. In winter we undressed for bed in front of the living room fire and had stone

The summer brought long lazy days and the freedom to roam the countryside enjoying innocent pursuits like pond dipping.

hot water bottles in our beds. Only if we were ill was the bedroom fire lit. I loved to lie and watch the flames, it was almost worth being ill.

In the spring we went looking for violets and primroses to take to the Mothering Sunday service and later we gathered armfuls of bluebells. We rode horses over Elstead common and picnicked and climbed trees at Heavens Gate on Milford Common.

The milk was delivered by horse and cart and the milk bottles had cardboard tops which, with the centres punched out, we wound wool around and made fluffy balls for babies' pram toys. My mother allowed us to ask the milkman if we could take the reins and drive his cart – but only in the road in which we lived, no further. We watched eagerly for him in the summer holidays.

The post was delivered by a postwoman on a bicycle. Always Mrs M, we never saw anyone else delivering letters, year in and year out. We were fortunate enough to receive food parcels, and sometimes outgrown clothes for us children, from American relatives. These caused great excitement, the postwoman would tell us there was one waiting for us at the post office and we went with my father to collect it.

Many Saturday afternoons were spent watching my father play cricket. And early memory is of my father, a fast bowler, running straight across the pitch and sweeping my mother and me under a wooden bench as a buzz bomb was heard. Within minutes the sound stopped and we were showered with clods of earth. The bomb had fallen in the garden of a nearby house. Several buzz-bombs fell in the Godalming area and several shop windows were boarded up.

I remember a neighbour calling to tell my mother that bananas had arrived at our local corner shop. To my amazement we set off straight away, not even stopping to finish our lunch, to buy some. I had never seen them before and I can remember wondering why there was so much excitement, they didn't seem all that wonderful even when sliced and covered in custard!

A HAPPY FAMILY

I was born in Charlwood. When the First World War came my father went into the army and when London was bombed by Zeppelins my mother moved to Charlwood where she had a friend. After the war was over my father worked in Horley, where he was a plumber.

We children played with tops and whips, also with wooden hoops, and we played hopscotch. We played in the road as there were only about three cars in the village. In the summer we were in the hay fields and woods, and we used to get a ride in the hay cart. We went acorning, picking dandelions for wine, and blackberrying for jam. We sometimes had visits from relations in London, they had to walk from Horley station as there was no bus.

We were a happy family. We all went to Sunday school, and later to church; my two brothers and sister were in the choir. We went on one Sunday school outing to the sea each year. That was the only outing we had, so we used to save our pennies to spend, and always had a happy time. We had a lovely Mothering Sunday service, when the rectors's wife gave us all a little bunch of violets from her garden. We all went to Band of Hope. Just before Christmas was Smith's Charity, when we went with a truck to collect a joint of beef and bag of flour; we always had the beef on Christmas day. And on 1st January we had free bread, that was Round's Charity. Sometimes gipsies used to call with pegs, also asking for food and clothes.

There was a village flower show each year and we children entered hand-writing, painting, pressed wild flowers, and twelve wild grasses on a board. Also there were races, sack races, running races, coconut shies and tilt the bucket which was a jolly good laugh. We had baby shows, dog shows and pony rides.

We girls went into service when we left school at 14 years of age. It was long hours and small wages, but we had good food. When I was in my teens I went to all the dances and socials in Charlwood, Newdigate and Rusper.'

110

SUMMER HOLIDAYS

'My fondest memory of living in Surrey in the early 1930s is when we had our summer holidays. There were quite a few of us children and not many went away on holiday. We were content to get together in the morning when usually we were given a halfpenny or if we were lucky a penny, with which we would buy a bag of broken biscuits and Mum would give me a bottle of home-made lemonade. We would go to the fields near us in Old Byfleet and play and watch the hay making. We would spend most of the day there, somehow we always knew when it was time to go home for tea, very tired but happy.'

THE SIMPLE THINGS OF LIFE

'Looking back, the simple things of life seem very vivid, wandering the fields and lanes, the wild flowers, bluebells, poppies, cowslips and scabious, white daisies everywhere, eating the wild strawberries and the blackberries. I remember playing for hours under a copse of trees opposite our house making fairy gardens between the gnarled roots of the trees. These were made with moss, stones etc and a piece of mirror to make a pond and any other little mini-figures we could find.

Then came winter, always with snow it seemed. We lived on a hill and many happy hours were spent sliding down the hill on our precious toboggan made by Dad, then walking up the other side to repeat the process. After all this activity, indoors we went to shed our mitts and scarves and hats, when Mum always dished up hot Oxo and a slice of bread. One day my friend and I were taken by her big brother for a walk on the Downs when a heavy snowfall came on and we became lost. We finally did find our way home, meeting my frantic father coming to look for us. I was taken home and tucked up into bed to warm up beside my mother who had just given birth to a new baby brother.

Perhaps the most vivid memories were the war. Sitting in the lounge listening to the voice of the announcer saying we were at war with Germany. Not really understanding, but sensing the fear and uncertainty of the adults. The horror of the gas masks, having to carry them everywhere, the big Mickey Mouse one for the baby.

In the garden Dad grew all the vegetables he could and part of the garden was used for chicken runs and rabbit hutches, not for pets I am afraid but to supplement our rations.

Then the shelters, the Anderson in the garden where we spent so many nights on the bunk beds. One night I recall my Dad taking me up to the entrance to see all the fires burning caused by the incendiaries. One fell on our house, came through on the landing and shot through into a bedroom. Fortunately it was put out before too much damage was done. At night there were the searchlights across the sky, the constant air-raids and sounds of guns and bombs. I saw a barrage balloon on the ground one day and the size was staggering.

I also remember the doodlebugs. The first night, hearing the strange noises, not knowing what they were, Dad sent me down to a friend's house to say I would not be going to school and instead of staying with my friend when the siren went, I was ambling up the road quite unconcerned with anti-aircraft guns banging away overhead and Father frantically waving and shouting from the door. One day an aircraft enthusiastically chased and fired at a doodlebug overhead – we all rushed for the shelters and afterwards Mum found a blanket which was folded on the line to air had eight bullet holes right through it.

The hospital trains used to come in at the local station and we young children used to go around to neighbours with an empty powder box collecting donations. The money was then spent on cigarettes and given to the soldiers.

Finally came peace and all the celebrations – a large bonfire behind our houses when shells were let off. The noise terrified me and I wandered off and hid in the cornfield.'

TWOPENCE WAS A FORTUNE

'We walked back and forth to school, going home for our dinner from twelve to 2 pm during which time I shopped for relatives and neighbours who lived near. We earned a little pocket money by doing this plus odd jobs. If we made threepence a week we thought we were well off. At the sweet shop we usually only spent a halfpenny or penny at a time – twopence was a fortune.

Depending on the time of year, our games included skipping, marbles and hopscotch. At home when we had friends in to play, it was usually post offices and shops, the stamps, postal orders etc for the post office having been made by ourselves. I remember using my toy sewing machine to make the perforations for the stamps. I think we enjoyed making the things as much as playing with them.

We had no television so we learned to sew and knit, played card and board games, shove-ha'penny, darts, read and generally amused ourselves in any way we could. Looking back we never seemed to be bored. We had a gramophone with a horn and loved to play our few records on a Saturday night. The machine had to be wound up for each record – no plugging in to the electricity like today.'

WANDERING

'We would often wander off down into Betchworth village by the church. In Church Street we would call in at Dray's the village baker's and see Eddie baking the bread – it always smelled so good. Eddie and his father used to call daily delivering the bread. From there and on the other side of the church opposite the Dolphin pub, we would visit Alec Stovell, our village blacksmith – Alec was also one of Dad's part time postmen, so we knew him well – he would mostly be busy shoeing horses, either farm working horses or hunters. Often Alec would let us help in some way, I recall he used to let us operate the bellows for him. Sometimes we would call at Home Farm to see the cows being milked and I vividly recall watching the milk cascading over the cooler; but I never fancied trying a drink of warm milk straight from the cow.

From here perhaps we would wander off down by the river Mole and if it were springtime gather a few primroses to take home. On the other side of the bluebell woods one day when we were in Gadbrook Lane I saw the wondrous sight of a kingfisher in flight over the pond at Swans Farm; the plumage was magnificent and I will never forget it. On other days, from the church we would go through Betchworth Park towards Brockham and if it were autumn we would gather pockets full of chestnuts on the way. Near to Brockham we would come to a place called Polands where there was a shallow boating lake and local children were allowed to take out a small rowing boat; this I remember as great fun. Afterwards we would walk on to Brockham Green and return home via Kiln Lane and maybe visit the old brick kilns on the way and make another picking, this time of hazelnuts – I wonder if they still grow there now!

At other times we would wander in the other direction and up over the main Dorking to Reigate road over the railway line into the hills; we knew our way up to Box Hill and around and also into the chalk pits. On these chalk hills we would often find bee orchids growing. I'm glad to report that even in the 1930s we were taught just to look at them and not to pick, which I would like to think had something to do with still being able to find them there today.

When I stop to think and look back, my greatest wonder now is that Mother didn't ever seem to be worried by us moving around the hills and village so freely. Maybe we managed to turn up for

113

meals on time! Nevertheless I cannot, unfortunately, imagine it being allowed in the present day.'

SEASONS IN THE PARK

'In the spring at Richmond we would visit the "Mini-ha-ha" – so-called – a tributary of the river Thames which meandered alongside in the Old Deer Park. We would go armed with a net and jam-jar, and return triumphant with either frogspawn or tiddlers, which could be transferred to an old enamel washing-up bowl when we got home.

Sundays in summer would be watching father play cricket on Sheen Common, and then in the evening we would walk into the Park where our parents would sit listening to the band which played from the band-stand at Richmond Gate.

We were not far from Richmond Park, and on crisp October Sundays we would walk over to the Plantation to pick chestnuts, which we would roast on the living room range and listen to them spit and burst!

On Saturday mornings in winter I would play hockey in Old Deer Park, and with bruised shins and dirty knees make my way home, calling in at the local grocery shop for a pennyworth of broken biscuits – making sure to have a fair share of the cream pieces!'

HOW BETTER OFF CHILDREN LIVED

'FRIDDY' THE GOVERNESS

'I was the eldest of six children and my parents decided that it would be sensible to have a governess to educate us until we were eleven years old and could go to school. Miss Fridlander ("Friddy" for short) appeared therefore and every morning the nursery became the schoolroom and she also taught us piano.

At Christmas time we children had to entertain the "grown ups" – that is our parents and various aunts and uncles. "Friddy" therefore spent a frantic few weeks before the big event trying to instil some sort of law and order into a programme of very mixed abilities. There were of course carols and poems, monologues and the usual piano pieces and duets. It was just as well that "Friddy" wasn't there on *the* day because there was one uncle who always found the duets the highlight of the whole programme. For some reason they could never be completed as a battle royal always seemed to break out! This uncle used to egg on the duettists – to the despair of my mother but we all thought that it was a wonderful conclusion to our agonizing evening – we were sent up to bed after that.'

NANNY AND THE NURSERY

'Life for babies and small children in well-to-do homes before the First World War was very different from today. Anthony was born in 1911 at home in Merstham, with a maternity or "monthly" nurse in attendance to look after mother and child. Mothers were kept in bed for up to three weeks after the birth, but by the end of a month they were expected to be ready gradually to resume their normal social lives. The maternity nurse was keen for the mother to be up by the fourth week and if possible for the christening to take place, as it was the custom for the godparents to tip the monthly nurse! The baby was handed over to Nanny, who, as the saying went, "took the baby from the month".

There were day and night nurseries presided over by Nanny. As there were already three other children in Nanny's care there was a nursemaid to do the chores and when one realises what clothes Baby Anthony would have worn, one can see the need. He would have worn a binder, a vest, a nappy, a long cotton lawn petticoat, covered by a long lawn robe, and both of these would have been hand-made, with pintucks, lace edgings and lace insertions. He would wear a matinee jacket of knitted wool over these and knitted bootees on his feet. When he went out he might have had a knitted bonnet or cap and a cape called a pelisse before being put into his pram, to be taken for a morning and afternoon walk with the other children. If he had been born in the winter he would have had a long flannel petticoat and a thicker gown, perhaps made of nun's veiling. At night he would wear a long nightdress, rather like his gown but with less trimming. All these garments would have to be washed and many of them ironed daily: there were no washing machines or electric irons, so the nursemaid would have had to wash them by hand and iron them with a flat iron, heated on an asbestos mat over a gas ring in the nursery. There were no plastic or even rubber pants, so the consumption of nappies was considerable.

The children lived, ate and slept in the nurseries. It was Nanny to whom Anthony would run when he fell in the garden and grazed his knee, it was Nanny who comforted him when he woke crying at night after a bad dream and it was Nanny who organised much of his social life. Walks, tea parties and picnics were arranged by Nanny, who invited other Nannies with their charges.

Thus Nanny was an important person in Anthony's life. She was a Lowland Scot and came from a good but humble family. She had probably had the basic education provided in schools up to the age of twelve or 13, but she had had no training for the job. She had worked for two families as Nanny before coming to Anthony's mother when her first child was born and probably had been a nursemaid before that. She had a fund of common sense and was devoted to the children, but she was a strict disciplinarian. She had a week's holiday a year, but for the rest of the time she was on duty virtually 24 hours a day. The children had a happy childhood, secure in the knowledge that Nanny was always there.'

SATIN AND VELVET

'The house in New Malden we moved to in about 1913 was much bigger than our previous home and my mother had to entertain a lot.

The nursery area was the whole of the top floor and Nanny had an under-nurse and a housemaid under her. She wore a very stiff apron and a cap. She ruled with a rod of iron! But we felt really safe with her as she was never unfair. Mabel, the under-nurse, would have been much softer with us if she had had the chance. The little maid had a hard time keeping the fires going, keeping everything spick and span, carrying the washing up and down to the line in the garden.

I can't remember what I wore in the mornings, but in the afternoons I was dressed in the most beautiful Liberty smocks or ones embroidered by my mother. In the winter Gerald had little velvet suits in dark blue. I remember the twins best in long robes and later in tiny satin trousers and satin tunics in which they looked adorable! Real silk satin, of course. My mother spent quite a lot of time in the nursery and came up for tea on the rare occasions when she had no visitors, but usually Nanny had to take us all down to the drawing room after our tea and every detail of our clothing had to be perfect. Once, at the bottom of the stairs my penetrating child's voice was heard to protest, "Company or no company, I won't be washed wiv spit".

Evenings in the nursery were lovely; there was a huge fire-guard right round the fire on which nappies were warmed before they were put on the twins, but in the evening everything was tidied away and we sat round the fire and had stories read or told to us in the firelight. There always seemed to be plenty of time, much more time than I seemed to have later with my own children. Staff in a house certainly make for a more leisured existence.'

BEAGLING AND BEATING

'I came to live in Surrey in 1930 at Russ Hill, Charlwood, which is now an hotel. There were about 150 acres, including fields, woods and a water garden, also large gardens, both floral and vegetable. There was a space for two tennis courts, but not enough space behind the back lines. My father had a hard court built near the gate to the front drive and one of my jobs was to pull the heavy roller, with a mat tied behind, after people had played.

The house also was spacious, and my brother and I had a happy childhood. My mother was WI President for many years, and in those days there were competitions each year for poultry farms. She won her class so often that she gave up entering.

My father worked in London, and used to catch the train from Horley. The rector's daughter and I were then driven to school in Reigate and my brother and other boys, till they boarded. We then picked up some more girls in Horley – so the journey was never dull.

Tradesmen delivered in those days, and we used to telephone the fishmonger in Horley (his son only retired a very few years ago) and often the fish was delivered. Butcher and village shops existed then in Charlwood. There was a troop of Girl Guides in the village, and I twice went away to camp with them.

When war came, I was the first casualty. Actually the war had not started, but we were expecting evacuees in the village and all hands were needed to help. I had some knitting with steel knitting needles and I sat on it in the car. One needle must have gone in about one and a half inches. I had to get my father to pull it out, and was then taken to the first aid post (set up for checking the heads of the evacuees) where the rector's wife coped with me.

Another memory I have is going beagling. I had a pony and went cubbing and hunting with the Surrey Union. As a covert-owner's daughter I could go free, but beagling was another matter. I went down to the village with my brother, got worn out running round the fields in circles and eventually decided to go home. My wretched brother, who was slimmer than me, stayed on, and eventually passed me going up the hill to home – and wouldn't wait. No more beagling for yours truly!

My father was in a shooting syndicate – various people in the neighbourhood shot each week on one of their properties, and I remember being a beater when it was at home. I first met my husband then, as his father was a syndicate member, and he brought him along in the school holidays.

Life was much safer and less hectic in Surrey even up to the end of the 1950s. Children were able to ride bicycles and horses in the lanes alone, and parents did not need to fear for them.

Before the war we actually had an early television set, but, of course, we were not wedded to it as is the modern child. I had a netball post in the garden and spent a long time practising shooting, and also a high jump. We read much more, of course, and I used to listen to Children's Hour on the wireless instead of getting on with my homework.'

THE GAMES WE PLAYED

'The seasons were marked by the games children played. Everyone seemed to know by some mysterious instinct when to change from hopscotch to skipping, or from hoops to whipping tops. The climax of the year was the conker season and an all-conquering conker was a great status symbol.' Some games were of local interest, such as the cries to 'Remember the Grotto', and the macabre 'Bogey won't be out tonight' surely had its origin in more ancient times.

REMEMBER THE GROTTO

'A particular way of collecting money by children in Mitcham took place in late July or August. Three sides of a square were made with earth about three inches high, the back of the square against a wall. Into the earth were pressed heads of flowers, wild or garden; in the centre of the square, ornaments or more flowers. The whole area covered was between two or three feet. The child or children then stood beside their "Grotto" asking for money. This was subsequently spent at Mitcham Fair.'

'We were fortunate in that we enjoyed unrestricted use of the streets around our home at Frimley, the traffic being not so much light as virtually non-existent.

An odd phenomenon was the "seasonal" appearance of certain games like the playing with glass marbles that were so beloved of boys, cigarette cards, and whip and top, each fad superseding its predecessor as though in a preordained sequence. On summer evenings, adults would occasionally join in our fun by stretching a rope across the entire width of the road, allowing several girls to skip in unison, chanting those chants that children know so well and adults forget.

One particular event may have been unique to the time and the place. It invariably occurred in August, and apparently with a kind of mass spontaneity, when the children of the neighbourhood could be seen gathering earth from the surrounding gardens, together with a few flowers and handfuls of pebbles – anything that could be pressed into service to decorate the intricate patterns we laid out on the pavements, the earth providing the primary material for these patterns. When they were completed to our satisfaction, we would call out to passers-by: "Please remember the Grotto". The origins of this strange invocation are a mystery to me, but presumably it was on a par with: "Please remember the Guy". I imagine also that all of this fell on deaf ears, and that we never actually anticipated gaining from the exercise, our pleasure deriving from the process of constructing the grotto – which certainly kept us absorbed for untold hours as we continually arranged and rearranged our patterns and decorations.'

THE GIANT STRIDE

'We were so free, even though we were growing up at the time of the First World War. We had the commons at Holmbury St Mary to play on. I remember a ditch that held water near the school and made a marvellous slide in winter, when frozen. We slid all of 19 feet, collapsing in a heap with great laughter. We also had our Giant Stride behind the school. It was a sizeable trunk of tree, embedded in the ground, with a revolving metal cap. From this hung four feet of chain, with extending thick ropes; at the end a smooth crossbar. Collecting our ropes, we ran like "Billy-oh" and jumped onto our crossbar, swinging out to shrieks of laughter. By modern standards, it was dangerous! We were quite adept at walking on stilts – not bought ones, they were cut from scrub oak. We could not afford pogo sticks (all the rage), but we had fun on borrowed ones. Later on we played stool ball.'

MY FIRST BALLOON

'I remember seeing my first toy balloon in the late 1930s. I was on a coach outing with the Sunday school from Millbridge, and one child got on the coach with a beautiful blown up coloured balloon. He pointed out the shop where it was purchased, and I dashed across with my money and was given a piece of coloured rubber; but I wanted a balloon! The shopkeeper said it *was* a balloon and I had to blow it up. I was so disappointed. I got back on the coach and found I couldn't manage to blow it up; no one helped me. I can still remember the "let down" feeling!'

WATCHING THE SOLDIERS

'The military tattoo took place about three miles from our home, at Aldershot. We enjoyed going to the main road to see the charabancs on their way. Some of the vehicles were rather ancient and liable to break down. If we knew it was getting near the time for the tattoo to start, we delighted in taunting them with the fact that they wouldn't get there on time, especially if we could hear the bands starting up.

A scene we also liked to watch was when the army were on a route march from Bordon to Aldershot, or vice versa. They would have a break for a cuppa and a bite and often the field kitchen would be set up near us and we would have a chat with the soldiers and see if they had any "fag" cards to give us as we were keen collectors.'

'During the 1920s and 1930s the army held torchlight tattoos at Rushmoor, near Aldershot. It was common for Wood Street families to sit on the bank opposite the Cricketers pub on the Aldershot Road, watching the charabancs go by. Some of the passengers threw halfpennies to the children. At night the torch lights could be seen in the village.'

THE BETTER BRITAIN BRIGADE

'My sister and I were in the Better Britain Brigade in Croydon in the 1930s, an organisation similar to the Brownies and Guides but attached to the Church Army. I went every Monday evening to PT and Tuesday evening to The Bs, as it was called. We started and finished with prayers, learned knots and first aid and put on a pantomime each year. Every year we went camping for two weeks to Wendover, where we joined with about 200 other children from around the South East.'

GIRL GUIDES

'I was 14 when I became a Girl Guide in 1924. I joined the 1st Kenley Company as some of my school friends belonged. I learned many things, from home nursing to the morse code, but my chief motive was to go to camp. For many years we went for the second week in August, and usually had lovely weather. In spite of sleeping six to a bell tent on palliasses filled with straw, cooking on an open wood fire, and digging latrines, there was something magical about being at camp, particularly the singsongs round the campfire at night and feeling part of the "great outdoors". When I returned home to Coulsdon I felt so claustrophobic that I slept in the garden while the weather remained fine.'

'In 1952 when I was twelve years old, I belonged to the 1st New Haw Guide Company. There were various things we had to do to gain Proficiency Badges, one of which was a six mile hike.

My friend Ann and I set off with one aim – to walk from New Haw to Shepperton and get the autograph of Barbara Kelly and Bernard Braden, who we knew lived in Shepperton but not where. This walk proved to be an initiative test too.

We arrived in Shepperton and found out that the couple had a boat and lived near the river Thames, so we sat by the river, eating our packed lunch, watching the boats go by and resting our blistered feet. When we saw a water rat we made a hasty retreat into the village. We asked at the post office cum paper shop if they could tell us where the TV stars lived, not really expecting them to tell us, but they did and we had been sitting very near to their house without realising it.

We duly knocked on their door, not knowing quite what to say if one of them came to the door. It opened and a man told us they were not at home – which was a bit disappointing as we wanted proof that we had reached there. We explained why we wanted the autograph and he suggested we left the books with him and came back for them the following week.

I did go back the next Saturday and it was Bernard Braden who opened the door to me. He was very nice and had signed the books for us. Needless to say, we did not walk on this occasion, but we did get our Badge.'

WALKING ON FLOWERPOTS

'We went to school in Goldsworth Road, Horsell in the 1930s. We still played with hoops and dolls and I had a doll's pram which my daughters played with later on – things were made to last in those days. We played hopscotch too, using a stone called a peaver; sometimes we made it smooth by sliding along with it under our foot. Another game we played was walking along on flowerpots tied on with string. We had whips and tops, and a yo-yo.'

'During playtime we played with whipping tops, cylindrical and mushroom types, whipping them with leather thongs attached to sticks. The tops were chalked in many colours to give a better colour effect when spinning. We were avid collectors of cigarette, chocolate bar and tea cards, which needed to be swapped to stick in books supplied by the local sweet shop. There were sets of cricketers, footballers, film stars, flowers, monarchs etc. On our way home from school, we passed the old smithy on Woodside Green. This was open fronted and we watched the blacksmith at work with his roaring furnace.'

SKIPPING IN THE ROAD

'I can recall skipping in Guildford Park Road, in the 1920s, now an extremely busy road in the town. Two children held the rope either side of the road, and laid the rope down flat on the road when a bus or cart went by.'

STATIONS AND JELLIED EYES

'At Christmas we, and all Father's family, often went to the grandparents in Wimbledon for a party. There were twelve grown ups and eight children. I remember Father taking half a bacon pig as a present one year. It was very heavy so the rest of us had to help with carrying the luggage. A favourite game – with we children – was "Stations". We each chose the name of a different railway station and sat in a circle round the room with a blindfolded "caller" in the centre. The caller said something like, "The train is going from Wimbledon to Waterloo" and the two who had picked these stations had to change places without being caught by the caller. If one were caught, then he or she changed places with the caller in the centre and the game went on. We children thought this was great fun – it certainly kept us amused and used up spare energy. A deliciously scary game we also enjoyed involved feeling objects passed around in the dark on a tray whilst one of the Uncles told a ghost story. I can still recall the feel of a "jellied" eye.'

BOGEY WON'T BE OUT TONIGHT

'One of the highlights of the year in our village on the Kent/Surrey border in the 1920s, was when the fair came. The real gipsies moved in with their caravans, and set up their swings and roundabouts on the village green. The lads would chase the girls with water pistols, and they would retaliate by throwing handfuls of dock or sorrel seeds in the boys' hair.

Another landmark was the coming of the tar barrels. Once a year the road would be resurfaced, and the children hung around watching the hot tar put down, covered in gravel and rolled flat. Any child suffering from a cough, particularly whooping cough, was brought to inhale the hot tarry steam. Steam rollers were a common sight in those days.

We drew our hopscotch patterns on the road with chalk, either round or breadloaf shape.

The best time of all, though, was when the hay was cut on the village green. Then the children played "Bogey won't be out tonight". One child would lie down and be covered with the cut hay. The other children then danced round singing "Moonlight, starlight, Bogey won't be out tonight", until they saw "Bogey" throwing off the hay. This would send them shrieking in all directions, while "Bogey" chased them until one of them was caught. That one then had to be "Bogey", and the game started all over again!'

TREATS, CHORES AND POCKET MONEY

Most children had chores to do which helped them earn a little pocket money. Some found ways to supplement their income, finding 'lost' balls on the golf course or picking whorts on Leith Hill. Even a penny could be enough to make a visit to the sweet shop a weekly occasion.

THREEPENCE A WEEK

'I had threepence a week pocket money in the 1920s and had to help my mother on Saturday mornings. She would teach me to cook etc.

I spent some of my pocket money on sweets and also saved some. When I had a shilling I would go along to the post office and put it in the Savings Bank. When I was eleven I had saved enough for a bicycle and was then given sixpence a week because I could go further delivering shoes for my father, who was a bootmaker and repairer in Betchworth.'

CADDYING AND 'LOST' BALLS

'On Saturdays the boys used to go caddying on the common at Copthorne. This was about 1924, the time of the Charleston. They got one shilling and sixpence a round, a sixpenny tip and sixpence for cleaning the clubs. The brook ran through the course and two or three boys would waggle their feet in it so that the golfers couldn't find their lost balls in the muddy water. With the help of a Jack Russell dog, the boys got the balls, hid in the bushes and then "found" them after making a show of looking. Of course, they knew who would be likely to reward them for their trouble. Otherwise they took the golf balls apart and made catapults out of the elastic. Arthur's parents ran the Artisans Golf Club at the bottom of New Town, now The Gables, and the Toffs played the working men once a year and invited them into the clubhouse.'

MILK AND RABBIT FOOD

'My mother bred goats for milk and to show and won several awards. Milk was of course on ration just after the Second World War and I had a small milk round in Woldingham, delivering the milk in little churn-shaped containers. I also delivered eggs, chicken, duck and goose. This service was given completely free of charge on my part. Imagine sending a six or seven year old out on her own nowadays! We also kept 50 or so rabbits, and I spent many happy hours with a wheelbarrow out collecting rabbit food from the hedgerows.

'For many years, twice a day (Christmas Day included), my father did a milk round through Capel village and we children always had to be on the milk float, drawn by a pony, to help with the delivery. It always seemed to be my turn to go to the almshouses. Today callers go to the front door, but in our time it was the back door for us. I didn't mind the first four houses, but the inhabitant in number five always reminded me of a witch. No doubt, she was a very sweet old lady really, but I used to creep by her door as quietly as possible, as through her window I could see her kitchen range on which was the largest saucepan I had ever seen and I felt for certain that I was going to finish up as "one for the pot". Milk was three pence a pint in those days and our speciality was Devonshire clotted cream at one shilling and three pence per half pound.

My sister and I for our help in delivering the milk and also assisting with household chores, washing eggs and milk bottles, received six pence a week, which we had to put into our money boxes to be later transferred to our banking account. We did also receive another two pence a week, though, which we were permitted to spend on sweets. I think we rather felt at times that we were overworked and underpaid, but with hindsight I realise what sacrifices my parents made and how they worked and struggled to make the farm a paying concern so that we could receive better education in later years. We did have our times of fun, though, especially when there was a considerable fall of snow and we could go tobogganing down our fields, and with a green adjoining the farm we had our opportunities to go on the swings and roundabouts. Birthday treats didn't cost a great deal of money, they just meant a picnic in the hay with various children from the village joining us.'

HASLEMERE MUSEUM

'The Haslemere Museum on Museum Hill, built by Sir Jonathan Hutchinson, one of those many Victorian educators and benefactors of their own particular village, was a favourite haunt on wet days and Sunday afternoons with my parents. Exciting and brave to see the toes of the Egyptian mummy which had escaped from those ancient wrappings!

In the Easter holidays when I was ten we were encouraged to follow Sir Jonathan's rather original idea about examinations. He thought students should be encouraged to study their papers before they sat for their examination. Accordingly, encouraged by our parents to take part, we went along to the museum and bought from the curator, Mr W.E. Swanton – dressed as always in a tweed Norfolk jacket and knickerbockers and brown suede leggings – a brown paper covered booklet of ten question papers, with ten or twelve questions on each paper. Then began the research for the answers.

Only one question can I remember: "I'd have you know that these waters of mine were once a branch of the river Rhine – what am I?" But not only papers were to be studied. There were also two large trays in the entrance hall, one had photographs of such celebrities as the local late Lord Tennyson, George Eliot and Bernard Shaw, and politicians and artists, the other had objects such as fossils and dried cuttlefish, which had to be identified from their counterparts in the museum and, hopefully, remembered. When we felt fairly confident that we had done our homework, we nervously approached the curator and asked if we could sit the examination. We sat in his office and pulled out one of the papers and wrote our answers, and with this done, we then had to name five of the photographs and five objects shown to us. I suppose I was lucky to get enough marks from this test for I was allowed to choose a book from the selection by a local donor – it was Palgrave's Golden Treasury – and this was duly labelled "presented to Mary Madgwick in recognition of having passed a meritorious examination", and in due course presented to me at a prize giving ceremony one Sunday afternoon after Easter that year by a local resident, Sir Algernon Geikie (an eminent geologist of those days).'

SMALL DELIGHTS

'Two things remain in my mind as the "ultimate" in small treats for me as a young child in the second half of the 1930s.

The first was to persuade my mother to allow me to buy a Japanese shell. Carried carefully home, costing only a few pence (two pence comes to mind), it was dropped into a tall tumbler full of water. Then followed a period of breathless anticipation, watching and waiting until – joy of joys – the shell began to open gradually and as if by magic paper flowers began to unfold and bloom in the water, followed sometimes by a tiny paper flag. The war obviously put an end to the import of this Japanese wizardry.

Another treat was to have a "Penny Stab". The going rate for pocket money at the time was a halfpenny a day, so with a bit of self denial, this was an affordable treat. On the counter of the sweet shop was a box with lots of small circles printed on the surface of its cardboard lid. You chose a circle and stabbed a hole through the lid, whereupon a tiny coloured ball rolled out. Mostly the balls were coloured and you just got your moneysworth – or less – in sweets; but it was possible to get a silver ball, in which case you received a two penny bar of chocolate. There was (reputedly) one gold ball. If you were lucky enough to punch the right hole you would get a prize worth sixpence. The gambling instinct came into play, and children were drawn like iron filings to a magnet to this. I never saw anyone get either a silver or a gold ball (though it was rumoured that a silver ball had appeared on one occasion). Despite a feeling of being cheated, it didn't stop us risking all.

All sweets in those days were sold from large glass jars. The sweets tended to stick together, and were shaken up before serving, thus by the time the jar was empty there was always a collection of chippings from the brightly coloured, highly flavoured boiled sweets sticking to the bottom of the jar. These the shopkeeper used to press together from all the jars – all the colours of the rainbow and all the flavours, from winter mixture to pear drops jumbled together. These were sold in half penny bags and were called "sievings". Second only to bubble-gum on my mother's hit list, and therefore highly popular and much prized . . . and simply delicious. Forbidden fruit really did taste the sweetest! Health and hygiene legislation must have destroyed for ever such tasty morsels.'

WHORTING

'In the summer months of July and August during the 1940s, my eldest sister and I used to get up very early on a Saturday morning to go up onto Leith Hill to pick about six pounds of whorts (whortleberries or bilberries), in time to send them on the 7.40 am bus to Dorking to the greengrocer to earn a bit of pocket money. After this we used to have to go wooding to get enough sticks for Mum to light and keep the copper fire going all day Monday to do the family washing.'

SCHOOLDAYS: THE HAPPIEST DAYS OF OUR LIVES?

Tables learned by rote, milk warming by the stove on a cold day, the ringing of the school bell, the new school dinners – memories shared by thousands of Surrey schoolchildren. By the age of 14 most had left school, thankfully or otherwise, to find work, though for the lucky few a university education was a possibility.

THE FIRST WORLD WAR AND BEFORE
'My first memory is of school, which I attended when I was three years old in 1898. We had sand trays with sticks to write and draw with, and the schoolroom I was in was tiered, which we called The

Gallery. We wore white pinafores and there were no backs to the seats. When we were doing nothing arms were always folded behind our backs.'

'We had the usual village school at Capel with a headmaster and three teachers and I went there before the First World War, at the age of five, to be given a good grounding in the three "R"s. This being a church school it was visited regularly by the local clergyman. The first lesson each day was Scripture. We were examined yearly by a diocesan inspector and if any class was not up to standard the class teacher *could* be dismissed. I remember getting a medal with "The Good Shepherd" on it, and I wore it round my neck. This exam was followed by a half-day holiday.

The next lesson would be arithmetic. I learned to count with small sticks, and tables were learned by rote, the class reciting them all together. Only when one table had been thoroughly memorised would we move on to the next. Then came reading, not by the phonetic method, but the "look and see" way. I found reading easy, but many found it really difficult – though these children were never neglected.

After that came writing. I believe much more use was made of the blackboard in those days than is customary now. We had to copy what was written there, and if we made mistakes the teacher would come and rap our knuckles with a thick blue pencil, but for really good work we would be rewarded with a blue G in our exercise book!

Drill was another morning lesson, taken out in the playground – arms up, arms down, hands on hips, knees bend etc. This was not very exciting and nothing like today's PE. In the infants' class we did have games such as "Two's and Threes", "In and Out the Window", "Fill the Gap" and so on.

When dinner hour came, local children would go home for a meal, but those coming from a distance (in some cases two miles or more) would have brought their own food – whatever could be afforded. No school meals or drinks were provided in those days.

Afternoon would be the time for handwork, girls learning to knit on large wooden needles, or to sew with red cotton on white calico; while the boys would be taught canework or gardening, each of the older ones having a plot of his own in the school garden and, in later years, in the recreation ground.

On some afternoons there would be painting and drawing for boys and girls, also nature study lessons, when pupils would bring specimens such as sticky buds or catkins to the class. School finished at 4 pm and some children then had a long walk home, there being no public transport in those days.'

'When I had been at school for a few months the First World War started. The commons around Churt were soon covered by Army camps, and the lanes resounded with marching soldiers and horse-drawn gun carriages. We had a long walk to school, so took sandwiches for lunch in what we called our "dinner bags". Mother made these like shoulder satchels out of some strong material. I wore a white starched pinafore over my frock, and had black stockings kept up by garters and button boots. My brothers wore knickerbocker suits, strong boots and caps.

We started the school day with prayers and hymn singing. Our first lesson was Scripture. We sang grace before and after the dinner break, and ended each day with prayers. In the winter we paid two pence a week and at dinner break were given a cup of cocoa made by the elder girls. If cold or wet we ate our sandwiches sitting on forms round the classroom fire. We were expected to sweep up any crumbs and leave the classroom tidy.

There was no sports equipment at the school, and boys would fashion a cricket bat and stumps out of pieces of wood. In those days boys had iron hoops, and the village blacksmith would make one – and a "skidder" – for about a shilling. We had seasons for games. In the spring girls would play ring games and the boys would play marbles. No marbles were played after Good Friday. We had hopscotch, skipping and hoops. There were conker fights in the autumn. Conkers came from the tree by the church gate.

There were only coal fires in the school rooms and if it was very cold we were allowed to wear our gloves in class. During the war slates were used for sums and tables to save paper. The scratching of the slate pencils was most unpleasant to the ear.

Once during the war we marched to the church green to a service when a Canadian Regiment laid up their colours in our church before going to France.

We picked blackberries for jam, collected acorns for pigs, and took pennies for the Red Cross, and wrote slogans such as "Don't Waste Bread" for the War Effort. We rarely had pocket money, and I can remember my brothers weeding a drive for a penny an hour. We had to remember to say "Sir" or "Ma'am" or "My Lady" when spoken to by the gentry, and to respect anyone in authority. Books were scarce, and as we all liked reading books were treasured. We took a great interest in wildlife, made up our own games, and had a healthy happy childhood.'

CHANGING TIMES

'My father, and his brothers and sisters who had also been brought

Serried rows of children at their desks learning by rote was the norm of infant school life right up until the 1960s and strict discipline the order of the day.

up at Meadvale in the 1870s and 1880s, first went to school in the village hall and my grandparents had to pay one penny a week for each child to attend. My elder brother and sister went to the new village school which was built in Somerset Road. There were two classes, one taken by the headmistress Mrs Robinson and the other by her assistant Miss Peat. At this time children were transferred to St John's at the age of eight or nine. Then by the time it was my turn the village children undertook their complete education at St John's school.'

ORPHANAGE CHILDREN

'During the First World War, the orphanage at Meadvale was at the bottom of Hardwick Road, in a large house now divided into flats for the elderly. One half of the house was for boys and the other for girls. In those days the two did not mix. I well remember those poor children in their drab clothes. Few in the village were well off in those days, but in comparison with the children from the "Homes" we were well cared for.'

'I had a somewhat different childhood from most folk in that I grew

130

up in an orphanage from a very early age until I was 18. We were well cared for and had a thoroughly good education. Our staff were all resident. I don't recall any love or an arm around a shoulder but neither do I recall any unkindness. There was the odd school bully, of course, but you soon learned to keep out of her way.

We had to learn to stand on our own two feet from a very early age and had to make our own beds, darn our stockings, sew on buttons and name tapes etc and clean our own shoes.

Shoes were the only thing I remember fighting over – needless to say we never had new shoes. The shoe-room was the only place I remember being in a scrum. Most of us fibbed as to whether shoes fitted, appearance was all important (little changes in this sweet life) and it didn't matter too much if toes were squashed – only now do I regret those fibs!

On 1st May, every year, we changed from gym tunics into summer dresses and from long, black thick woollen stockings into socks. With the shedding of the black stockings we could also dispense with those ghastly liberty bodices and attached suspenders – a great joy! I detested those frightful liberty bodices and frequently hid mine, together with my knicker linings (essential, I was led to believe, for use with navy blue "ETBs") under my mattress.

Gym tunics were worn at a regulation four inches above the knee. We had to kneel on the floor for the seamstress to measure the hem. My grandfather always commented "By Jove, she has some good understandings!" and as I was in gym tunics until I was 18, who was I to complain about the mini skirt when it came into fashion?

We had an excellent library and were greatly encouraged to read. We had to read four books every term before we were allowed to do any handicrafts. We were questioned on the book which we said we had read and a list went up in the classroom. This was checked from term to term so that we could not repeat the same books.

School was routine and no one had any options. We all did the same things and games were compulsory every evening from 4.30–6pm. Next we changed for tea and then went off to "prep", which was done in our classrooms with either a prefect or the duty mistress in charge.

If we stepped out of line, naturally we were punished – usually given a hymn or a psalm to learn, or some poetry or a goodly chunk of Shakespeare. Writing lines was not "done". It was considered a gross waste of time and paper, and having nothing we were all taught, from a very early age, to abhor waste. Sometimes we were given an unpleasant task to do such as sweeping the playground or helping to clean the playroom or the common room or ironing the Guide uniforms – we had our own Guide company and Brownie pack. If we talked after "lights out" in the dormitory the prefect in charge made us get up and dress and run around the playground to tire us out.

As routine we had assembly and prayers morning and evening. We went to the local church, in crocodile, every Sunday morning. Walks, again in crocodile, were compulsory every Sunday afternoon. On our return we had to write a letter to our next of kin. All letters were censored by our form mistress.

I had no parents but I was well cared for with a lot of others in the same boat. We were grateful for small mercies and most days were filled with fun and nonsense and always there was someone up to mischievous pranks to make us laugh.'

THE MISSES OUTRAM

'In 1922, at the age of five, I started my education at a school called "Miss Outrams" in a room at The Institute, Leatherhead. The school was run by three elderly spinster sisters known to us as Miss Flo, Miss Edie and Miss Winnie. It comprised abut 30 boys and girls from the ages of five to eleven. Most of the boys left when they were eight and went on to preparatory schools. We sat on benches at long tables covered with brightly checked tablecloths. We didn't always sit in the same places and I well remember how the girls avoided sitting next to a boy called Roger, as he was prone to pinching us!

After roll-call, prayers and hymn singing followed. We learned the catechism, and I was forever mystified as to why the answer to "what is your name?" was "N or M"! Bible stories were made interesting and various matters were learnt in rhyme such as:-

"Joshua the Son of Nun
And Caleb the Son of Jephunneh.
Were the only two
Who got right through
To the land of milk and honey."

The three "R"s were tackled every day and each child was carefully monitored to make sure that they were learning. Reading was taught phonetically and we really did start with "The cat sat on the mat". For writing, we began with copy-books which had parallel lines between which we formed the letters of the alphabet. Pencils had to be held in the correct manner and with their blunt end pointing towards the centre of our shoulder. In arithmetic lessons we chanted our tables parrot-wise and we did our sums in graph paper exercise books.

132

English grammar was given great importance and gradually we learned how to parse a sentence. We were encouraged to write stories from our imagination and read them out loud. We listened eagerly to the books which were so well read to us. One beloved poem about "Leary the Lamplighter" would bear no relevance to the children of today, but there was a gas street light outside my nursery window and I watched out for "Leary" at dusk.

Gifted as they were, the Misses Outram could not have been artistic as Miss Bell came once a week to teach us Art. I fear that I shared their lack of talent, as the highlight for me was that the class was taken in another room from where one could see passers by, specially horse drawn vehicles and motor cars.

Ball games were not played but we did set exercises, and also those with dumb-bells and clubs. During "break", we played around in a yard at the back of The Institute.

We always had a holiday on Derby Day and for weeks beforehand, we watched the colourful gipsy caravans being pulled along by horses up the Epsom Road.'

GUILDFORD COUNTY SCHOOL FOR GIRLS

'When I was at school in the 1920s, my day started by leaving home each morning at 7.30 to walk through fields and woods in all weathers to catch the eight o'clock steam train from Horsley station to Guildford. There was only one train an hour so I dare not miss it. Spring was quite the nicest time of the year to walk through these woods, which were a mass of anemones, primroses and dog violets.

Each morning we assembled in the hall for prayers, wearing navy blue box-pleated gym slips – four inches from the ground when kneeling – with white long sleeved square-necked blouses, long black stockings and black house shoes; plimsolls were allowed only for gym and games.

One could hear a pin drop when our headmistress, Miss Wright, tall and dignified, gracefully walked through the assembly and on to the stage. On one occasion I remember her wearing a long bottle green wool gaberdine skirt with a deep cream long sleeved high necked silk blouse. Her hair was swept up with a small bun at the back. After prayers, a hymn and notices, we would leave the hall to the music of a stirring march, played by dear Mr Seal, the music master, or by one of the staff and occasionally by one of the senior girls.

Rules were strict, uniforms must be worn at all times – navy velour or felt hats in winter and plain white straw or panama in summer –

both with the navy and red hat band and badge with the monogram GCS. This badge was also worn on the pocket of our blazers.

Hair should be bobbed, tied back or in plaits, never loose or over the face. No jewellery whatsoever. House badges only were allowed: blue for Anglo Saxons, dark green for Britons, orange for Danes and white for Normans. These Houses during the year competed for various trophies for work, sports, gymnastics, national savings etc. The House contributing the most articles for the annual sale was rewarded with a cheap tea on the day of the sale.

And yet another rule. Girls living in the Guildford area were allowed into the town after school. For those travelling by train permission was granted only if one had to attend the dentist or for any other good reason and then only if a letter had been received from the parent with such a request.

During one of our gymnastic lessons we were told with straight knees to bend and touch our toes. One poor girl was unable to do this and sprightly Miss Gill in her short gym slip hopped off the stage to help her. She cried out, when she found the poor girl was wearing a boned corset, "Don't come to school again wearing those. What do you think your ribs are for?" Most of us were wearing liberty bodices.

We always looked forward to our school party, which was usually held in December. Then we really could let our hair down and wear our crepe-de-chine and velvet frocks and dancing pumps.'

EOTHEN SCHOOL, CATERHAM

'I only went to one school – Eothen School, Caterham, which I attended from 1920 to 1932. It had been founded in 1892 by Catharine Pye, a fine woman with a real vocation for teaching. She had read History at Newnham, but I suspect that many of the other teachers were unqualified. However, they were dedicated women, who worked as a team under an exceptional leader, for whom they, and all the pupils, had love and respect.

Our curriculum included English, History, Geography, Scripture, Arithmetic, Geometry and Algebra (taught as three separate subjects), French, and Latin from the age of about twelve. Science was Nature Study and Botany until, at about 14, we had Chemistry lessons in an ill-equipped lab in a disused stable. We had to pay for any test tubes we broke and, as I was clumsy, it became expensive, so, after one term, I abandoned Science in favour of Greek!

I enjoyed all academic subjects but Needlework was always taken by the current Mademoiselle and we were supposed to talk French during the lesson. As I was shy and nervous about talking French and my sewing was abysmal, needlework was not my favourite subject! Art was called drawing and was taught by a forceful lady who soon realised my inadequacies. PE was two half-hour periods a week of gym in the school hall, where we had a vaulting horse and a horizontal bar, but no other equipment. I was fat and clumsy and always found myself at the back of the class, partnered by an unfortunate girl called Nancy, whose nickname, for obvious reasons, was Beaver. I did not shine at netball or lacrosse, which we played in the winter terms, but I did achieve the first VI tennis team in my last two summers. For matches the team wore white dresses coming well below the knee and white cotton stockings. We went as a deputation to Miss Pye to ask if there could be any alternative; after consideration she agreed that we could wear flesh-coloured thinner lisle stockings, provided we all bought them at the same shop, so that our legs would all look the same!

At the age of 16 I took School Certificate, roughly the equivalent of O Level or GCSE. Each subject involved two or three papers, usually of three hours each, and there was always a three hour essay.

Our classes were arranged by the pupils' ability rather than by age, so there was often a range of two years between the oldest and youngest in a form. I was in a group of about a dozen and was always one of the youngest, so all the others, some of whom were 17 or 18, left after School Certificate. I, however, wanted to do what was unusual in those days, especially for a girl – go on to a university. Accordingly I was alone in my glory in the VIth form, studying Classics, for a year, though the following year two others joined me.

At 18 I took Higher Schools Certificate (A Level) in Latin, Greek and Ancient History and then, the following autumn, I had to take an exam for entrance to Cambridge, involving two three-hour papers each day for a week, followed by an interview. Luckily I was accepted, but the competition was great, as there were 6,000 men at Cambridge, but only 600 women!'

GIRTON HOUSE SCHOOL

'I must have been about three and a half when we moved from London to a new house in Mitcham. In the 1920s developers built long straight rows of identical houses but didn't make up the roads first, as they do now. I can remember walking beside my mother, who was pushing my brother in the pram, over wooden sleepers with thick sticky mud oozing up between them.

But it was our first very own house, and it was in the country. My mother was pleased and worked very hard to make the house

135

comfortable, while my father cleared the builder's rubble and dug the heavy clay, with the help of his brother, my uncle, to make a large garden where we could play, and grow flowers and vegetables.

There were all those houses and no school anywhere in the vicinity. So two enterprising ladies started one in an ordinary three-bedroomed house similar to those many of the children lived in. They called it (rather grandly) Girton House School and that's where I went when I was five. There were hooks for our outdoor clothes in the kitchenette, and milk was heated on the cooker there at playtime when we played in the garden in fine weather. The back room, with a French door into the garden, was empty except for a piano, and the floor was covered in shiny brown lino. It was in this room that we had morning assembly, singing and dancing lessons. The front room downstairs and two bedrooms were furnished as classrooms, and the third and smallest bedroom was where the "big girls" studied. There were two of them, and they must have been all of 13 or 14. Sometimes they helped with the younger children, among whom there was great rivalry to stand next to them and hold their hands! As one was my mother's cousin, I always felt that privilege should be mine!

This idyllic and unconventional schooling lasted until the council school was built. We called it the "tin-can school" because its walls were of corrugated iron. Eventually a "proper" brick school was built to which I went for the rest of my elementary education. A secondary school was afterwards built on the site of the "tin-can school".

However, I never attended that school as when I was ten I won a scholarship to Mitcham County School for Girls. So for the next several years I, with three or four friends, walked every morning right across Mitcham Common, passing Seven Islands Pond on the way. The journey took us about 50 minutes and we did it in snow blizzards, in dense fog, and in lashing rain as well as the heat of summer. Not something today's children would contemplate, I feel, but our parents didn't have cars, very few girls had bicycles, and there was no bus route then. But on the whole we were healthy, the exercise did us no harm, and we walked to school amongst golden gorse bushes with larks soaring and trilling above our heads on summer mornings. The pond was a source of delight on our homeward journey. In winter we tried to reach as many of the islands as possible on the ice, and in summer attempted to reach them without getting our feet too wet!'

NAPS IN THE AFTERNOON

'No school dinners were available in the 1920s and everyone walked home at midday, and then back again in the afternoon, which was no hardship for the older children, but was a little wearying for the tinies. The teachers were aware of this, and as camp beds were few and far between, the following ingenious method was applied so that we could get a much needed nap. At a certain time in the afternoon, the tables were turned upside down, to display a heavy screw embedded in the end of each leg.

Then oblong pieces of canvas were produced, with a large ring in each corner, which was hung over the screws, forming a hammock, into which each child crawled. Necessity was certainly the mother of invention in those days.'

DRESSED IN VELVET

'My first day at school in Sanderstead in the early 1920s was an anti-climax. I was sent home again until a week after term commenced when I would then be five. I wore button boots, a white pinafore trimmed with lace, and a blue velvet dress trimmed with swansdown; presents from maiden aunts. My mother soon changed all that. Sandals or lace up shoes and drill tunics or cotton dresses with knickers to match. Hair cut to semi-shingle with fringe. Other children soon followed the fashion, long hair and plaits disappeared overnight. We had long periods in class when we had to sit with hands on heads or folded behind our backs reciting times tables. We were not allowed out of our seats and desks were in twos or long forms. My first day at school I sat next to a boy called Philip. He was rather plump and dressed in a brown velvet suit with a lace collar. The impression I received was that he had outgrown it.

Those early days of my childhood were overshadowed by the recent war. My father came back, many did not. One of my friends, a war orphan, had to deliver clean washing to the better off houses. Her mother had to "take in washing". When her shoes were being repaired she stayed away from school. At school we learned plenty of Scripture. I already knew a lot having been to Sunday school from age three. Also at day school we learnt much about the British Empire, the Royal family, and many of the works of Rudyard Kipling. There was no question of new books, they were given out at the start of lessons and collected at the end. A much coveted job was of monitor; book monitor, ink monitor, and much later when older, to be allowed to ring the bell for school, which was housed in a belfry with a long rope attached. It was quite an art, ringing the school bell.'

GETTING THERE

'I lived rather off the beaten track – no chance of a car – we had to walk everywhere, whatever the weather. It took us between half and three-quarters of an hour to reach school, depending on the conditions. If wet or snowy it meant sore legs where wellies rubbed and tired socks that went down inside. Often fingers and toes were so cold – a sure recipe for chilblains. On reaching school we went into the classroom with a fire in the corner behind the guard (the milk was put round it to thaw out ready to be drunk at playtime). We kept our coats etc on to keep warm. There was often a pool of water round our thawing feet.

Concentration was guaranteed as windows were either obscure glass or so high that it was impossible to see out. Lunches were not served at school so this meant another walk of about a quarter of a mile on a path to the Grafham Room where all food had been delivered in insulated containers, (which meant that the menus were rather rigid).'

THE SCHOLARSHIP

'I was born in 1925 so by the time I started school the Depression was really biting. Being an only child and with an excellent housekeeper for a mother I was well cared for. My socks were always washed and darned, my blouse was always ironed and I always had plimsolls for drill (PE nowadays).

My father was the village postman and his wages were less than £3 a week. Money was so tight that on Sunday afternoons he would cycle from Merstham to Chipstead to empty a letter-box at 3.30 pm. It was a round trip of six miles and for this he earned an extra threepence a week.

In the summer evenings he worked hard on his allotment so we had plenty of fresh vegetables, but it was winter evenings which I enjoyed most. We didn't have a wireless and after tea my mother and I would sit at the table playing Snakes and Ladders, Ludo or a card game, while my father sat in his big armchair and read the *Evening News*. On his way home from work he would call in at the station and buy his paper for a penny. It was his only extravagance and he read every page before his bedtime at ten o'clock.

I coped quite well at the little village school and when I was ten the headmaster sent for my mother and said he would like to enter me for a scholarship to the grammar school. My mother agreed, but realized my chance of passing would be slim as it was seven years since a local girl had won a free place; this was before the days of the eleven plus and the vast majority of places were for fee-paying pupils.

Well, I managed it.

Then came numerous forms to fill in to apply for various grants based on my father's income. I can see him now sitting at the table with his steel-nibbed pen and a bottle of Stephens Blue-Black ink. It was not an evening for playing Snap or any other noisy game. My mother read a book, probably Dickens, and I lapped up an Enid Blyton.

As the result of all the form-filling I was awarded full fees, free dinners, a bus pass and a grant for uniform every two years, so it was decided I could accept the place.

Next followed an interview with the headmistress, a tour of the school and a prospectus giving the names and qualifications of the staff, certain rules such as the production of a Health Certificate on the first day of term, and a little note to say that every girl was expected to contribute twopence a week to the charity which the school supported each term, a penny a week for flowers for the assembly hall and so on, making a total of sixpence!

This caused much consternation. Fourteen shillings a week went for rent, a set amount went in the gas and electricity meters, so much was put aside for insurance, the panel and the hospital fund (no NHS in those days), a shilling or two was for clothes, my mother would never buy on credit from the tallyman. There was food, coal and household goods to allow for, and nowhere was there a spare sixpence. I went to bed at eight o'clock and I could hear my parents talking downstairs. They couldn't say no to the scholarship after all, could they?

The next evening my mother and I cleared away the tea things and washed up. As we sat down at the table my father pulled up a chair too.

"What are we playing to-night?" he asked.

He had found the much needed sixpence a week. He had given up his beloved *Evening News*.'

'Having survived the Second World War, I passed the scholarship and went to Dorking County (Grammar) School. I was one of the first of the non-fee paying children at the school; free education came in in 1945. The teachers and some of the upper school were none too pleased about this – instead of having only those rich enough to pay, they had to put up with the likes of me . . . poor but bright. Unfortunately, due to the snobbery I soon became very unhappy at school and left in 1949 without any qualifications.'

TUNIC. Dark Navy blue serge or woollen gaberdine with velveteen yoke 2 ins. deep, three equal box pleats back and front (not stitched), to fasten with buttons under the left arm, **and in no other place.** Length to clear the ground when kneeling, **but not shorter.** Ready made **tunics (serge and alpaca), blouses and Science overalls or materials for tunics or overalls** must be bought from Messrs. Chiesmans, who supply these at specially reduced prices.

KNICKERS. Navy blue serge, gaberdine or alpaca to match tunic, to fasten with elastic above the knee, and not to show below the tunic.

GIRDLE. Navy blue military braid. Quantity required, 2 to 2½ yards. Separate from the tunic, and to be tied in a bow.

WHITE BLOUSE to be worn with tunic; ordinary shirt pattern to fasten at the front with turn-down collar of the same material, cut so as to be suitable for wearing with the School tie, with **no trimming or ornament of any kind** (such as feather stitching).

TIE to be bought at the School, price 1/-. It should be fastened with a plain gilt safety pin brooch.

STOCKINGS. Black, not openwork.

In the Summer Term, the serge or woollen gaberdine for the Tunic and Knickers may be replaced by navy blue alpaca. The alpaca tunic should not have a velveteen yoke and the girdle of military braid should be replaced by an alpaca belt, 2 in. wide, and fastened in front by two navy blue buttons.

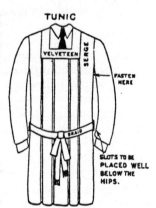

NOTES.

I.—Strong leather, laced shoes, with low heels, and pads are required for hockey.

II.—At all times the hair, if not cut short, must be tied back with navy blue ribbon.

III.—**No Corsets or Stays** must be worn for Gymnastics and Games. Corsets or Cotton Stays must be replaced by a woollen "Liberty Bodice," obtainable at most drapers.

IV.—No petticoats must be worn with the School uniform.

V.—No ornamental hair-slides or jewellery of any kind, except a small plain safety-pin brooch, may be worn in School at any time. If other jewellery is brought to School it will be confiscated until the end of the Term.

[P.T.O.

Details of the exacting uniform requirements of Lewisham Girls School in 1928. It was probably a relief to many that 'no stays or corsets may be worn for games' although the dreaded 'liberty bodice' had to be worn instead.

SWIMMING LESSONS

'One memory I have of Shalford school was learning to swim in the river Wey. We would all march down to the Three Oaks – the nearest shallow point for non-swimmers. To get there we had to walk round the back of the cemetery, across two fields and then it was everyone for him or her self to find a suitable place to undress. The boys would creep around the trees or bushes to try and catch a glimpse of the girls' underwear, and heaven help the girls if the boys saw their knickers. For days afterwards they would shout out at school, "I saw your green (or any other colour) knickers." We were always shouting out to the boys, "I'll tell my Mum you were looking at me." However, came the dreaded moment when, in our locknit costumes, we had to run across the field to the river, dodging the cow pancakes, thistles and nettles and enter the cold dark muddy water. Once I saw a dead dog floating by, but we still had to go in. Surprisingly enough, I managed to get a Swimming Certificate for 25 yards, but one foot must have been on the bottom. The worst part was getting out and running across the field to get dry, trying to get the wet locknit costume off, with towels never thick enough to dry and the same boys still peeping at you. Then the march back to school.'

WANBOROUGH SCHOOL 1930s

'I attended Wanborough school from 1935 to 1939. In those days there were two classes, one for five to eight year olds, the other for eight to 14 year olds. The young ones were taken by a Mrs Summers and the older ones by Miss G.E. McDougal. Lessons did not follow a set pattern, but I remember the weekly swimming lessons during the summer terms for the twelve to 14 year olds, involved a two mile walk across fields to the Normandy Scouts swimming pool. Boys on one day and girls another.

Cooking lessons were held in Ash Vale. This meant a one mile walk to Wanborough station, a train ride to Ash and another mile's walk to the cooking centre. The boys did the same trip for their woodwork lessons. There were at the most only four of us who went at a time, there being only between 20 to 30 pupils of all ages attending Wanborough school at any one time.

After morning prayers on Empire Day (24th May) we used to have a small ceremony of raising the Union Jack on the school's flagpole. Then we had the rest of the day off from school. The flagpole was in the school "field", no cut grass in those days. We did have a garden. It was looked after by the older pupils. The boys worked the vegetable plots and the girls looked after the flowers.

We had a wind up gramophone and a few records, to which we did PT (physical training) and country dancing. Other lessons like geography, history, maths, English, spelling, art and needlework were also covered.

Looking back our teacher had a real task, but we were given the will to learn, and respect for others. When my younger sister left in 1945 there were seven pupils left and one teacher. The school closed soon after.'

INGRAM SENIOR SCHOOL 1930s

'It was 1933, I was eleven years old and had just sat the dreaded "scholarship". My loved ones and mentors knew I would pass, but, contrary to these affectionate but biased high hopes, I failed! Auntie Ivy led the wails of protest at the rejection of this wonder child's talents, but secretly my thoughts were: "Oh good, I can still roller skate to the Senior School, it's only just down the road!".

Miss Payne, the headmistress, was a diminutive lady of five ft one inch and although lacking in height oozed authority and competence. Her hair was, as the saying goes, "black as the raven's wing". Was it dyed? Probably, but beautifully coiffured in the Marcel wave style of that era. She had a flawless complexion, very little make-up, grey eyes that could quell the most rebellious pupil and scare the living daylights from the rest of us. She had a curvy but petite figure and always wore black silk or crepe de chine. Peeping from her elegant dresses were an exquisite pair of ankles and tiny feet encased in high heeled, black patent leather court shoes. In summer, the only deviation from her "uniform" was her enormous cartwheel hat of scarlet straw. It was a magnificent creation. Our Mums, who were so much younger than Miss Payne, didn't dress so stylishly; it never occurred to us that Mum lacked the wherewithal and only at Christmas did she appear in anything new!

She was an exceptional lady. For all her fierce exterior she had our interests at heart, particularly with regard to education. I think that she realised that some of us had missed out on higher education. She encouraged, bullied and cajoled us and saw that we sat the examinations available at that period. I still have my Royal Society of Arts certificates in various stages of Arithmetic and English. I also possess and treasure what was, from Miss Payne, a glowing reference.

The 1930s was a very sporty era. It was almost as though athletics was a new discovery, which to some extent, it was. We discarded

142

our navy blue pleated tunics for sport and frolicked around in our navy fleecy lined bloomers, white ankle socks and black plimsolls. On went the tunics for netball and, as captain, I sported a white girdle. I did enjoy swimming but Violet was the best swimmer in the school. To everyone's mind, she was Olympic material. What a hope! She came from a very poor home and there was little or no sponsorship.

Our last year we attempted to learn how to cook. The lesson took place in a grand new building with all the latest "mod cons": electric cooker (very new) and of course gas, and a huge electric mincing machine. The lunches we prepared were for the very poor pupils. We were poor, but always there was plenty of the necessities of life. Some of the children were in very poor circumstances. My friends Nellie, Margaret and Doris had "school dinners", not "lunches" as they are called nowadays. What shocked and worried me was the size of the portions that "the powers that be" considered sufficient to sustain good health. Nellie had a perpetual cold, sores and nasty flaky patches on her arms and legs. The food was beautifully cooked; Miss Newton saw to that. She was a perfectionist, and woe betide us if we failed her culinary standard! But she was carefully rationed by the School Board. The result was, and the menu never varied, one tablespoonful of mince, a little less of potato, cabbage or dried peas. For pudding, a spoonful of boiled rice or a gill of milk. The rules were strictly adhered to, after all, it was FREE! But, if I could take an extra turn at washing up instead of serving, I would do so. I just could not face these poor unfortunate friends of mine.

It was about 1935 when the craze for bandeaus became fashionable, along with the games of biff-bats and yo-yos. Bandeaus were of bone or tortoiseshell, half circles to wear almost as a tiara. They came in various colours and so we saved our farthings and ha'pennies for weeks! There was a tacit understanding that no one wore theirs until we all had one. The great day came and we arrived in class resplendent in our bandeaus. None of us had much but this was something glamorous and within our reach. Miss Robbins looked us over in breathtaking silence, carefully studying each of us as we simpered and smirked and waited for her words of admiration and praise.

At last, and staring at no one in particular, Miss Robbins said quite slowly and succinctly "You look like a troupe of chorus girls!" The bandeaus disappeared, never to be seen en bloc at school again. Such was the awe and respect we felt for our "betters".'

SURBITON 1930s

'Until 1937 we attended the local St Andrew's school in Surbiton built about 1860 with very high windows and one open fireplace. It was customary to have milk mid-morning then and the elderly teacher with the fireplace instructed the girls in her class to place the bottles round the fender to warm the milk in winter. There was a wooden partition separating one classroom and a whitish curtain divided the main large room. This was used for assembly.

Playground games went in cycles but skipping was very popular with lots of rhymes for doubles. Two of the rhymes were modern featuring Charlie Chaplin and another R. White's gingerbeer. We also played marbles periodically and collected cigarette cards but it was only boys who played flicking the cards and conkers. Some children played in the side street but we were not allowed to. We also played various types of "he" with rhymes for commencing the game. In 1937 I went to Tiffins Girls School at Kingston, then just moved into new buildings. Hopscotch was the only game played. It was played on every available patch not yet planted with flowers and on a bank where the grass was struggling to grow. I had never played it before and played it for two years. Three years later when I left it was still being played on the same sites.

One of the biggest differences between now and then must be school dinners. It is true I lived in an urban area, but virtually everybody went home to midday dinner. The school day went from nine to twelve and two to four in the infants and to half past four in the "big girls", giving a two hour break. One teacher stayed and got a girl to buy her rolls and cheese and apple and very occasionally one girl who lived near the school asked if she might stay the next day. The new Tiffins Girls School was on the outskirts of Kingston and it was not expected that so many would be able to get home so the lunch break was shortened and dinner could be bought for one shilling. It was also accepted that you could take sandwiches but nobody was allowed off the school premises unless they were going home. In the autumn of 1940, lessons were scaled down from 40 minute periods to 30 minutes enabling us to finish school at 1 pm. This of course was because of the bombing. It was probably in the spring of 1941 that we reverted to afternoon school but the lunch hour was shortened again and we finished at 3.15 with 3 pm for juniors. More children were staying to dinner and the price was reduced to eightpence because a government subsidy was introduced for the first time.'

144

CLOSED FOR ASCOT

'I went to the local school at Egham and as Egham in those days was on the main route to Ascot, lessons were disrupted during Royal Ascot Week when the school was closed. It was said it was because the increased traffic in Egham High Street would be dangerous for the children – we went home to dinner at twelve o'clock and that was peak traffic time. We used to go and watch the traffic go through and see the fashions. Every year right up to the Second World War there was a man who came through on a penny farthing bicycle. He always got a special cheer and it was rumoured he cycled from London.'

MERROW SCHOOLS 1930s

'We had to walk to Merrow school, roughly one mile, and come home to lunch and back again in one and a half hours. There was a bus called the Merrow Swinger, which plied between Merrow church and Guildford Park but we rarely had money to spend on it, if we did we would rather spend it on a sherbet fountain or aniseed balls. If we stayed at school for lunch, which was rarely, we had to either sit in the playground on the tarmac, or if wet in the cloakroom on the floor. When I was about 13, hot chocolate was introduced for schoolchildren, and one of my school friends and I were detailed for making it for eleven o'clock. We had to make it in an urn, add water and boil it over a small gas ring on the floor. When ready the class would come with their mugs and we would dish it out to them.'

'I also went to school in Merrow. It had two rooms heated by open fires, a rough playground and outside lavatories. One piece of wood left ready for firelighting was used as a cane. I was caned when I was five for getting three sums wrong on my slate. We had cowrie shells for counting. The fire warmed the room, dried our wet clothes and heated our milk (if our parents had paid for it!). On Sundays I returned for Sunday school – I suspect my parents had a well earned sleep.'

OPEN AIR CLASS

'As I was a poor little thing I went to the open air class in our school at Mitcham; a permanent marquee with duckboards for a floor and ordinary desks. If the weather was cool we wore our coats in class. In the afternoon we lay down on some sort of stretchers to have a nap. In the winter we went into the main school building. Every pupil had a third of a pint of milk a day, the crate sitting in the corner of the classroom near the radiator and in very cold weather the milk was actually put onto the radiator. The tops, made out of cardboard, had a hole to put a straw through – It really was straw, not paper. Your parents could pay for you to have a spoonful of cod liver oil and malt, which was dished out by teacher, the alloy metal spoons being put into an enamel bowl to be washed.'

THE SCHOOL OUTING

'Our annual school outing from Great Bookham was a great day as the whole school went to Polesden Lacey for tea; all the younger ones and the girls went by horse-drawn waggons, but the boys had to walk. There were large swings put up in the trees, and long trestle tables were laid up in the courtyard in the front entrance. It was a wonderful tea and I remember large bowls of very big red ripe gooseberries. The staff of the house looked after us. There was always an entertainment of the Punch and Judy or conjuror type after the tea, and before we went home we all had to walk past the large entrance where we had to curtsey to the Hon Mrs Ronald Grenville who was waiting to give us each a new silver sixpence. We also lined the streets with plenty of flags to wave to the then Duke and Duchess of York arriving to spend part of their honeymoon at Polesden Lacey in 1923.'

THE GORDON SCHOOL

'In 1948 I remember visiting the then Gordon Boys School (built in memory of General Gordon of Khartoum) on their Open Day. In the carpentry room there was on display a farm wagon complete with shafts and wooden wheels – a beautiful thing. They also had a cobbler's section and the tailor's where they made their own uniforms. The fabric was much thicker than it is today and they had to wear their uniforms all the time. Now their "blues" are worn on special occasions only, and their uniform is grey trousers and green blazers. They now have a tuck shop in the school, but before they all used to get their sweets and pop from "Johnnie Bull's", as they called the little shop on the corner of the road by Windlemere Golf Club. Mr Bull had a long, flowing white beard.'

THE WORLD OF WORK

LIFE IN SERVICE

The **Upstairs Downstairs** way of life was, for many Surrey young-sters, the only choice when they left school. 'Big houses' such as Shillinglee Place and Wotton House demanded a large staff, and middle class homes were not complete without a servant or two, a situation which lasted until the Second World War. Perhaps the epitome of the overworked servant class was the 'tweeny', the little maid of all work.

THE 'TWEENY'

'I left school at 13 to go into service. The Rev Thomas said he knew of a "good" job with the Wakefields of Wilcot House in Bisley. (Wilcot House no longer exists, but a housing development – built in the 1960s – known locally as "The Wilcots" stands on the land.) The house was built when Mr Wakefield was single. He married late in life – after recovering from a severe illness he married his nurse. They kept a cook, chauffeur, house parlour-maid, and I was supposed to be the between maid . . . or "Tweeny". All I know is I was the maid of all work, scrubbing floors from 7.30am often till 10pm at night – and then I had to walk home in the dark! All the bedrooms had jugs and basins for washing which had to be filled and emptied – and chamber pots too! All for seven shillings and sixpence a week. My employer had been a big game hunter, and the walls of the house were covered with the heads of animals he had shot, and glass cases containing huge spiders which used to frighten me even though they were dead. If he was in a good mood, Mr Wakefield would talk about his trophies. The largest of these was a huge moose head, which he waited in a swamp for over seven hours to shoot. Another "trophy" which he brought home from abroad was his tombstone, which was kept up in the loft in readiness! This can now be seen in Bisley churchyard, inscribed "William Burbeck Wakefield".'

'I left school at 14 years of age, when Mother accepted a job for me as 'between-maid' in a nurses home at a hospital.

My trunk had to be equipped and every piece of clothing marked with a name tape. Two vests, spencers, petticoats, four pairs of bloomers, four pairs of black stockings, two woollen, two lisle, two morning dresses, six white strapped aprons, two black afternoon dresses, six frilly caps and aprons, two pairs of shoes, lace up for the morning and strapped for the afternoon, a hair brush and comb in a linen bag, a clothes brush and shoe brushes and twelve sanitary towels. These were made from layers of old sheeting, about three layers thick, ten inches square, neatly sewn all round. With a loop of tape fastened on the opposite corners diagonally, these squares had to be folded so you could wear them attached by tape or elastic through the loop and tied around the body. Of course, they had to be washed and went through the laundry like the rest of the clothing.

I worked from 6 am to 9.30 pm each day with one half day off each week and a full weekend every three months. One hour off on a Sunday to go to church. All this for ten shillings a week which was a good wage at the time. But the work was very hard, I had to give it up after 15 months as I got so run down in health with a continual sore throat. They, the powers that were, considered I was a health risk.

Whilst in this job I used to cycle home each half day, 13 miles each way. My half day started about 2.30 pm after I'd cleaned the kitchen range, two fires, five ovens with black-lead and scrubbed the kitchen floor. I had to be back in the nurses home by 9.30 pm and many miles I cycled in the dark with just a little oil lamp on my bike.

At this job I had to work in the laundry one half day a week. I used to hate the ironing. The irons heated on a six-sided coal burning stove with two shelves around it. One stood the irons on these shelves, flat bottoms to the stove. There were rounded irons also for ironing the Sisters' frilled caps. All the nurses wore striped dresses and after ironing several of these one couldn't see straight.

I did enjoy putting the sheets through the big wooden mangle. The weight used to drop with such a clonk it seemed to relieve the tension.'

'My mother took in washing and also worked in one of the big houses in Merrow in the morning, one or two days a week. I started work at 14 as a between-maid at a house called Woodlands in Horseshoe Lane. I had to start at 6.30 am and finish at 3 pm. I had so much scrubbing and kneeling to do I got housemaid's knee, so only lasted there about two weeks. I then worked as a packer at Cow & Gate in Stoke Road, and after two years went back to service (which was hard work) until the war came in 1939, when I got a job as an assistant in a grocery shop.'

'When I was in daily service I was taught by the butler. At breakfast one morning I was told off for taking the boiled egg out of the cup to finish it. That was not the right thing to do. Always leave the egg in the cup I was told.'

'There was no work in my mining village in Wales and, through an agency, a job in domestic service had been arranged for me in Walton on the Hill. With me on the train travelled my tin trunk, its transit costing one shilling. I was warmly welcomed by the family for whom I was to work, and I appreciated my pretty uniform, the extra clothes and the good food. In fact, I have nothing but happy memories of my days in service and of my eventual marriage to a gardener also employed at the house. They were certainly not "the bad old days".'

THE JEKYLL HOUSEHOLD

'I went into domestic service when I was 14, in 1920. I went to the local vicar in Bramley, the Rev David Green. It was not compulsory but it seemed to be the idea that young girls stayed about a year or 18 months to get a grounding; then they were expected to get a better position with some other household, which of course happened with myself.

After several posts gaining experience I obtained a post with the Jekylls in Munstead. I worked with them until I got married. That is how I knew Gertrude Jekyll, because her brother, Sir Herbert, for whom I worked, had the old house when their mother died and Gertrude built or was building her own house in Munstead Wood. They were on opposite sides of the road so they were in and out of each other's houses all the time.

Gladstone gave the Jekylls a parrot, called Polly. The housekeeper would let it out of the cage and it would go running through the corridors and if the phone rang it shouted at the top of its voice "Aggie! Aggie! The phone!". "Aggie" was Lady Jekyll and it was telling her to come to the phone in the servants hall! It rather terrified the younger members of the staff. I once saw it get on the back of a chair behind a visiting chauffeur and nip him, right through the ear. It was rather vicious really. The footman and the groom, who lived in the house, used to get it into the downstairs bathroom and tell it all sorts of things to repeat, so you can imagine what it was like! Sir Herbert had a little dog, Jock, a lovely little Aberdeen. He was terrified of the parrot, of its getting on his back. Oh yes, it was a real horror, but I always got on alright with it – as long as you were very, very careful.

When I was at Munstead House, you started at half past six in the morning and you were lucky if you got to bed at ten o'clock at night.

150

If you were lucky you might get an hour in the afternoon to sit down or go shopping. You got out for half a day; they called it an afternoon and evening but sometimes it had got to three o'clock before you got away. You got this once a week, and every other Sunday. You were expected to go to church Sunday morning and then you got the rest of the day. And we had one week's holiday a year, when you usually went home to see your people.

In the beginning I used to get £12 a year, paid only once in three months. Out of that you had to buy your uniforms, so you did not get very much, but you managed. I paid my mother half a crown because she did my personal washing when I wanted her to. That was about once a month. The household laundry used to go to the Godalming laundry.

You had a good living if you were with a good household. Munstead House was excellent. Their social life there started about Friday until Monday or Tuesday. The house was full of visitors and it was an entertaining time. I was able to meet very interesting people, in the art world in particular. One of the nieces, Margot Post, was married to Mark Hamburg, the pianist, and I also met ballet dancers. Lydia Lopkokova, wife of John Maynard Keynes, used to come – the idea of inviting such people was that they entertained the other visitors. We had an enclosed yew garden where all the yew trees were carved out and marble figures stood in them, and in the centre was a lilypond, and I saw her dancing there many times at weekends.

In the household we had three staff in the pantry – a butler, a footman and the boot boy. There were three housemaids, three in the kitchen, a chauffeur and a groom outside, plus the gardeners.

I was in the Jekyll household for about two and a half to three years. Then I got married. If I had not, I should have gone with Sir Herbert's sister, Mrs Eden, whose husband had been the planner and maker of the Garden of Eden in Venice.

My husband was chauffeuring when we got married. He had always been on agricultural work, tractors, horses etc. He went to Eastwater House, which was bought by a Mr Mackenzie-Grieve, to drive their car. I remember when they had the first Lagonda, they had an awful job coming out by the lake and turning into the road there. The driver was in a dickie seat behind, so the whole of the bonnet of the car was across the road before you could see!'

IN THE NURSERY

'On leaving school before the First World War there was little choice of employment in Headley. Men and boys could work in the sandpits on the common splitting flintstones, or there was gardening. Women and girls mostly went into service. Hetty loved children and wanted to be a nanny, but her mother had other ideas – start at the bottom in the kitchen as a scullery maid, then kitchen maid and upwards to cook. But at 17, Hetty became an undernurse at Fourfield Close. Up at 6.30 am, light the nursery fire, taken nanny her tea, then clean and tidy the nursery. Their uniforms were grey suits and, when they went out, black bonnets with bows under their chins.'

'When I left school at Merstham, I went as undernurse to a titled family, hoping that they would travel, which they did. I was paid 30 shillings per month and out of this I had to provide myself with cotton dresses and aprons, a grey coat and skirt, white blouses, a black hat and black shoes and stockings. My day began at 6.30 am and finished at 10 pm. I was expected to be in the nursery all the time, to fetch and carry for Nanny, and not to mix with the other servants. The day and night nurseries, a bathroom and my own room had to be kept clean and meals fetched from the kitchen. There were walks outside morning and afternoon and prams and shoes to clean, and washing and ironing to be done. In between times the children were played with and dressed and, when they had gone to bed, there was the finest of sewing to be done on little frilly dresses. I had half a day off each week, after the lunch things had been washed up and tea laid, and half a day on alternate Sundays, but if one of the children was indisposed, then I would have to forego my time off.'

THE LADIES COMPANION

'Father was a clerk in the Goods Office of the Southern Railway Company at Guildford station. Mother did not have a job outside the home after she was married, but looked after our house at Merrow. Before that she had been companion to a lady, and she had lived in the "big house". She had to read to her mistress – *The Times*, and from a serious book each day. She had to look after the collection of stamps, birds' eggs, butterflies, moths etc and to be generally "there" when required. She accompanied her mistress on drives out each day. Her father was the lady's coachman.'

IN THE KITCHEN

'I left school at the age of 14 in 1928, and although I had passed an examination for Guildford Commercial College, my father could not afford to send me as there was no help in those days for bus fares or books etc; so I went into service as a kitchen maid. My duties were to help the cook. The staff consisted of cook, parlour-maid, house-maid, laundry maid and myself. We had one afternoon and evening a week off and alternate Sunday afternoons, but we had to be in by ten o'clock. I think my wage was ten shillings a week. The house where I worked was called "High Weathesell" and is near Pitch Hill, Ewhurst.

There was no electric or gas stove; cooking was done on a large range and a three burner oil stove. My first job in the morning was to black-lead the range, polish the steel fender and fire irons with emery paper, and light the fire. Once a week I had to clean out the flues – what a filthy job that was.

Milk was brought from the farm each day and put in large pans in the cellar. When the cream had set it was skimmed off and we made our own butter in a wooden churn which we turned by hand.

No frozen chickens then – my job was to pluck and draw any birds that were needed, also skin the rabbits. No washing up liquid, but large tins of soft soap.

The family had a cottage at Bembridge in the Isle of Wight. I was not quite 15 years old when I was told I was going with the housemaid and I would be doing the cooking. I remember I cried as I thought I would never manage it, but off we went and I did manage and had many happy days there. On my 15th birthday the family gave us the day off and we visited Carisbrook Castle.

Although we worked very hard, I had some happy days in service and I think we were more content with life than some of the young people today.'

'Monica came down from Durham at 14 years of age because there was no work in the north after the 1926 strike. She had to go into service. To get into service she had to see Lady Hedlam. A week later her mother was told that she had found her a place at Wotton House, near Dorking in Surrey. They could not afford a uniform as her father was out of work so they had a "club out" paid weekly and bought aprons, etc, and she was put on a coach to Kings Cross.

Monica was not allowed to eat in the kitchen, she had a seat in the scullery, although she had to lay the table for the housekeeper's meal. She worked from six o'clock in the morning (she was woken by the nightwatchman walking his dog), and black-leaded three stoves before starting anything else. She had to make sure the staff dining room was laid, clean the door step of the dining room, and clean the housekeeper's room before breakfast. She had then to start on the vegetables, draw and featherpluck chickens, and prepare hares (she got a gardener to take the blood from the hares). All copper saucepans and kettles had to be cleaned with sand, vinegar and salt. Monica's hands were always in water and she thinks this is the reason for her arthritis now.

Queen Mary and Queen Elizabeth were entertained at Wotton House. All Wotton came to see them. The butler normally used to prepare the tea but Monica was told to cut the cucumber sandwiches as he couldn't cut them thinly. John Evelyn's sister, Susanna, thanked Monica but Miss McLeod the housekeeper said she had done them! As a scullery maid she earned five shillings a week, half of which went home to mother. She had to pay two and sixpence insurance when she was 16. She had to walk into Dorking and back to save money – this must have been three or four miles one way.

There were 14 staff indoors, eight gardeners, a bricklayer, carpenter, and the plumber. Mrs Evelyn ran Manor Farm with the first Jersey herd in the South of England and there were a lot of staff in the dairy.'

'Just after the First World War, Daisy worked at the Abinger Hatch, which was a hotel in those days. She went there after leaving school and worked there for twelve months, but got the sack for laughing too much. She worked in the kitchen. She was one day carrying a pile of plates and dropped the lot. She lived in the attic with two other maids and that night one of them sewed up her nightie and they made a lot of noise laughing. In the morning she was told to go and pack her clothes and clear off home. This was in the winter at seven o'clock in the morning.'

'One maiden aunt used to live with us between jobs. She was a jobbing cook, what would now be called a temp. Some of her appointments lasted a year or more. She worked for the aristocracy. She liked winter jobs in London and the country in the summer. When she worked in Scotland we used to receive parcels of salmon wrapped in heather and once we received a box of venison. No fridges in those days, so everyone in the road received a bit of venison. Boxes of apples arrived in the autumn – it was a great life. But mostly we liked it when Aunt Ada was between jobs and she stayed with us. Her stories about the "gentry" held us spellbound. Before she retired one of her positions was at Chartwell cooking for the Churchills. She was working at Chartwell during the time Sir Winston was building his famous brick wall. She was always admiring him in those days when he was not popular elsewhere. Aunt Ada remarked that he liked his steaks underdone.'

ON THE ESTATE

'In the 1920s and 1930s Chiddingfold was a completely rural village with a two-class society: the gentry in the large houses and the village people who mainly worked for them. The most notable estate owner was Lord Winterton at Shillinglee House. With very few exceptions the men were employed as farm workers, gardeners, grooms, keepers, copse-cutters or in the three village industries – ie two brickyards and two walking-stick factories and Gauntlett's Nurseries.

Farm workers worked extremely long, arduous hours – carters feeding the horses at 4.30 am and cowmen starting the hand milking at the same time. Acres of hoeing was done by hand, and during the bitter winter weather, mangolds were pulled and trimmed for cattle feed, which were then chopped in root-cutters operated by a hand-turned wheel. Milk was delivered twice daily in two churns drawn in a pony and trap.

All livestock was driven on foot along the roads, even to Guildford market, and chickens and ducks roamed the village green. Cart horses and wagons were always outside the forge on the green. The men had dripping and onion sandwiches with a bottle of cold tea for their lunch.

At Shillinglee there is an ice-house excavated into the hillside. This had to be stacked with ice from the ponds in winter. It would last for several months and was mainly used for storing game.

When the girls left school they nearly all went into domestic service. The scullery maid was up at 5 am to clean and light the range and make the cook her morning tea. They had one afternoon a week and every other Sunday off. To visit their homes often meant a long walk there and back again. The staff at the big houses were generally very happy, and their employers treated them well. There was considerable rivalry between the different households.

On Sundays the coachmen drove their employers to church, and waited for them in The Crown.'

'Large estates, of which there were several in the Lingfield area, employed five or six gardeners, had their own stables with grooms in charge, estate carpenters, and many upstairs/downstairs staff – these were usually members of local families. Men skilled as carpenters, plumbers, painters etc often worked from home. Ivy's mother was a dressmaker, her father was a painter and decorator and her grandfather was a tailor, making clothes for the local gentlemen and the male staff employed on the estates. Marjorie's father was an estate plumber, and met her mother in the private laundry of the estate, where she worked.'

155

'My grandfather was a shepherd at Gatton and every Christmas Lady Colman presented my grandmother with blankets made from their own sheep. These were cream coloured, with a navy blue stripe at the ends.'

ON THE FARM

Surrey has a strong farming tradition, supplying fresh produce to the great city on its doorstep. It is not long since dairy herds held up the ever increasing traffic on the roads, and haymaking was the highlight of the year.

THE DAIRY FARMER

'Richard Balch, my grandfather, came to Erne House, Whyteleafe in 1910 and set up as a dairy farmer assisted by his three sons Harry, Dick and Ted. Cows were housed in a large barn near the gas holder opposite the Rose and Crown. Also two Jersey cows grazed in a field at Well Farm, on which now stands the Rank Organisation's offices. Other supplies of milk came up by train to Upper Warlingham from Oxted, Cowden and Hever. The eight-gallon churns were rolled down Station Road with a little man called Bibby. Twice daily supplies of milk were delivered by horse drawn milk carts. Each cart held two eight-gallon churns, from which milk was drawn into two-gallon hand cans onto which hung one pint and half pint measures. Housewives brought out a jug, basin or jar to collect it. The gates over the level crossing at Whyteleafe were manually operated by a little man called Jock.

My father set up a small dairy at 44 The Green in 1927 and carried on until his retirement in 1950.

One of the milk roundsmen always wore a bow tie, a bowler hat in winter and straw boater in summer. One Christmas morning he became the worse for wear, through too many glasses of home-made wine and lay outside the Harrow Inn in deep snow with horse and cart standing over him. My father had to leave his Christmas dinner and go out to rescue them.'

'I was born at Bullhousen Farm in the 1920s, which is situated out on the common at Bisley, where I still live and where my family continues to farm and provide a milk round for the villages of West End and Bisley. The farmhouse dates from 1757, and is unchanged structurally from the time it was built.

Memories of farming in my childhood are of the large amount of staff involved by comparison, bearing in mind that we had far fewer customers and far less cattle to look after. We used to employ at least eight full-time staff as well as casual labour. The men all used to milk before going out on the round. Despite this it was quite a lonely life for a child, tucked away out on the common away from the mainstream of village life. My parents were too busy to take us for outings, and we never had a holiday. Few village children had holidays away from home in those days – most were in their 'teens before they had the opportunity to go away.

Life did have its compensations, however, and though haymaking was hard work it was great fun in those days – much more fun than it is now! The men used to come home for their meals, but I remember taking tea out to the haymakers, and in the evenings village men who were not farmworkers used to help out.

The milk used to be delivered twice daily, and was bottled in the evenings. One of my jobs as a child was to polish all the brass on the churns every night. All the little hand churns with brass bands round and brass measures had to be polished. I also had to polish Dad's leather leggings to a high sheen.

Old Grand-dad Elliot of Ramsbrook Farm in Bisley used to go out twice daily with two pails slung from the wooden yoke on his shoulders delivering milk. He used to walk so slowly, "like a snail", presumably so as not to spill a drop of the milk, which was ladled into jugs on the customer's doorstep. It was sometimes as late as 10pm when he arrived at the last houses. Before the days of refrigeration, it was common practice to put a ten gallon churn down the well to keep the milk cool.

Most farms in the area had a pond, fed by underground springs. This was the only water available for the cattle. It was customary to keep one goat with every herd of cows to prevent contagious abortion (brucellosis). I hated the goat – and the feeling was mutual – and one day when I was little it chased me upstairs. It was common practice for local people to keep goats on the common for their milk, and three horses roamed the common too – Gwen, Maisie and Dick. Dick had mange, and used to rub against the post box, until eventually he knocked it down. Cattle used to be driven from the market in Guildford (where the new Law Courts are situated now) along the roads to Bisley and Chobham.'

157

'My father was a dairy farmer. Milk was delivered around Millbridge with a pony and cart from a large churn, from which milk cans were filled and the milk ladled into customers' jugs. Later bottles were used. Surplus milk was separated for Mother to make butter, and cream was also sold. We kept pigs, chickens, and turkeys for Christmas. These, with fattened cockerels, were plucked and dressed – feathers everywhere! The chickens scratched in the farmyard and eggs were collected from all sorts of odd places.

All the farm work was done by our three horses. Long hours were worked at haymaking and harvesting. Threshing day caused quite a commotion, with the big steam engine to drive the machinery and all the windows closed against the dust. When grass was cut for hay it was turned several times, then made into small cocks with pitchforks, carted, and made into ricks which were thatched for the winter.

We lived in a 16th century timber framed farmhouse. It had a large kitchen/living room and originally there had been a large open hearth, where bacon could be smoked in the chimney. When gas arrived in about 1927, a gas stove was fitted in the scullery and all the cooking was done in there. Until a gas geyser was fitted, water was heated in a copper and carried upstairs once a week for a bath, otherwise we had a jug of hot water and a good wash. The toilet was an earth closet outside, and chamber pots were used upstairs at night. Most of our relations visited us at weekends in the summer and there were large parties for dinner and tea. Mother did all her own cooking and there was a plentiful supply of food for any unexpected guests. There was always a lovely warm smell of baking.'

THE POULTRY FARMER

'In 1924 my family moved to Great Bookham. My father bought the land with the idea of developing it as a poultry farm, and by 1927 it was taking shape. I left school that year and stayed at home tending the poultry and working up an egg round in the village for which I received the grand wage of five shillings per week. Most of the eggs were sold commercially in bulk from the farm. Dorking and Guildford markets were favourite haunts for poultry farmers who seemed to meet for a day out and a good gossip. My father's plan was to give up his work in London as soon as the business was able to support the family, and it was at this time that he took the step. As things progressed he increased the size of his holding. Later, when we had large incubators for hatching the chicks, we found that the oil heaters were unreliable and it became clear that electricity should be brought to the farm. This was not done without some frustration, because by this time other people had started to build and move in and it seemed to us that they might like to share the cost of having an electricity supply brought to their homes. Nobody was interested, however, until we, of necessity, went ahead and got it installed at our expense. They all wanted it then! For us, however, it was wonderful to have lights that didn't soot up and a cooker that didn't need fuel that had to be laboriously carried in by hand.

Christmas was always a busy time, plucking birds for sale to a butcher in Leatherhead or directly from the farm. An interesting feature of poultry farming were the poultry shows and egg laying trials held at Chilworth. We frequently did well on these occasions.

By the mid 1950s Bookham was beginning to take shape as a dormitory town and our land was sold off for development as a bungalow estate – so my father was able to retire.'

BORN ON THE FARM

'I was born on a large farm in Surrey and my earliest recollection was at the age of four years being pushed from the station by my mother. I was very cold and my mother had wrapped a rug around my knees, but my feet were frozen. I imagined that if I moved to a different position the rug would feel warmer, but of course it was much colder. I believe that this was the beginning of my determination, in a different sense, never to have cold feet again. My life held many dangers, but I grew up never to be afraid of life.

Haymaking was the highlight of summer – my mother would load the wagons and Dad drove the steam engine. I was in the coal bunker singing from my heart, totally carefree. I was desperate to help, so my father made me a miniature hay rake and when they "stacked up" I did also. Back at the farmyard Dad would say "Round or square?" for the shape of the stooks, and I was allowed to choose. I grew to love and know every thing about farming.

My brother was two and a half years older than me. It was six years before my sister was born. About this time war was declared. All the children around had to help on the farm gathering eggs and helping with the milking. My job was to hold the cow's tail to prevent my mother being flayed. Butter was made in the dairy. In my mind I see the gleaming marble slabs and huge attractive bowls. The cream was separated and everything done by hand. I would take my turn to churn the butter. Nothing was refrigerated but everything was perfect.

One day I was left in the charge of my father who was lining out the wheels of his engine. He asked me if I had a paintbrush, which

I hadn't, so he said "Your hair would make a fine line." He cut a little piece of my hair from one side only and bound it together and painted the wheels. When my mother saw my ruined hair she was furious, but Dad said "It was a perfect paintbrush" and I was very proud to tell everyone that my hair was used for the lining out.

There were no combine harvesters in those days but all the children helped with the stooking. It was my job to keep the horse which drove the elevator walking in circles. One day I walked away from the horse and my skirt got caught in the gearing, pulling me towards the cogs. No one was near to help me as I was pulled in. I tugged at my skirt which tore but released me. My mother, who realised the danger, did not mention the state of my dress, knowing I would have lost a finger at least.

With so many dangers, I had only one real accident when a cart horse backed suddenly and trod on my foot. There were no X-rays but Mum, who had some nursing training, bound my foot tightly, but the fact that my toe will move up but not down proved that no bones were broken.

My father was bailiff on the farm. At the end of the war the owner started a market garden and we had one last adventure in a much smaller farm. We were threshing beans and a stick caught in the machinery. My father said "Crawl in and see if you can pull it out", which I could not, and so he very slowly started the steam engine whilst I pulled out the stick. All was well despite the danger.'

HOP PICKING

Although Kentish hops are those which usually spring to mind when hop picking is mentioned, Surrey once had a strong hop growing tradition in the Farnham area. School holidays were arranged to coincide with hop picking, when whole families joined the visiting Cockneys in a well loved custom.

'During the First World War, I lived in a charming old village situated amongst the fruit and hop picking fields. Fruit picking of strawberries, gooseberries, black and white currants, was hard work and had to be done with care, but hop picking was our delight!

160

Our day began with a three mile walk to the fields where we commenced work at 8 am. There we met with the Cockney families from London, who adopted one of us for the day to pick with them – all earnings going to them. Most of the Cockneys regarded this work in the fields as a holiday away from London. They were provided with a hut to sleep in, and a large communal brick fireplace to cook on. They had large families, all doing work of some kind, no matter how young. During our dinner break we had lots of fun playing amongst them, learning games and songs and how to do all manner of useful things.

My first introduction to one of their mid-day "snacks" was the biggest hunk of bread I had ever seen, topped with a huge piece of cheese, topped again with a Spanish onion – oh boy! How they used to tease us about eating this and a mug of hot sweet tea was very gratefully received to wash it down with.

Hop picking became a very sleepy job during the afternoon owing to the contact with the lovely smell of hops and sometimes we children were allowed to sleep awhile on a hop sack.

Work went on till 5 pm when we walked the three miles back home, rather dirty and hungry but with memories of a wonderful day spent in the countryside.'

'Our school summer holiday at Farnham was a month in August. There were no seaside holidays but days spent playing in the nearby fields and woods. Then it was back to school for two weeks, then two weeks hop picking holidays. Whole families went off to the hop fields each day, arriving by six o'clock in the morning, rain or shine, then everyone, adults and children alike, picked hops for the princely sum of a halfpenny a bushel. I well remember the year when the whole field went on strike, so they upped it to a penny a bushel.'

'Many people went every year for the same growers. The price varied according to the state of the hops and pickers would try and get a higher price if the hops were small as it would of course take much longer to fill the large bushel basket. I think the rate would have been somewhere around twopence a bushel.

The woman who had taken the basket would generally pick straight into that and the children and anyone else who would lend a hand occasionally liked something smaller, maybe a bucket, basket or box. Woebetide you if you knocked against the big basket when it was nearly full! Arms would be thrust into the hops to lift them up to touch the seven bushel mark. When it did the tally man would be called and the hops were tipped into a surplice – a canvas sheet which when fastened would be put into a cart and this would go off, when full, to the kiln for the drying process. There were quite a few kilns in the town as there were a number of fairly small growers in the area.

Children would naturally soon get tired of picking and enjoyed playing with the many others around when let off, though the small amounts they earned were most acceptable.

Picking hops stains your hands a browny green and the smell is not easy to get rid of. Hop bines are very hairy and if you weren't careful could give you most unpleasant scratches.

Before the hops were quite ready we enjoyed watching the gipsies coming through the town on their way to a nearby village where there were some facilities for them. What a colourful lot they were in their horse-drawn caravans, loaded up with all their goods and chattels.'

'Aldershot is on the Surrey border and in a corner of this garrison town a few hundred yards from the Surrey villages of Ash, Tongham and Runfold, I lived from birth in 1924 until marriage in 1946. Looking back, many memories are based in Surrey – the unexplained pleasure of standing one foot in Hampshire and one foot in Surrey, the excitement of speedway and greyhound racing in Tongham, and the hop picking in Runfold.

Summer holidays were a month long and after about two weeks back at school another fortnight's break was hop-picking holiday. Many families went from the council estate where I lived. Fathers took their holidays then from work (if they had any) and the money was a God-send to many of the poorer families in the area. From the warmth of my bed I used to hear the rattle of pram wheels on the road very early in the misty autumn mornings. Children crying, squealing and shouting, their elders hurrying them along on the long walk to the hop fields. Later on in the day if it was warm and sunny I would get my bike and join one of the local families and pick a couple of bushels of hops for them. I can still visualise the hordes of children, all but the toddlers, having to do their share of the picking, mothers in their pinafores letting the hops trickle gently through stained fingers from the bushel baskets to the seven bushel bin at the end of each row of hops. Sometimes strikes took place for an extra farthing a bushel because the hops were so small, "shirt buttons" they were called.

I can hear the wails of a child having been given a really hard smack for knocking against the bin and making the hops sink. Father's belt was in evidence often when boys were not doing their share. The calls for the tally man to empty the bin and the shout of "No more bines" when the oast house was nearly full.

I remember the pungent smell of the hops and sometimes above it all, wafting from the bakery nearby, the aroma of lardy cakes straight from the oven. Never since then have I tasted lardy cakes to match those greasy sugary delights.

I never waited for the packing up, I never had to trudge miles back home, I never got to the fields to find it was too wet and no picking was to be done that day. My new winter shoes didn't depend on hop picking. I was lucky.'

'For generations my family were on hop and fruit farms, and all my childhood in the 1940s was spent amongst the orchards and hop gardens.

Before September the farmers and labourers were busy putting the final coats of white-wash on the hop-pickers' huts and making up the beds of tree branches and wheat straw. The Cockneys liked their huts as cosy as possible. They booked the same ones each year and often came down in the summer to check that there was no mistake over bookings.

Sharp at 7 am everybody got out in the hop garden. "Oh Gawd Blimey, we've only just cum darn", they called to my grandmother. "What's the tally this year Guv'nor?" they shouted to my grandfather as he drove round the field in his pony and trap. My mother was Bookie and she started by taking down the names of the bin occupiers. She recorded each picker's daily pickings and also controlled the amount of hops that could be picked in one day. There was a limit to the quantity of hops that could be dried in the oast house.

The smell of the hops was marvellous, and an apple laid in the hops in the bin was truly delicious.

Varsity students came down to the camp every year and organised surgery, canteens and concerts. They had their own ambulance and brought tea and coffee out to the pickers. There was great hilarity all day; the lolly-man came with huge baskets of sweets, the ice-cream van came ringing its bell, and the fishman came with his kippers and bloaters.

At the end of the day my father patrolled the hop garden and ordered the measurer and bin man to get the hops ready. The special basket formed the "tally" and this decided the rate the pickers would be paid. Sometimes the next farm had better pickings and fights would break out. The sacks of hops called "pokes" were taken to the oast, and I loved to ride on top of the load and go into the oast where the hop drier would be spreading the green hops into the kilns over a horse hair carpet. The hops were dried over fires of charcoal, Welsh coal and a dash of brimstone for colour. The dried hops were pressed into pockets by special machines, and we used to sample the billy-can tea and baked potatoes from the hot ashes of the kilns.

The hop-picking season usually lasted about five weeks, and every Sunday visitors came down from London to see their families. There was dancing and singing at the pubs every weekend, and I remember lying in bed listening to the "hoppers" making their way back to their camp. There would be singing round their big open fires and jostling round the water pumps. Near the farmhouse I remember the stamping of heavy feet as twelve magnificent greys champed at their oats.

Everyday the marvellous smell of hops was all around, and everywhere there would be carts of hops or apples coming from the orchards.'

JOBS FOR WOMEN

Work for women tended to be in the traditional fields, such as going into service, nursing or the fashion world, even for those with a university degree. It was accepted that a woman gave up full time paid employment when she married – beginning instead the life-long, and unpaid, task of running a home and a family.

A WOMAN VET

'A friend of ours, Miss Groom, lived with her mother in a large house at the top of Park Road in Kenley – now a nursing home. She was a qualified vet, but at that time, just after the First World War, women vets could not work on their own, so Miss Groom helped the local RSPCA man. Her great love was cats, so she had plenty of work to do. She went everywhere on a very old bicycle, and she had a basket fixed to the front of the bicycle and another to the back. When it was raining she wore a huge macintosh cape which covered her and both the baskets! She also wore a fisherman's hat – a wonderful sight.'

APPRENTICE TAILOR

'My father was killed in the last big battle at Passchendaele in Ypres in 1918, after being in the Territorial Army from the start of the First World War. He was posthumously awarded a medal for gallantry as he was killed trying to save another officer. It left my mother with two small children and she was expecting another, that was me. At the age of 26 it must have been a very gruelling time for her.

My grandmother came to live with us to help us out, and she decided to go into the tailoring trade with a Mr Cotterill, so a tailor's shop was opened in North End Croydon, but the workshop was built in the back garden of the large house that we lived in.

My mother always said that if we were left in the same position that she was, we could always sit at home, look after our children, and earn a living at the same time, so whatever our qualifications at school, into the trade we had to go.

You did as you were told in those days. My sister and I were paid apprentices. It was a civil and military tailor's shop and we made all the livery for the staff that stood outside the Croydon Town Hall. We also altered the Mayor's coat every year, taking off the ermine

Women employed in Department stores sometimes had as restricted a life as those 'in service' as they often lived above the shop. Here the ladies of Alders pose for their staff photograph.

165

and having the coat cleaned, and then shortened or lengthened it according to the height of the Mayor. As a little girl I remember parading up and down the workshop in the Mayor's gown before it went to the cleaners, feeling like the cat's whiskers.

At the age of 15 I went into the trade, and I hated it! There were about 32 tailors and tailoresses in the workshop – aunts, uncles, family friends, even some of the girls I went to school with became apprentices.

As I was the youngest, I never minded making the morning tea, at least I got out of the monotonous tuition of the buttonhole making, the felling and basting that had to be perfect.

I saved my first and last button hole, and it has been entered into the living memory quilt that has been designed by Jean Hammond, a professional quilt designer, reflecting the lives of the people in Croydon.'

APPRENTICE DRESSMAKER

'In 1936, at 14 years old, I started my life's work as an apprentice at a dressmaker's at the bottom of Wimbledon Hill. It was a narrow building which stretched back from the road quite some distance. Two maiden ladies, Miss Carter and Miss Scorey owned the business and ran it with cast iron rules. Below them were three hands, then three improvers, then, lowest of the low, one or two apprentices. My father paid a premium for the first year, and my pay was five shillings for the next year, he also had to provide scissors, tape, needles, and pin cushion. On my first morning I had no thimble (I had never used one) and I was told to bring and use one on the next day or not to come back!

The ground floor was used by an optician, and our front door opened to a corridor the length of the building. The back door (used by staff) was at the end together with the steps to the cellar.

Turning sharp right before these, one walked the width of the house, and then turned left up two flights of stairs. The corridor ahead led to the fitting room which was large and comfortable and looked over the street. There were screens down the centre with cheval mirrors on one side and armchairs, a table and magazines etc on the other. Halfway back along the corridor, steps led to a landing where there was our one telephone and pad. Turning again, more steps led to the top corridor, and turning left yet again there was Miss Carter's and Miss Scorey's sitting room and bedroom. Above the fitting room was the workroom. This had large windows overlooking the street and gas lighting. Two long tables ran the length of the room with dressmaker's dummies scattered around.

Three treddle machines lined the wall in front of the door and in the fireplace opposite were gas rings and flat irons. Bowls of water and cloths for pressing were next to them.

An apprentice was expected to answer the front door bell; it took three minutes going full pelt to get down there to show up the clients. We had to answer the phone, pick up pins and be general dogsbodies. No-one was allowed to talk in the workroom except about work. The thought of a wireless would have sent Miss Carter and Miss Scorey completely mad. Miss Carter ran the fitting room and saw clients. Miss Scorey did most of the pattern making and cutting. We were lucky to be taught all the work, some places only had skirt hands and bodice hands etc and never worked on the whole garment. If you were lucky and Miss Carter liked you, you would also be taught fitting and cultivating clients, and some of them were very hard work! If there was a death in an important family we would work all night to finish the mourning outfits. No bereaved lady could go beyond her front door in those days except in full black. We made Court presentation dresses and the three-feathered head-dresses. I completed mine to get my Court Dressmaker's certificate before the war stopped the "drawing rooms". To do this I had to complete a five year apprenticeship in three years.'

APPRENTICE MILLINER

'After leaving school in the 1930s I eventually obtained an apprenticeship as a milliner with a family firm in Hanover Square. We were very well looked after. There were girls called "matchers", who would visit shops and wholesalers matching up ribbons and straws for hats. In the millinery workshop we sat at long tables with white cloths. The milliner sat at the top of the table, then came the copyist, the improver, and last of all, the apprentices. I well remember I had to make 50 hat linings every day by hand fly running, and I would use a large magnet to drag around the floor to collect all the pins that had been dropped.'

THE SEAMSTRESS

'"Tribie", a much loved friend from my childhood came to our house in Sanderstead weekly to do sewing jobs. My mother used to think up tasks for her to do to keep her in employment. When all else failed she would ask her to make a tennis dress, and when my mother died a pile of almost unworn tennis dresses was found. Miss Tribe was

167

expert at making loose covers and curtains, and turning shirt collars, but not so hot at fashion.

Times were hard for Miss Tribe. She walked to our house in Sanderstead and earned five shillings a week for her work, later this was increased to six shillings. Her terraced cottage with no mod cons backed onto the railway. She bought coal one bag at a time.

We always had a big dinner on Tuesdays, Tribie's day, as my mother thought she needed a good meal, and she did love her food. She usually stayed in our house some time after her work was finished to save fuel at her home. It did not seem to occur to anyone to raise her wages, but she did receive a good many perks and did not seem to feel patronised by it.

It spite of her hard life, Tribie had endless patience with us children and always radiated good nature, though I do remember her saying "It's all or none, Nora. All or none," ie the well off want for nothing, the poor have nothing. She was not far wrong!'

NURSING

'It was a raw and gloomy November day in 1935 when I found myself looking up at Tredegar House, the four storey building being the preliminary training school of the London Hospital. The door was opened by a trim maid in a pink striped dress and frilly mob cap. Standing close by, a formidable figure in an attractive pale blue dress with leg of mutton sleeves and a beautifully goffered lace trimmed head-dress with long streamers trailing down the back. Janet Scott, the Sister in Charge, greeted me. Although she ruled with a rod of iron, under her ample bosom was a heart of gold and kindly help for any of her flock that was in trouble.

"Don't use the lift unnecessarily – it's good for you to run up and down stairs" rang through the building. What stairs! Four flights up if you were unlucky enough to have a bedroom on the fourth floor.

For the next six weeks, one's feet barely touched the floor. Up at 6 am to place jugs and bowls in each bedroom, cleaned until they sparkled, then a dash to the broom cupboard where serried ranks of brooms and dust pans awaited breathless student nurses to grab and race back to sweep under beds and linoleum covered bedroom floors. Breakfast at 6.45 am, bowls of steaming porridge passed quickly down long tables. The food was plentiful and good and after the first day or so was thankfully eaten by all as our bodies needed every ounce of energy that food provides. Our arms and bodies ached as we struggled to strip a bed as we had been shown by Sister and Staff Nurse – envelope corners, the middle crease of the sheet exactly in the middle of the patient. Rubber life-size models of male, female and child were blanket bathed and sat up, limbs bent in various positions, as we dressed and bandaged their bits and pieces. A welcome break was tea served in the sitting room – what a benison, a hot cup of sweetened tea and a large piece of sponge cake! A glance through the windows where we saw endless funerals winding their way down the road, black horses tossing their plumed heads as they pulled flower-laden hearses to the cemetery.

Twice a week we donned our outdoor uniform and raced to the underground to arrive at our Alma Mater. Here in spotless clean kitchens, we concocted dainty dishes to tempt jaded appetites and to memorise nutritional values. Before we realised, exams were on us and we cajoled our brains to bring forth the facts and data we had tried to learn.

Then the Pass List – oh joy of joys. I had passed, I was no longer a "Tredegar".'

'I was born in 1919, one of six children. I knew from a very early age what I wanted to do for a living – I wanted to work with children. My mother had a niece who was a teacher in Manchester and she knew of a day nursery that trained nursery nurses. The fees were £50 per year and you had to buy your own uniform. I was accepted for this training and my mother and sister took me along on the day I was to commence my training. I had never been away from home before, and knew that it would be six months before I would see them again.

There were five of us in training, plus a Sister and the Matron. I was shown my room, which I shared with two others – an iron bedstead, lino on the floor and several old chests of drawers and a large wardrobe. Although the girls were all very friendly, I must say I felt very homesick for some months.

Our day started at 6.30am. We spent three months in each department: tiny babies up to one year; toddlers from one to three years; and older children three to five and three months kitchen duties where you assisted the cook, shopped and prepared meals. Our first job was to light the fires in the nursery and sweep and dust and generally tidy up. Breakfast was at 7.30am and the children started arriving at 8am. You were served at meals in order of seniority – Sister first right down to me – newcomer!

When the children arrived they were bathed in a mild disinfectant, as many of them had fleas, then put into nursery clothes. Jumpers and trousers on the bigger children, and the babies in knitted matinee coats and dresses. The nappies were huckaback cloth, and these were put into a bucket and washed and scrubbed by hand at the end of the day. Our hands were red raw with harsh soap. The washing was done in a large cellar that also had to be scrubbed out afterwards.

The children were collected between 5–6pm. Most of the fathers were on the dole, but the mothers worked in eiderdown factories, and some of them came to breast feed their babies during the day. They paid one shilling a day, and the children had dinner and tea for that money. After the last child had gone home, we had to rake out our fires and re-set for the morning, scrub the floor and make up the cots for next day. Our own supper was at 7pm. After supper on three nights of the week we had to report to Matron's room for a lecture and make notes on all she said – this was for study for our final exam at the end of one year.

We were only allowed one bath a week – two had to bath on Tuesday and three on Thursday. We had to wash our own undies, but our uniforms – dresses, aprons, caps and cuffs, went to the laundry. I was left with just Matron at weekends as it was possible for the four other girls to go home, and this is when I was very homesick and tired, as I had never scrubbed a floor in my life before this. When I first went home it was quite a wrench to go back – however, I knew this was my bent in life and I loved the children. Some of them were very poor and dirty, but very lovable. As time went on I enjoyed the training, as strict as it was, very much. Occasionally one of the girls invited me to her home for the weekend – this was a real treat to get right out of the building.

The end of training came and exam time. A five hour exam, and I am happy to say I passed with credit. We could leave at the end of one year, but I still didn't feel confident to go out into the world to earn my living, so decided to do another year and gain an advanced certificate. I was then promoted to staff nurse, and felt quite important and was given quite a lot of responsibility.

War was now looming on the horizon. I got my first job at Dolphin Square in London as a staff nurse to very monied families – some serving abroad and some divorced. This nursery was on the ninth floor and very luxuriously furnished – the opposite extreme from my training days.'

SECRETARIAL WORK

'I graduated from Cambridge in 1935, aged 22. My Classics degree did not specifically fit me for anything except teaching Latin to little girls, who probably did not want to learn it anyway and I did not think that I would be very good at it, so I decided to take a six month secretarial course at Mrs Hoster's.

This was considered one of the more up-beat secretarial colleges.

As well as learning the basic skills of shorthand and typing we were instructed how to address, say, one of HM's Ambassadors or the Archbishop of Canterbury, as it was felt that this information would be of great value to many of the students. At the end of six months, armed with certificates showing a reasonable competence in typing and shorthand, I went to see the Secretary of the Cambridge University Women's Appointments Board. She was Miss Sybil Campbell, a large cheery Scotswoman, like anyone's favourite aunt and I shall never forget what she said, when I asked her if she had any suggestions to make. She said "Well, dear, I ought to say that because you have a degree you should not accept a job at less than £4 a week. However, having said that, no one is going to employ you for £4 a week as you have had no experience. Go away and get *any* secretarial job you can and come back and see me again in six or nine months' time, when I am sure I shall be able to help you".

I managed to get a job with a well-known firm of stockbrokers in the City for 45 shillings a week. I was the third of a small group of three who worked for the Partner and his team, who were responsible for giving opinions on shares to would-be investors. We worked in the same room as the typing pool of girls who worked in the general departments of the firm and we all had to wear cotton, wrap-around overalls over our ordinary clothes. They were provided by the firm and were changed every Monday – green one week and brown the next. The only occasion when we were allowed to leave them off was if there was a heat wave in the summer and the temperature soared into the eighties. That was the signal for the men to be allowed to remove their jackets and work in their shirt sleeves!

I did not go back to Sybil Campbell, as I had two rises with the stockbrokers and after about 18 months I left for a job with the John Lewis Partnership at, I think, the princely sum of £400 a year, which was riches indeed. My salary may seem low, but one has to take prices into account. My third-class season ticket for three months from Merstham to London was £5 10s 0d.'

171

JOBS FOR MEN

THE JOCKEY

'My father-in-law Ted Finch had become a prominent jockey by the turn of the century. He started his riding life when he ran away from home and became an apprentice with a horse trainer in Malton, Yorkshire. He moved to various parts of England and eventually arrived in Epsom, where he became a retained jockey to the Nightingale Stables. In the course of his career he also travelled through Europe, riding horses in Ireland, France and Eastern European countries. To keep down his weight for riding he regularly "walked the hounds" from Epsom to Worcester Park and back, over what then was open country.'

THE BRICKMAKER

'My father was a brick moulder at the local brickworks in Red Lane, in the southern area of Limpsfield/Hurst Green. Bricks used to be hand-made of local clay. The clay was dug by the brickmakers, called "homicking", mixed by a steam-driven engine, taken out and manually worked into a mould. It was left to dry, then piled onto "ack" ground and surrounded by other bricks, and the whole was set alight to "fire". The local school in Hurst Green was built of these bricks, as was most of the Merstham council estate. The bricks were of a mottled colour.'

'At Meadvale during the First World War, Brown's Field led to Brown's Brickyard, one of the main sources of employment for men from the village. They made bricks and a large assortment of clay pots and the kilns were always firing. The clay was dug from an area adjacent to the towers and the subsequent hole was made into a pond and stocked with carp. Mr Brown charged two or three pence for a licence to fish in it.'

THE CARPENTER

'I remember Grandpa as a stocky, older version of my father, except for his grey hair and bushy moustache, and his headgear. He lived and worked in Sanderstead.
    Dressed in his blue serge suit and best boots, Grandpa always

172

looked slightly like a fish out of water. In his element he wore a long white apron with a rule protruding from the pocket, had a pencil behind his ear and carried some sort of tool in his hand. He was a carpenter and joiner, as were his father before him and my father after, and his memory is inextricably linked with the smell of sawdust.

His apprenticeship indenture, which I have, is dated 16th February 1893, and it bound him "with the advice and consent of his father" as apprentice to a local builder, in consideration of the sum of £10 "part of the monies of the Charity of the late Archbishop Laud for binding out Poor Children of the Parish of Croydon Apprentices." He promised to serve his master; keep his secrets; do him no damage nor see it be done by others; not waste his goods nor lend them unlawfully; nor absent himself. In return his master undertook to teach and instruct him in "the Art of a Carpenter and Joiner", for the wages of seven shillings and sixpence a week during the first year, twelve shillings and sixpence during the second and 18 shillings during the third. To complete the agreement, my great-grandfather undertook to find and provide the boy with "good and sufficient meat, drink, lodging, clothing, washing, medical attendance and all other necessaries".

My husband now uses some of the tools which belonged in later life to that young apprentice. When I look at them I may not be able to visualise the 17 year old who signed his indenture, but I can quite clearly see myself, sitting on the old man's knee, delightfully dreading the damp and bristly kiss of his walrus moustache.'

'One of my most treasured possessions is a book of signed photographs of many film stars of the 1930s, all dedicated to my father who worked with them. He was quite a small cog in the great wheel of movie making – he helped to build the sets. So wherever the film was made Dad would go. Sometimes we did not see him for weeks when the film was on location and once he had to guard the giant octopus seen in an action adventure film (it was actually six inches across and kept in a bucket).

His favourite actress was Jessie Mathews and he was involved in a number of films she made – even on one occasion holding the door as she stepped from a taxi in a film. In those days everyone helped out. In *Lorna Doone* starring John Loder and Margaret Lockwood (1934) he donned a Puritan hat and rushed round firing the village of the Doones. All very stirring stuff and I loved to hear him talk about it.

He was a superb carpenter and made most of the toys I played with as a child – a tiny Welsh dresser, a tiny three piece suite, and various puppets! There was little money to buy toys in those days.

Teddy was one of the few bought toys I possessed and he is still with me. This period was quite a short one between 1934–38. Every time a film finished Dad was out of work until he signed on again with a new one. It became increasingly difficult to find work so eventually he moved to work for London Transport to build the tube trains. The magical time had passed and although he was happy in his new work his passion for the cinema never varied and we always went at least three times a week during the war.'

THE BREWERY DRAYMEN

'Just after the First World War, my family and I were living in a flat on the Surrey side of the Thames supplied by the New London Brewery, who employed my father as the foreman horse keeper. He was responsible for the welfare of about 20 horses, comprising the Shire variety and a few cobs. Also, he had to allot the daily jobs to about 15 draymen, who delivered the barrels of beer to various establishments and public houses.

On return from their daily duties, the men had to groom their horses of the day. They would lead them to a cobbled lane (part of the brewery yard) where they were tethered to a wall. I can remember being terrified, as, too, was my sister Violet. There was only about three feet space between the rear of the horses and the other wall.

We had to go past these horses to get to our home and we were always aware of the restlessness of these animals, after having been out working, they were hungry and tired. However, the draymen were always very kind to us 'kids' and they would stop grooming and escort us to the bottom of the stairs leading to home. Of course, not all the horses were there at one time, usually about eight. One of my father's duties was the cleaning of the brasses on the harnesses and to make sure that the bridles and saddles were in good order.

In about 1920 my father, with two of the draymen, namely a Mr Thompson and Mr Spratt, decided between themselves to enter a pair of Shire horses in the Regents Park Royal Horse Show. These events always took place on a Bank Holiday Monday. They acquired permission from the New London Brewery and they then set the wheels turning.

This meant a terrific amount of work. Extra special care was taken on the grooming and extra shine on the harnesses, in which my father took great pride – so much so, he got us all "at it" as we helped to polish up every buckle and my father cleaned the leather work.

The horses were decked up with coloured braids (mostly red white and blue) which were plaited in the manes and tails. They really were beautiful creatures. Their thick white spats were brushed and combed over and over again. The cart, or dray, was also well cleaned and decorated and seats were erected for the passengers who went along on the occasion.

Passengers included all my family and Grandfather too. The folk belonging to Mr Thompson and Mr Spratt were there and others. I must say, our 'carriage' was completely full. It was a jolly day and the weather was perfect. We all wore our 'Sunday Best' clothes for this Cockney jaunt.

My mother had made two dresses. Mine was white crepe-de-chine with green spots, and my sister's was similar, but with red spots. Mother also trimmed our white panama hats with a strip of the materials with a streamer and bow. We felt so proud of ourselves.

Our horse entry won a first prize, so we had to join the procession of winners through Regents Park. A spectacular event indeed. The parade stopped every now and again, as each entry received the prizes and medallions, which were presented by HRH Princess Mary. When our turn came for presentation, we couldn't but help noticing the eyes of HRH focusing on our hats and dresses. Of course, this was a proud day for my mother and father too. Just seeing Princess Mary at such close range, was such a privilege and a lovely memory.

My family left the dray and the other folk at a point where a Lyons Corner House emerged. What a joy to finish the day with tea at the Corner House. We had a large plate full of cream pastries, chocolate eclairs, cream slices etc, etc. It didn't take long for my family to see these off. This was a real luxury in itself at that time.'

LIVERY STABLES AND GARAGES

'I was born in 1910. My father Albert was head groom and coachman to Mr Walter Raphael at Holmbury St Mary. He had been born in Norfolk, and the job in Holmbury was for a married man – so he hastily proposed to Emma, who tossed up between Albert and the local policeman. Albert won, and their honeymoon was spent driving to Surrey from Norfolk in a trap.

Our home was over very smart stables. We moved out when I was 18 months old to Livery Cottage, where my father went into partnership. He later ran his own business of "Cabs and Carriages" to Gomshall station at the princely sum of three shillings and sixpence for the three and a half miles. We stayed here for 73 years, and at one time it was one of the oldest businesses in Surrey. The business after the First World War progressed to "Hacks and Hunters and Children's Lessons".'

175

'My father was a qualified motor engineer, and upon his marriage to my mother, an upholsterer by trade employed in her uncle's firm, they moved to Crawley to manage a garage and filling station with associated tea-rooms. Shortly after they moved to Gaston Gate, a hamlet on the borders of Cranleigh and Shamley Green. Gaston Gate had been a toll gate on a turnpike road. The cottage is still there, but hidden behind a high hedge, and I have never discovered the origins of the name "Gaston". The first bus service to Guildford had started in the garage before my father took it over. It became a coach firm – Gaston's Coaches.

Cars in those days were mostly owned by the moneyed class; the sort who went to the horse races, returned and said "What do I owe you?" and peeled it off a wad of winnings!

The four pumps were operated manually, and oil was pumped into special cans – a rather messy process. Father was independent and sold petrol grades he chose, but never Esso. He and my mother served the petrol and oil; he repaired the engines, with the help of boy apprentices – one at a time.'

THE WELDER AND BLACKSMITH

'Originally from Folkestone in Kent, I followed my parents to the village of Hersham about 1936, eventually to get married and find work at the Hackbridge Transformer Works.

For a time I had been employed at the Weyburn Engineering Works at Elstead, near Godalming, where they repaired lifeboat engines and made parts for Rolls Royce aircraft engines. This gave me a good grounding for my new job at the Hackbridge Works. Hundreds of skilled men were employed in this large factory, which was reputed to build some of the largest transformers in the world. We were quite proud when these huge tanks containing electrical coils were lifted on to vast special lorries and trailer. One lorry at the front, the other pushing at the rear. In those days roads had to be closed off and diversions planned to enable the transformer to reach the docks and eventual destination. It was quite a sight in the 1930s when the factory opened and closed each day to see the hundreds of cyclists swarm through the village as the employees went to and from work. These would include those people employed at the ABC works which employed dozens of workers over many years. It is claimed that during the First World War some of the very first army tanks were made on the old Hackbridge site. This is now of course occupied by the modern complex of Air Products Ltd.

When I first started my business as a welder and blacksmith just after the war in Brown's Yard, it was my good fortune to start the

176

first private enterprise there after the small factory on the site, which also had been engaged in war work, vacated the yard. I was quite thrilled to be able to rent one of the lockup garages that had been used as a steel store. There were six of these in a row, and later I was able to turn them all into one large workshop and employ men to assist me. My very first job was for Mr Mackey up at Burvale Farm, when I was asked to repair some farm equipment that was in a bad state of disrepair after the war. I remember how proud I felt taking my welding equipment into a field behind the farm to start my very first job as a self employed person.

My only means of transport at that time was a trusty Austin Seven, with which I was cruel enough to tow a small trailer in which to transport my oxy-acetylene equipment about. Many years later, a lorry is now required. As you can imagine, the springs on my small trailer eventually needed attention. At that time it was beyond my experience. It was then that I had the good fortune to meet the wonderful and elderly Mr George Welland.

He was the original Hersham blacksmith and wheelwright, a truly wonderful old gentleman. He lived with his wife in the little Forge Cottage in Bury Lane just opposite our present doctor's surgery. His forge was situated at the rear. In 1945 when I first met him he must have been well over 75. We became great friends in spite of the age difference and he taught me a great deal about blacksmith's work in the form of wrought ironwork. All his work was carried out in the forge fire. As a very small recompense I was able to show him how modern welding could save time, in the joining of metals, but he was never really convinced that it was as good as the old method. Who was I to argue? He was famous in a way that I never felt that he appreciated. He was chosen, while the war was still on, to repair Florence Nightingale's coach, used by her in the Crimea and which stood during the war, until it was badly damaged by bombing, in the vestibule of St Thomas's Hospital in London as a kind of symbol to the nurses there. It was brought down to Hersham, and I would often visit the forge as work progressed by Mr Welland and his assistant. He made new wheels, using aged timber on his steam driven bandsaw and lathe, rolled new iron tires and shrunk them on the finished wheels by first expanding them by heat and the age old method. It was quite an experience to stand and watch.'

THE LENGTHSMAN

'My grandfather was a ploughman for most of his working life but the last years, from the 1920s, he worked as a lengthsman on the A3 London to Guildford road, starting at 7.30 am and leaving off at

4 pm. He walked the two and a half miles from home to work and did two miles of road, which was his length. Not being allowed to leave his tools and barrow in the hedges, he used to leave them at his sister's, which was at the back of the Green Man, Burpham, now the Harvesters and West Court. He wore an Oxford shirt (heavy white drill with blue stripes), corduroy trousers tied with string just below the knee, and a tweed jacket and black oilskin coat for bad weather. He always took a very large umbrella and carried his lunch in a red and white handkerchief on the crook of it. A quart bottle of cold tea was his drink. He retired at 81 years of age and kept his large garden dug and planted.'

TRAVELLING IN SWEETS

'In the 1930s my father was a commercial traveller in sweets and chocolates, working from our home in Thornton Heath. He owned a large Ford van, the back of which was fitted out with shelves. These were often piled high with boxes of sweets and chocolates of all descriptions, and large jars of toffees and boiled sweets. When I grew older, a special treat was to be taken to the factory to watch Mr Bucknell "pulling" the humbug mixture. The smell was delicious!'

AT THE FACTORY

'My father worked at the Staines Linoleum factory in the 1920s. There wasn't much industry in the area – Staines Lino, Lagonda cars and one or two small light engineering works. For women there was the Wescot Overall factory, making all kinds of overalls. It was still agricultural, with two quite large farms and an agricultural engineer who hired out traction engines to farms at harvest to work the threshing machines. They also had steam rollers for road works. All of these have now gone.'

THE TAXMAN

'My father, born in 1895, worked for HM Inspector of Taxes. This fact was never mentioned in front of my sister and myself, consequently we thought it was distinctly shameful to be in that line of work.'

WAR & PEACE

THE GREAT WAR 1914–18

Air raids, searchlights, prisoner of war camps – all came to Surrey during the 1914–18 war. It is remembered as a time of fear, hardship and sorrow by the older generation, when the Zeppelin airships brought warfare to families in their own homes for the very first time and every village and town in Surrey experienced loss and the sadness of seeing men return who were wounded in mind and body.

SOLDIERS ON THE COMMON

'During the war two regiments of soldiers were stationed on the common at Meadvale. On Earlswood Common, at the end of Clarence Walk, was the Royal Field Artillery Regiment, and on "little common" was a Welsh regiment. The soldiers were billeted in the houses of the village and the horses were grazed on the common tethered to ropes stretched across the grass about three feet off the ground. Several of the young men from the village went to fight for their country and some did not return. Meadvale should be especially proud of George Knight of Somerset Road, who was awarded the Victoria Cross.'

'Soldiers came to Virginia Water; where the 14th tee on the East course now is, there was a searchlight on the hill and on the lower ground there was an anti-aircraft gun. Soldiers were billeted in houses that had room. We had two. The Canadians were in a camp on Smith's Lawn in the Park. They were lumberjacks and they cut a lot of fir trees down in what is now Wellington Avenue.'

PRISONERS OF WAR

'I was four years old when the Great War started, and before it ended we had a German prisoner of war camp on our common at Holmbury St Mary. Their occupation was to fell the fir trees for timber, so at each end of the village were sawmills. Huge shire horses pulled the trees to the mills. The prisoners stayed two years.'

ZEPPELINS AND AIR RAIDS

'I was born in Purley just before the Great War and can remember an air raid. I was put under the table, over which was a cloth with a fringe hanging down all round and I remember playing with that fringe – it was great fun undoing it. My father was not fit to be sent to the Front but was in a kind of Home Guard. I asked him what he did. He said he and his friends were digging trenches to send to our soldiers in France. He had great trouble putting on his puttees and used to get Mother to put them on for him.'

'I was born in 1915 in Carshalton, which was then a village. Our house was at the edge of the village, two minutes from one of the lavender fields where Mitcham lavender was grown. One day during the war I must have been playing in the hall when I heard my mother calling from upstairs, and my brother came running, picked me up and half carried, half dragged me to the back bedroom. I was lifted onto a chair and we all gazed at a bright ball of fire over London. It was a moving ball of fire from which pieces broke off and fell. I remember my brother shouting "It's a Zeperline!"

I also remember a tram ride to Croydon to "see the tanks". It was about a mile's walk down to the trams and some of the neighbours came with us, very excited. We arrived in Croydon and all lined up at the edge of the pavement and waited – and waited. Some heavy, ugly great things rolled by, everyone cheered, then the crowd started to move away. I said "But where are the tanks?" and everyone around turned to look at me and laughed. I had no idea why.'

'The air raid alert in those days was the discharge of maroons from the local fire brigade. As we lived within a few yards of the station the noise was quite frightening and set our nerves off before the raid even started! The "All Clear" was sounded by a Boy Scout riding through the streets blowing a trumpet.'

'My parents moved to Surrey when I was six. We had one of a block of twelve houses, the only houses then in Wallington, between South Beddington and Waddon. Croydon Aerodrome was only a couple of fields away.

Years later, when war broke out, Croydon Aerodrome was a training centre for the Royal Flying Corps. I woke one Sunday morning and a plane was coming straight for my bedroom window. Fortunately we had a very high wooden swing at the end of the garden and the left wing tip just caught this and swung round, the plane ending up nose down in our potato patch. I went into

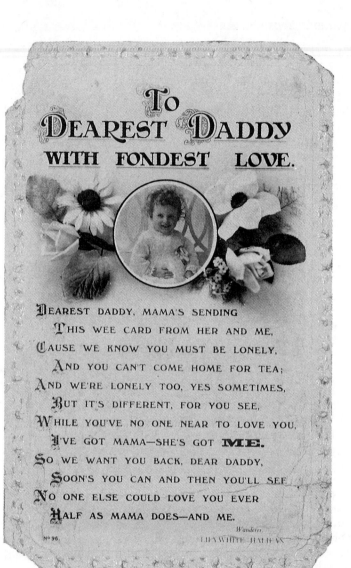

To DEAREST DADDY
WITH FONDEST LOVE.

DEAREST DADDY, MAMA'S SENDING
THIS WEE CARD FROM HER AND ME,
CAUSE WE KNOW YOU MUST BE LONELY,
AND YOU CAN'T COME HOME FOR TEA;
AND WE'RE LONELY TOO, YES SOMETIMES,
BUT IT'S DIFFERENT, FOR YOU SEE,
WHILE YOU'VE NO ONE NEAR TO LOVE YOU,
I'VE GOT MAMA—SHE'S GOT ME.
SO WE WANT YOU BACK, DEAR DADDY,
SOON'S YOU CAN AND THEN YOU'LL SEE
NO ONE ELSE COULD LOVE YOU EVER
HALF AS MAMA DOES—AND ME.

Wanderer.

Nº 96.
LILYWHITE HALIFAX

Cards like this sent to fathers away at the front helped to keep up the family's spirits in time of war.

my parents' bedroom and told them. "Oh yes, dear! We know it's April Fool's Day", which indeed it was. The noise of hundreds of people swarming in our garden convinced them something was up.

How so many people could appear from nowhere at seven o'clock in the morning was beyond us. They stripped that plane to its bones. The Adjutant was furious, it was a new one and had only been flying six hours. The pilot – a Captain Berry – was doing his sixth solo flight. He only broke his nose on the joystick but was grounded for six months, this being their lot if they pranged on the sixth flight. We couldn't grow anything in the kitchen garden for years. My brother, confined to bed with mumps, was given the propellor – the Adjutant said there was no use keeping it, the public hadn't left much else. The brand new plane was a write-off at a cost of £1,000 plus, a lot of money in those days.'

LIFE AT HOME

'A mobile kitchen was set up in the yard of Town House, Chobham, where children could buy a threepenny dinner with sometimes a slice of suet pudding with treacle. This was perhaps a forerunner of the British Restaurants of the Second World War.'

'Most families were encouraged to keep a pig to help with the meat and everyone grew their own fruit and vegetables. If we swept up a sackful of acorns we could earn sixpence from the farmer for them to feed the pigs. We could always pick mushrooms in the early morning, then go home and have them fried for breakfast. I can vividly remember at Limpsfield the air raids by German Zeppelins and how frightened we were when the sky was lit up with searchlights and the guns firing at them.'

'My father was a regular soldier in the RAMC and was whipped off to war before I knew him, so I grew up a child surrounded by female relatives. I recollect delightful family walks over the recreation ground by the old Monument Hill School at Woking, near Granny's house, through woods (gathering cones and bits of wood for burning on the old kitchen range, or open fires), and out onto the golf course round which blackberries could be garnered. Sometimes my father's sister, a teacher in the East End of London – anxious to gain a respite from the threat of Zeppelins – would come to us for a few days, bringing a little nephew or niece, and then we would walk from Maybury, down Sandy Lane (now East Hill, but then a narrow rutted track, flanked by sweet chestnut woods), through Pyrford, past the Old Church on its hill and on towards Ripley for tea.'

183

'Having signed on for the Army on the day I was born, within a month Father was called to join the East Surrey Regiment in Kingston and before the year ended he was at the front in France. So my mother was on her own for the next two years with her three small daughters.

This was a difficult time for all mothers and children. The food rationing started later, so my mother planted potatoes and cabbages in the small back garden. Along with her neighbours they took turns to walk to Sutton on the off chance to buy butter at the Home and Colonial Stores. They shared whatever they could find to buy. Banstead was a small village with only a few shops. There were large houses which were self-supporting with their own fields and cattle. Some of them sold skimmed milk to poor people for a penny, and you took your own container to collect it.

Early attempts at Welfare were organised by the landed gentry in the Church Institute with the District Nurse in attendance. Here a large jar of Virol was purchased to sell off to the mothers at low cost. Of course everybody walked, and so it was a case of loading up the high pram with babies, shopping, etc. When I was a year old I had no teeth, so my mother asked advice from the doctor about weaning me as there was no appropriate food. He suggested baking an apple in its skin and giving me the pulp from inside. My sisters sometimes had a meal of lentils or split peas cooked until soft and then spread on bread, as that was the only food in the house. People managed somehow. We all survived the flu epidemic of 1918.'

'In the first week of June 1916 I was a very upset little girl. Everyone in the house had been frightened by a dreadful thing called a "Jutland". My mother in hysterics, Grannie in tears, Cook in a temper, and my best friends the two young maids would only tell me to run away and play when I asked questions. At tea-time my grandfather came home with the newspapers and latest news of a huge naval battle. My father, a young Gunnery Officer in a battleship of the Grand Fleet, had left Scapa Flow under the command of Admiral Jellicoe and gone into battle off Denmark. Luckily they had suffered no damage.

On leave my father took me down to Southampton Common to see the horses at the Remount; an enormous collection of animals ready to embark for France. I was put up on one which seemed the size of an elephant, and had a most enjoyable ride. Once my mother took me to a convalescent home where I gave out little green packets of "Bines" (Woodbine cigarettes), chocolate bars and apples to the wounded soldiers. Some were in wheelchairs or on crutches in their bright blue suits and red ties; others bandaged and in bed.'

'During the First World War my father was Head Gardener at a big house called "The Homestead", and we lived in one of their cottages just across the road. He was not called up for the Army as he suffered with bad legs.

Mr and Mrs Du Chalice, the owners, lent their house to the Army as a Convalescent Home for Officers wounded during the war. Although I was only six or seven at the time, I can still remember one of the officers coming over to our place to buy some of our lovely big Victoria plums, also the black plums. Instead of money he gave our Mum a lovely solid silver-topped walking stick. I can't remember what happened to it, but I expect Mum sold it as money was very short.'

NEW WORK FOR WOMEN

'Come the First World War, my father volunteered for the Royal Marines, expecting to go to sea. Instead he had three and a half years in the trenches of France. At the time he was engaged to my mother, who decided to go on munitions. She and one of her sisters walked from Ewell to Cheam and back each day. They left home at six in the morning to return about half past six in the evening. In the winter it was evidently so cold they had ice on their skirts, and as they were involved with explosives they had no heating, buckets of hot water being brought in so that they could warm their hands.'

'Gwen was born at Haslemere in 1897, and the family moved to Sutton when she was three. Although she gained a scholarship to go to high school, there were by that time two other children, and so Gwen was put to service with a local family. Not enjoying the work of a "tweeny", she applied for the job of ladies companion in the home of a Persian family. Here she worked happily till the Great War started.

Gwen wanted to do her bit, so she went into munitions. Life changed dramatically. For the first time she was her own woman, earning real money and paying her mother for her keep. She is proud of the fact that she was one of the few workers who could use the finest drill in the factory, and produced 1,000 drillings in a day with no broken drills or drillings. The workers took it in turns to do the dangerous job of filling special shells, for which they had to wear masks and gloves. The horrible stuff would be deep on the floor, and they had to stand on duckboards.'

'During the war, Holy Trinity Church School at Richmond was asked if they could find a girl to go on the buses (they were all open-topped

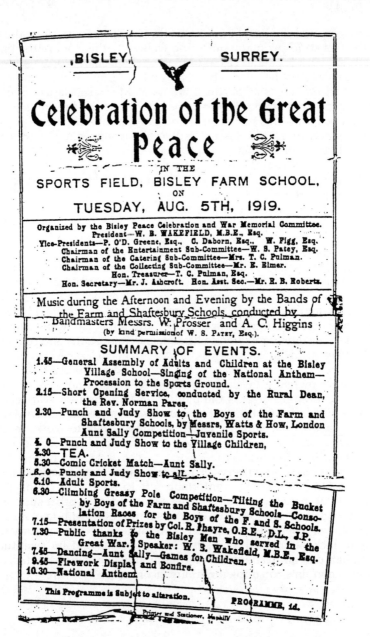

BISLEY   SURREY.

Celebration of the Great Peace

IN THE
SPORTS FIELD, BISLEY FARM SCHOOL,
ON
TUESDAY, AUG. 5TH, 1919.

Organized by the Bisley Peace Celebration and War Memorial Committee.
President—W. B. WAKEFIELD, M.B.E., Esq.
Vice-Presidents—P. O'D. Greene, Esq., C. Daborn, Esq., W. Figg, Esq.
Chairman of the Entertainment Sub-Committee—W. S. Patey, Esq.
Chairman of the Catering Sub-Committee—Mrs. T. C. Pulman.
Chairman of the Collecting Sub-Committee—Mr. E. Elmer.
Hon. Treasurer—T. C. Pulman, Esq.
Hon. Secretary—Mr. J. Ashcroft.   Hon. Asst. Sec.—Mr. R. B. Roberts.

Music during the Afternoon and Evening by the Bands of
the Farm and Shaftesbury Schools, conducted by
Bandmasters Messrs. W. Prosser and A. C. Higgins
(by kind permission of W. S. PATEY, Esq.).

SUMMARY OF EVENTS.
1.45—General Assembly of Adults and Children at the Bisley
    Village School—Singing of the National Anthem—
    Procession to the Sports Ground.
2.15—Short Opening Service, conducted by the Rural Dean,
    the Rev. Norman Pares.
2.30—Punch and Judy Show to the Boys of the Farm and
    Shaftesbury Schools, by Messrs, Watts & How, London
    Aunt Sally Competition—Juvenile Sports.
4. 0—Punch and Judy Show to the Village Children,
4.30—TEA.
5.30—Comic Cricket Match—Aunt Sally.
6. 0—Punch and Judy Show to all.
6.10—Adult Sports.
6.30—Climbing Greasy Pole Competition—Tilting the Bucket
    by Boys of the Farm and Shaftesbury Schools—Conso-
    lation Races for the Boys of the F. and S. Schools.
7.15—Presentation of Prizes by Col. R. Phayre, O.B.E., D.L., J.P.
7.30—Public thanks to the Bisley Men who served in the
    Great War. Speaker: W. B. Wakefield, M.B.E., Esq.
7.45—Dancing—Aunt Sally—Games for Children.
9.45—Firework Display and Bonfire.
10.30—National Anthem

This Programme is Subject to alteration.   PROGRAMME, 1d.

Printer and Stationer, Maphill V

Programme for the Bisley Celebrations to mark the end of the First World War.

186

then) to record the number of times the conductress came to the top of the bus and how many times she walked to the front of the bus. I sat in the back left hand seat and made the specific recordings. I was put in charge of the conductress of the No 33 bus, which I boarded in Richmond. We had our meal break at Mortlake Garage and my mother met me at the end of the shift, when the bus returned to Richmond. I did this for a week, and bought myself a new hat with the money I was paid. As far as I recall we never had a wet day, which was lucky for me.'

CASUALTIES OF WAR

'Leading from The Avenue was a school for officers' children, with extensive grounds adjoining Wandsworth Common. During the First World War, this was converted and came to be known as "The Third London General Hospital".

As a child I used to stand outside watching the ambulances coming and going. Sometimes the "walking wounded" would come outside for a stroll over the Common. I can still remember their bright blue uniforms and red ties. I don't know whether I watched out of childish morbid curiosity or out of sympathy! After the war the hospital was finally restored to its former school status and re-named "The Patriotic School".'

'My father owned a toy factory. All toys at that time were made of wood. As he did not pass the medical examination for war service, he was made to close the factory and work as a foreman in an aircraft factory in Chelsea, which entailed a long journey to work. In 1919 my father died. The long journey to work had proved too much for him.

There were no social services in those days. Our lifestyle changed dramatically from being comfortably off to having to count every penny. Our maid became our housekeeper and my mother supported us three girls by working in a draper's shop. She got home at seven o'clock every evening except on Saturdays, when she returned at nine o'clock. She joined the Early Closing Association and eventually got a half day off in the week. Our large house was now partially let off into two flats to supplement our income.'

COPING IN THE DEPRESSION

Times were very hard indeed between the wars as the Depression brought unemployment and poverty. Nobody was immune, and a letter at the breakfast table could bring news which brought the world down around the ears of even the most respectable of families. Barefoot children were to be seen in the streets, and there was always the threat of the workhouse for those who could no longer cope.

POVERTY AND CLASS BARRIERS IN SURBITON

'There was a considerable amount of poverty in the Surbiton area in the early years of this century. According to my mother, men would queue up at three in the morning in bad weather to be taken on for snow clearing. I remember in the 1930s the pink food tickets – value I believe five shillings and not always spent as wisely as possible.

The social barrier was trade or profession. There were two regattas on the river at Kingston. Wednesday was for tradesmen and I can remember being taken to see the fireworks that finished the day; Saturday was for the professional classes. In the 1930s several schools in Surbiton would not take tradesmen's children. Surbiton High School refused until, I think, 1958 although they accepted daughters of bank clerks.'

BAREFOOT IN CROYDON

'In the 1920s, wet mornings were really welcome because my father drove me to school in a Sunbeam open tourer, which must have been the size of a mini-bus because once 14 children were crammed on the back seat.

It was sitting in this car that I had my first lesson in compassion. My parents and I were driving through the old town of Croydon, near the parish church, and I saw some barefooted children. In those overdressed days, the only outside place I went barefoot was on the beach, so I asked where was the sea? It was explained to me that these children's parents had no money for shoes, possibly not enough to feed them properly. I often think about this when people talk about the good old days and how hard up we all are now.'

'Before I was born my mother worked as a cook in the Surrey Drovers in Croydon and Granny as a maid in one of the hospitals, which by all accounts way back in 1915 was not particularly hygienic. The staff weren't very kind to elderly patients said Granny . . . with a sigh . . . as she told us tales about old Croydon. She would often take my sister and I to visit her brother in The Dwellings – a block of flats with communal sink and tap on each landing. He and his wife had just one living room with a small bedroom opening off it. There was also a communal toilet serving the flats on his landing. A primitive style of accommodation in which to raise a young family – and not very unusual for the working classes at that time.

My grandmother used to mend all our shoes – she learned the trade from her father who was a shoemaker in the French quarter of East London in the 1800s. Leather was very expensive and not easy to acquire but Granny was not easily defeated. She even made little hand sewn shoes for our dolls, from an old kid glove that someone had given her. Nothing was wasted.

As a child I can remember food, fuel and clothing being very scarce. The Relieving Office came to see if we had any goods to sell before we were given any "relief" – either food tokens or boot tokens. We got some Oxo cubes and lace-up boots – not a lot really. My mother was so upset and helpless in the face of authority. She had nothing to sell. My mother was widowed when I was just two, my sister was four. People had to work at all manner of things to feed the family – some took in washing, others managed the milkcarts. My mother became a lamplighter and later on she took on man's work of shovelling coke for the gas works boiler. We were in dire straits without a man's wage coming in.

There was a great division between the poor, the not-so-poor and the more privileged. There was an invisible line. From a very young age I knew where I stood.

Children used to have to earn their pocket money in different ways: collecting jam jars and selling them to the grocer. The chemist would also pay for clean empty medicine bottles. Another way to earn money was to clean door steps. I got a sixpenny piece for doing one house but I had to clean it well!

Following the great flu epidemic at the end of the First World War there was a street party to celebrate peace. Pianos were wheeled out, trestle tables set up, and night lights in coloured glasses strung along the windowsills. Each family was given a memorial card with all the flags of the nation on it, brilliant colours splayed out like a fan. On that day food was somehow found for us children but after that there was hardly anything. Everything was scarce and what there was we couldn't afford.

Coal was one shilling and sixpence a hundredweight. Most could only stretch to half a hundredweight. We went to bed to save fuel, and to stop the hunger pangs. Bread was fourpence ha'penny a loaf, half a pound of bacon pieces cost a penny, whiting were two pence a pound and sugar was fourpence for two pounds.

Lack of funds didn't always mean lack of fun though and many of us made our own amusement, dressing up, drawing, just pretending. The public library was a sanctuary and the most wonderful place I knew then.

Between the wars life was very hard. Shop assistants worked an appalling twelve hour day, five and a half day a week for the princely sum (in 1928) of five shillings, with which, more often than not, you had to buy "respectable and suitable clothing" to wear in your job. That was my sister's lot as a shop assistant. But she was a marvellous manager and scrimped and saved to buy little things to make a home.

I became a live-in domestic servant. Very long hours but at least I was assured of three decent meals a day and a bedroom of my own. Heaven! I didn't get much money, and only one half day a month off, but I loved the freedom.'

SENT TO THE WORKHOUSE

'In the late 1920s and early 1930s, the Depression caused much hardship in Chiddingfold. Many families were evicted from their cottages because they could not pay the rent, as they were out of work. They were sent to the local workhouse at Hambledon where the men were segregated from their wives and children.'

THE GENERAL STRIKE

'In 1919 I left school and went to work in the accounts department of a film company in Wardour Street, where I was during the General Strike of 1926. It was quite hazardous getting from Richmond to London every day, waiting for a lift in a private car or getting on a "private" bus, run by volunteers, mainly university students. Twice we were stoned by strikers in Hammersmith Broadway.'

'I have a memory of the General Strike in 1926. I was one of a number of children who went by train to schools in Guildford. When news came out that there would be no trains running until further notice our parents persuaded our local general carrier, Mr William Shelton, and owner of a small van, to put benches in the van and drive us to Guildford in the morning and bring us home in the afternoon – some 13 miles each way. It was, I remember, a somewhat decrepit, asthmatic van, and we rattled off through Grayswood – a noisier load than the owner, who usually carried parcels and fodder to local estates, was used to, but his passengers were in for a nasty shock when at the foot of Brook Rocks he ordered the grammar school boys to get out and walk as his engine wasn't strong enough to cope with this extra load. He would wait for them at the top. This performance was continued each day until the trains were brought back to action by local volunteer drivers and firemen, and finally the strike ended and we could once again resume our usual train journeys to and from school.'

'During the troubles in the coal mines with strikes and lock outs, our coal was rationed to one sack per week. My brother fetched this in his home-made cart on a Saturday morning. On fine days my sister Dorothy and I and local children walked across the fields to Burgh Wood. We played climbing trees, swinging on branches, making little houses, then we would take home bundles of dead sticks and bags of twigs from the ground and any fallen branches which could be used to supplement the coal.'

THE CRASH

'I lived in Kingston Market Place over 60 years ago, where King Bros. shop was until just recently, as my father was the manager of Farrows Bank. One day just before Christmas we were having breakfast when the post arrived. There was dead silence as a letter was passed round. I knew something awful had happened when my mother said "Never mind, you will still have your doll for Christmas".

What had happened was Farrows Bank had smashed and we, with many others, had lost all our money.

I don't remember whether I did get my doll, but I do recall that the vicar of the parish church sent us a joint of meat for our Christmas dinner.'

THE SECOND WORLD WAR

Its proximity to London meant that Surrey suffered a great deal during the Second World War, bombing and strafing being the almost daily lot of towns and villages throughout the county. Many local people worked in London and they also witnessed the terrible scenes of fire and destruction in the city. Memories of that time have stayed sharp, not only the dangers but the effort of carrying on from day to day. Those who were children at the time have their own special memories, in particular of evacuation and disruption to schooldays. Life went on, though, until at last VE day brought relief and celebration.

THE AIR RAIDS

'I remember that when the siren sounded for the first time – a false alarm – we all rushed into the cupboard under the stairs and waited for the end with our gas masks on. Later we had an air raid shelter built in the garden. After a while we stopped using it as we were more in danger from shrapnel from the dog fights overhead while dashing down the garden.

My brother left and went to France where he was taken prisoner and remained so for five long years. He and my sister were older than myself and she stayed at home but worked for the Ministry of Defence and was also a Fire Fighter. This meant patrolling the road and having a bucket and stirrup pump at the ready! My father rejoined the Army so our family was reduced to four females. Due to the size of our house the Billeting Officers decided we should take an evacuee from London and a friend of my mother's came to live with us. On nights during the air raids we would sleep downstairs in the dining room. The mother's help always slept under the kitchen table – the old wooden type with a metal top, where she felt safest.

After the evacuee returned to London, it was decided that we must have Canadian soldiers in our house. My mother always said she wouldn't spoil them but after the first few days, she would ask them down to join us in the evenings and in the end she would even take them tea in bed at the weekends! I suppose, in a small way, it made up for the absence of my brother.

During this time, the Women's Institute Hall was used by the WVS to run a canteen for the Canadian soldiers. My mother, as did many other women, helped to run it and twice a week we went up there to serve teas, sandwiches, etc for the men and tried to make them feel more at home. Once a week, there was a dance with a band and the girls in the villages went. What a time they all had. I well remember being escorted home with my mother during a raid, with the searchlights from Merrow lighting the skies and thumps and bumps from the anti-aircraft guns. We weren't brave, but one got used to it, and life had to go on.'

GETTING TO WORK

'Travelling to London each day after the bombing on London started was very difficult. Trains and stations were so disrupted and one never quite knew how to get there and back. It sometimes took four hours in the morning and four hours at night and as I left home by 7.30am and did not leave the office until 6pm it was a very long day.

There were no lights in the trains, just a blue "glow" in the roof and even that was switched off in a raid. One of the worst journeys was one night in autumn when a raid had started by the time I left the office near Charing Cross at 6pm. Waterloo station had been closed for some time after bombing so it was necessary to go into the Strand to catch any bus going towards a railway station on the route to Bagshot. I think I eventually got to Barnes and then Twickenham station where we were turned out of the train with bombs falling not too far away. There was nothing to do but wait on the platform. I settled for staying outside against a wall where I could run, rather than crawling under a seat. When things quietened down the train went slowly on to Ascot, where we again had to wait on the platform for another train to finish the journey. By that time we were a small group of about five passengers and I was the only one getting out at Bagshot. All praise to Southern Railway for running a service at all in those circumstances. From Bagshot station – locked and deserted – it was a long and lonely walk home in pitch darkness. Not a chink of light showed from any window; my footsteps were the only ones on the village streets and up the hill on the main road. And, of course one started again at 6am for another day and another journey. But, this was not nearly as bad as for those left behind in London.'

THE END OF CROYDON AIRPORT

'On a fateful Thursday evening in late August 1940, planes had been circling for an hour. We were only a mile and a half from Croydon

Airport with Kenley and Biggin Hill nearby. My father was restless and stayed in the garden while Mother was setting the table and about to serve the evening meal. Suddenly Father shouted "Quick, bombs!" We all three and dog raced to the shelter as the first bombs hit the ground. The thunderous noise of bombs, guns, planes and machine-guns deafened us. There was a shaft of light through the nearly closed door, and when a shadow fell across that light we all thought our moment had come. Then after about 40 minutes the noise subsided and the warning sounded, as up till then there had not been a warning. Then sounded the All Clear and we emerged from the shelter to see to our surprise the house still standing tall and proud. Then we turned to look to the north and a huge pall of smoke rose into the evening sky. That was the end of Croydon Airport and the Evening in Paris scent factory next door, where the poor girls perished.'

DORKING CAVES

'Opposite the back door of a neighbour's house was a boarded up entrance to the Dorking Caves. There is another entrance up by the war memorial. These caves go right under the High Street and were used as an air raid shelter during the war. It was quite large down there, with room for lots of chairs and beds. The caves were dry as they were all sand and sandstone.'

THE POSTLADY AND THE PARACHUTIST

'In the spring of 1941, my husband had gone off to the war in the Army and I had to find myself some work; the Army allowance for a private's wife was 25 shillings a week! So I took on being the local postlady.

Hascombe postal area then was spread out over quite some lonely places, and the only way to get to the places was on foot.

One big house I delivered to was called "Nore", at one time home of the Godwin-Austin family, over the fields and through the woods.

At this stage of the war the Germans were bombing London at any odd time, it was not the "Blitz". Well, the Home Guard knew a plane had crashed locally so had been searching for it. Most of the wreckage and one body was found along the Guildford Road area of Cranleigh, but they couldn't find the second body. So it was on the morning of 18th April 1941 on my way to "Nore", that I noticed something pure white partly hidden by the undergrowth, down in a valley. I wondered what it could be, so on my way back I decided to investigate! Fighting my way through the bushes I came upon this white object, which was a parachute. I thought "Oh, good" – lovely white silk to make something, clothes being rationed.

As I stood looking at this I noticed a heap of greenish-khaki coloured straps and things, then I suddenly saw a leg with a black flying boot on caught in a blackberry bush – the "heap" was a body!

I was so frightened I couldn't move. It dawned on me it was the German airman the Home Guard were looking for. I rushed back down to the village policeman who had to send for the police to come from Godalming, then I had to take them to the place.

One didn't know at that time of the war what the Germans would do to you, it was frightening. I wondered if the young man was still alive, but it was not so – he had baled out of the plane which was flying too low.

I was really scared, only 22 years old, and that was the end of my postlady job. No one would take it on then to deliver to those lonely places. It was taken over by a postal van service after, which had to go around the lanes from Cranleigh way.'

THE DOODLEBUG

'The day that is imprinted in my memory must have been in 1944 when the "doodlebugs" were beginning to make an impression. It was early afternoon in New Malden and we had just finished lunch. The dreaded droning could be heard and Dad, home on leave, kept a careful watch to see if he could spot the "bug" before it silenced and began to drop. He did, and ran in shouting for us to take cover.

With just the kitchen table and the bodies of my parents as shields, Eileen, Freddie and I waited for the bang. It missed our house but landed halfway along the street. Several people were injured.

I remember hearing the bang and then the voices giving advice; a damp cloth on my forehead and the suggestion that a cup of tea with lots of sugar was a good remedy for a faint. I can still remember the horror of that cup of tea. I have not taken sugar since.

My parents had always resisted sending us away but, this time, it was felt that we had had a lucky escape and they would have to be parted from "their girls". Once the decision was made, we were soon on our way to Wales as evacuees.'

LONDON ON FIRE

'After a disturbed night with my friends in their Anderson shelter, I went and caught the bus for work. I was told no buses were going beyond Aldgate, but I could walk from there if I could find a way through. I started off from Aldgate – I don't remember how I got to St Paul's churchyard, but I arrived at the east end. I started to sidle round the stone wall surrounding St Pauls. On the left warehouses were on fire, burning freely. Firemen were just standing there watching, so tired many of them seemed to be asleep on their feet. I have never seen such hopeless exhaustion. There was no water. The Thames was at its lowest tide level too. I continued to walk round. I particularly noticed one leaded dome roof open up and peel back and flames come bursting through like some hideous flower. My shoes were awash with oil and water by this time. I looked back at St Paul's, still standing but ringed by fire. I pressed on down Ludgate Circus and I got to Lincoln's Inn Fields via Grays Inn Road – which I realise must have meant a big detour. Grays Inn Road was well alight but it was a wide street and no one stopped me. I arrived at work to find the windows blown out (again!) and little piles of sand bags on the pavements where fire bombs had been smothered by Fire Watchers. The men in the office had to take turns doing this. My mother and I did it at home. Finding food after this big raid was difficult, no water and no deliveries. I remember I had soda water and a very pink sausage in Woolworth's in the Strand.

After this raid the Partners in the firm decided to have part of the office and the valuable documents evacuated to offices near their homes, and I was sent to Virginia Water. Our office was in the parade of shops. There was a baker next door who made wonderful doughnuts.'

'WHEN IT GETS NOISY, PULL YOUR FEET IN'

'Before the arrival of our indoor air raid shelter we had an underground dug-out in the garden. In my innocence I thought this great fun. I loved to check through the emergency stores and replace the drinking water bottles. I loved the smell of the hurricane lantern and longed to try out the little cooking stove and portable toilet. It was fortunate that we never had the need to use any of these facilities. I can remember my brother vaulting the sand bags at the top of the steps and excitedly describing the "dog fight" he had seen whilst on Fire Duty. I can also remember our consternation when my mother insisted on returning to the house "to turn over the roast potatoes and check the pie for dinner!". "Those Germans are not going to spoil our dinner", she said, "the meat ration is small enough without losing what little bit we do have by burning the pie". How did she manage to feed us all I wonder? Three hungry men as well as myself. She worked so hard in the garden and we always had plenty of fresh vegetables and fruit. I can see the jars of preserved plums, tomatoes and apples lined along the cupboard shelf and the big tub of salted runner beans now in my mind's eye, and later the sound of the contented cluck of six hens we were allowed to keep. We supplied two neighbours with eggs and forfeited our egg ration. The sound of chickens clucking always reminds me of home.

When the doodlebugs, or VIs to give them their correct name, came they were even more frightening. The awful sound of their engine, the even more frightening silence when it cut out, the waiting for the explosion and the relief when it was over and we were safe but wondering where it had landed and who had been hurt. One day I had left for school – life had to go on – when a doodlebug came over and the engine cut out. It looked as if it must surely land in our road. A teacher from my school catching up with me pushed me down and held me as the explosion shook the ground beneath us and slates and tiles flew off the garage roof above my head. She was always my heroine after that. I later learned that a Spitfire pilot had tilted the descending flying bomb with the wing tip of his plane to lift it just over the row of houses to explode in a field with no loss of life. We had a collection for him in our road and some attended the presentation at his RAF base. A few weeks later we heard he had been shot down over the Channel. There were many people unknown to him who were deeply grieved to hear this news.

When London was so badly hombed we had an evacuee to stay with us. Our Anderson shelter had been installed then and we felt safer, especially at night. However, it was difficult to sleep us all in the conventional way in the shelter so we slept in a long row along its length. "When it gets noisy," my mother said, "pull your feet in", and so we did all in unison. We thank God we were all spared to laugh about that together for many years to come.'

DANCING ON THE CHEESES

'The war gave us a chance to earn money. We could get eight shillings for a large sack of conkers, which we took to school and in October we went carrot pulling at ten shillings a sack. We children always pulled the largest carrots in order to fill the sack quickly. The Land Army girls soon spotted this and swore at us, but we did not care. In turn, my sister and I did a paper round, covering some 57 houses.

Nutfield was host to London evacuees and Canadian soldiers. With such large numbers in the village, we only had a half day's schooling and the evacuees the other half. We all quickly became cooty (lousy) as a result. When the sirens sounded we descended through a trap door to the cellar of a cheese warehouse store – still there and used by a local auction rooms. The strong odour of whole cheeses was overpowering – we have never liked cheese since. Some of us danced on the cheeses and we sang. "The Quarter Master's Stores" which includes the words "cheese, cheese, wafting on the breeze".'

A LAND MINE IN CROYDON

'Although I had been bombed out twice during the war, my most bizarre experience was witnessing the destruction of a land mine in Croydon. The District Valuer, a clerk and myself were the first team on the War Damage Commission and had been kept busy since the daylight raid on the Purley Way, Croydon.

The land mine had fallen overnight on a tree opposite the Town Hall and it had been found impossible to remove it other than by detonating. This was done in the morning and our team was placed as far away as East Croydon station. We heard a tremendous bang and then the shock waves came down the High Street, taking out every other window of the large stores each side, almost to where we were standing. The glass debris to be cleared up was amazing.

Subsequently I became friends with a highly qualified lady chemist, who beat the Germans at their own game. She had the idea of dropping millions of tiny pieces of silver paper, which disrupted the radar to such an extent that the planes were unable to find their way.'

LIFE MUST GO ON

THE FIRST SIREN

'The first indication of war in Bletchingley was when the siren, situated at Clerk's Croft, sounded a warning at eleven o'clock on 3rd September 1939. However, it was followed shortly by the "All Clear". The following year on 14th June, all the village road signs were obliterated. On 18th August German planes made a bombing raid over Kenley, Caterham and the surrounding districts.

A Heinkel was shot down on 25th August, the fighter crashing in South Godstone. Mr Bamforth remembers playing tennis while the Battle of Britain was being fought in the skies above. Players saw many planes falling in flames.'

NOTHING WAS WASTED

'Living in Caterham between the Guards barracks and the RAF base at Kenley, the grim realities of war very soon became apparent. I can still recall the unique damp musty smell of the school air raid shelter where as one of the "infants", I spent so many hours learning to knit, progressing from dish cloths in garter stitch to pixie hoods in stocking stitch and thence to either socks or balaclavas for the soldiers. On bad days when the bombing was very noisy we sang at the tops of our voices – Ten Green Bottles was one of our favourites.

My father had a smallholding and kept chickens and pigs so we had to give up our ration of eggs and could give up many weeks' meat ration for part of a pig. I remember taking one of these unfortunate animals to the slaughterhouse on the back of an open truck and then having the whole carcass on the kitchen table to be carved up. I can't remember how many people were involved in this enterprise but it was quite a number of ration books which had to be given up.

Eggs had to be sent to the packing station and were collected weekly. They had to be washed and put in egg-trays. We were allowed to keep soft-shelled ones and, of course, the broken ones, but the number of eggs sent to the packing station had to be in a strict ratio to the number of chickens kept, otherwise the chickens' ration books for meal etc were cut. I couldn't even hazard a guess at the thousands of eggs I must have washed. As the chickens (and turkeys and geese for that matter) were fed on what was available, the number and quality of eggs produced was much more variable than is the case today. Day-old chicks were sent by train from one end of the country to the other. Carter Paterson (the carrier) was much more efficient than BR. Refrigerators were unheard of luxuries and eggs were preserved in isinglass in huge earthenware crocks in the larder.

We also kept goats and by the end of the war I had become an expert milker. The kids were very pretty but the billy goats – how they smelled. Everyone grew vegetables; lawns and flower beds were dug up and planted with potatoes, carrots, etc. Digging for Victory became a way of life. The local park became a hay-field and the hay was cut using a horse-drawn machine.

There was a great art in harnessing the enormous cart-horses to the machine. They had to be "paired" as some would not work with others and if harnessed in the wrong order, they would indeed "kick over the traces" and it was extremely difficult to extricate horse, harness and shafts when this happened. If the All Clear had gone when I got home from school I would be sent out with the hay-makers' tea and as a great treat be allowed to ride on the huge horses.

Nothing was ever wasted and to this day I cannot throw anything away without wondering if it will come in useful for something. All clothes were passed down, made over, etc. Summer cotton dresses became skirts, skirts became aprons and aprons became dusters. Parachute silk (off coupons) was much prized for wartime brides' trousseaux and being chosen to be a bridesmaid depended on whether or not you could fit into the dress.

All signposts, road/street names were removed and we all became adept at finding our way about in the black-out. It was very many years before signs were replaced and directions were always given by reference to churches, pubs, farm gates, clumps of trees, etc. Very many years later I was amazed to find that some of the lanes actually had proper names.'

FIVE CREE INDIANS

'Three days before war was declared the family went up to London Zoo. Father hired a car full of petrol for 15 shillings. We were lucky to see many animals and reptiles before they were put to sleep.

The soldiers took over one of the big houses just on the border of Forest Green and Holmbury. The house was called Pratsham Grange. This changed village life, with always plenty of activity and entertainment. I used to go to the ENSA concerts, almost all the village did. Most people welcomed the troops into their houses. We made friends with five Cree Indians, brothers and cousins. One was an Indian chief; he was wounded and he walked four and a half miles from Ockley station on his crutches to visit us. We used to go to Burchett Lane where the searchlights worked from. One night a cow was killed after the guard said "Halt – who goes there?" He got no reply and so opened fire.'

YOU MAY TELEPHONE FROM HERE

'Most people had a Morrison shelter in their bedrooms and after the war it was quite common to see parts of them used for chicken runs. I remember going to the village hall at West End to collect our gas masks. We children had Mickey Mouse orange ones with a flap which fluttered with your breathing. The lady who was giving them out was also our postlady, and she used to greet Dad with "It's alright . . . they're alright!" before he had a chance to read his mail for himself.

Two stray planes crashed in the orchard of a big house in our lane (Halebourne), which made two huge craters side by side. I've never seen so many people in our lane at once either before or since, as everyone marched down to see this spectacle.

The house next door to us had no drains, a bucket lavatory, no electricity, no bath and no hot water, *but* he had a phone because he ran a taxi service with a huge Dodge car with a beautiful shiny curved bumper – which we all used to look in because it made us look dumpy like in the "magic mirrors" at the seaside. There was a blue and white sign nailed onto a telegraph pole outside his house which stated "You may telephone from here", but which his wife had taken down as the Land Girls used to be always phoning their boyfriends!

There was a prisoner-of-war camp at Brick Hill on Chobham Common fairly near to us, and when the war was over the Nissen huts were allocated to local families until the council houses were built for them to move into. Several of the German prisoners used to visit us for tea and I can still remember all their names. Four or five of them corresponded with Mum and Dad until my parents' deaths. At that time my younger sister was a baby, and one of the Germans loved her as he had not seen his wife and baby since he was captured.

My Dad was in a reserved occupation, so he was in the Valley End Division of "Dad's Army". Once he went on duty with his rifle barrel full of cornflour as Mum had dropped it from the larder shelf above where Dad leaned his rifle when not in use!'

THE BOMBERS' MOON AND THE BLACK MARKET

'Everyone knew that the "Bombers' Moon" would bring over squadrons of German bombers, and the following morning further parts of London would be flattened. The morning following one night's bombing of the docks in the East End, it took one lady four and a half hours to get from Clapham to Waterloo, such was the scale of the devastation.

The Lingfield racecourse was a camp for German sailors, and was surrounded with high netting and floodlit at night. POWs were generally well liked, keeping themselves busy with their native crafts like wood carving. Many remember them mending shoes for the local people.

Most people can remember the Black Market, which was rife. Also the strange appearance of long-lost "Uncles" who seemed to turn up when the dads were away, but who disappeared like ghosts on their return!'

WHAT DO YOU KNOW ABOUT HORSES?

'In the early days of the war, the baker's boy called and told me it was his last week as he had joined the Air Force. I enquired who would be calling and he replied "Dunno, Mr Eatwell can't get anyone".

I went indoors and thought "What about me?" My husband had been called up and I had an aunt living with me who had been bombed out so my young baby would be no problem.

Having enquired about the job, Mr Eatwell said "What do you know about horses?" I replied "Nothing, but if those lads you employ can manage I guess I can". He agreed to take me on the round for one week's trial and I got the job. It would take a book to relate all my adventures in the years that followed, but I guess I'd call it "The Horse and I".

The following little tales stand out in my mind. The first is of a dear little old lady who came up the drive each day with a basket with a white cloth spread over it. She would then have her Hovis placed in and covered over the basket. Unfortunately, on this particular day, Molly, the horse had stopped short with a jerk and the back door of the van flew open and out shot her Hovis – that was bad enough but Molly decided to back and the wheel went over the little loaf! I got down and straightened it as best I could and placed it in the proffered basket.

An air raid on the village caught Molly and I in a lane in Warlingham and a sudden burst of gunfire overhead caused her to bolt. We tore along the lanes at a speed she had endeavoured in the past to assure me she was *quite* incapable of! At last I managed to pull her up and got down to stand by her head to calm her. Of course, the instructions from the Ministry were "In the event of an air raid, unharness your horse and lead it to a nearby field". One wonders how many terrified horses they had practised on!'

MOCK-STEAK AND FIR CONES

'In the inter-war period Hindhead, often called "The Switzerland of England", was a popular holiday resort for the middle aged and middle class and in consequence there were many hotels. Many of these were taken over as offices while others were used for accommodation of adult evacuees in 1939 and 1940.

We did not suffer from shortages of food. Living in the country meant friends often supplemented the egg ration and when Mother was given more than a dozen she would "preserve" them so that she could be sure of having some for cake making at Christmas and for my birthday. I used to enjoy the method, where using a pair of tongs I dipped them in a sticky substance, let them drip, then laid them on trays. The trays were placed under the wardrobe and at regular intervals it was my job to turn the eggs. Mother also used the other method of keeping them in a bucket of preservative but the drawback with this method was that the first to be preserved were the last to be used unless they were transferred from a full bucket into another one.

We were never short of meat. We lived next to a butcher's cashier and were registered at the shop. My father, an ironmonger's manager, worked next door to the other butcher. Our official ration was often augmented by the one and father often brought in a gift from the other – his payment for having found an extra packet of soap powder! It would cost my father a pint of beer at "The Legion" for a rabbit shot by one of the regulars. On Wednesdays lunch was a "scratch" meal. My favourite was Marmite spread on bread, dipped in milk and fried and known in our household as "mock steak". It was half-day closing for father and he always brought home some fish which he cooked for "high tea".

I never went short of sweets as the Canadian soldiers stationed in the area would go to "The Legion" and for the price of a drink willingly gave away packets of sweets sent from home. How I remember those fruity sweets with "the hole in the middle" known as life-savers. Obviously we were never short of household cleaning materials, toilet requisites or toilet paper as these were sold at the shop. The coal ration was supplemented by going into the woods to gather twigs and fir-cones and dragging home fallen branches in order to saw them into logs. The cat was fed the same as we ate except in very dire times when he might have to have a slice of bread soaked in gravy. In addition to our regular weekend meat order there was always "two-pennyworth of lights" for the cat.

As far as clothing coupons went, these were spent on Father's clothes for work, shoes, outdoor wear and material for mother's friend to make up into dresses for herself and me, but even here there was the occasional supplement from the Canadian soldiers. They would receive presents of gloves, scarves, shirts, ties and handkerchiefs and trade them for drinks. The barter system was well and truly in vogue, or should it be called the rural black market?'

CANADIANS AND BOMBS

'Troops occupied Boothlands Farm and, after Mrs Janson's death in 1941, also Newdigate Place. At Boothlands Mr and Mrs Cripps ran the NAAFI canteen and did the cooking. Lots of Nissen huts were erected in the fields of Boothlands Farm to house the troops and after the war these were used to provide housing for many people, some of whom later moved to Winfield Grove when that was built. At first the troops stationed here were British, but later various regiments of Canadians, who had previously been under canvas, moved in. I know that one Canadian regiment were Highlanders. They sometimes wore kilts and they had bagpipes. They used to walk up the road playing them. Mother hated bagpipes!

We children got on very well with the Canadians, who gave us sweets and chocolates. We knew many by their Christian names. They got lots of food parcels from their families and once Mother received one, with dried fruit in it, which she made into a cake. Mother did the laundry for the officers and sometimes at week-ends she would put up wives of the British officers.

The troops had sentries at each end of Dukes Drive – at East Lodge and West Lodge – and we all had to have passes so we could get through to go to school. At first we had to keep showing these, until the soldiers got to know us. Later we changed our route and went via Partridge Lane and Cudworth. The guards were necessary because ammunition boxes were piled up under the sycamore trees on either side of Dukes Drive from East Lodge as far as the lakes. After the war we found many cartridges lying around from boxes that had broken open.

At the time of D-Day the troops suddenly went without warning. We didn't know they were going and one morning they had all gone. They had done a lot of damage to Newdigate Place, for instance chopping up some of the furnishings for firewood. A lot of the lovely panelling was all damaged. It was a bit of a wreck after they left and was never lived in again.'

WHERE THE RAILINGS WENT

'In common with many other residents of Court Hill, Chipstead, the members of my family were deeply saddened when all the iron railings from around our properties were removed to help the war effort. We just had to make do with alternative, or no, boundary markings.

Many years later, during the tidying up process of peacetime, the Emergency Water Supply tank at the top of the hill was drained, preparatory to being removed. Imagine the chagrin of the whole neighbourhood when all the railings, earlier removed, were discovered in the bottom of this tank! My father was so very pleased that he had hidden his!'

PIE DAY AND JAM

'The Bisley WI took part in the Pie Scheme for agricultural workers. Pie Day was the highlight of the week. The meat pies were made at Bagshot and cost fivepence each (they were extra to the rations) and were sold by the ladies of the WI from the butcher's garage.'

'In wartime the WI was ready and willing to organise help wheresoever needed. Our biggest job was the jam making scheme. Much fruit was being wasted in the countryside when sugar rationing limited home preservation, so WIs founded Jam Making Centres. The Ministry of Food issued sugar, local people provided fruit and cooking know-how.

Our little WI at Grafham and Smithbrook made a ton of jam and not one pound was rejected by the Ministry Inspector who then took it away to the national store. So don't let anyone get away with sneering at Jam and Jerusalem!'

SILK STOCKINGS

'When war broke out my sister and I were travelling each day to London to work. The rail fare from Bagshot to Waterloo was, I think, 14 shillings a week; pay was not much more than this, so there was not a lot left over.

But, a beautiful fitted camel hair coat bought in Camberley was £5; good suede shoes from Dolcis, with the fashionable wedge heel, were 21 shillings and a reasonable rayon dress was about £2. In 1941 a 'Hershelle' model coat in tweed with a low bodice and a box pleated skirt, bought in Windsor, was £10 and it lasted me and then Mother until after the war.

When clothes rationing started I had built up a small stock of some dozen pairs of pure silk stockings, which we then wore. These were washed, rolled up and sealed in the Kilner jars used for fruit bottling. The stockings were reluctantly brought out to use from time to time; they were darned and darned and darned until after the end of the war. I never had to resort to the painted legs with seams drawn up the back. But, of course, three and a half years in uniform did help!'

A CHILD'S WAR

FROM RICHES TO RAGS

'I was the third child born into a family living comfortably in a beautiful five bedroomed house, built by my father in Beechwood Avenue, Weybridge. It was 1935. We had a car, a boat on the Thames and everyone was very happy. My mother had every modern convenience including a Hoover vacuum cleaner, a refrigerator and a washing machine. We had a large beautifully laid out garden to play in. I even had a Swiss nanny for a while.

My father owned a small building firm, A. Lake Builders, and was in demand building houses around Walton and Weybridge. Everything changed for us in 1939. Building houses was no longer a possibility and the men were all being called up to fight. My father was too old at 38 and not very fit, so he was in the Walton-on-Thames Home Guard.

In 1940, when I was four, I moved across the river with my mother, brother and sister to a sparsely furnished, two bedroomed, top floor flat, above a wireless shop. My father sold the Weybridge house with all the furnishings to a doctor. I saw very little of him from then on. This didn't seem at all strange to me as all the fathers were away during the war. It was tragic for my mother to discover he was using the war as an excuse to go off with another woman.

The inevitable shortages, caused by the war and the fact that we had no regular money coming in, meant life was very hard for my mother struggling to bring up a young family. She had to look after us all on the £2 maintenance a week which my father was supposed to send and sometimes did, if she was lucky. I know this because we children had to cash the cheques at the bank as she was too ashamed. After a while she took a part-time job in the local grocer's, but this was alien to her nature as women then believed their place was in the home.

All our clothes were handmade and usually handed down. I remember one grey skirt I wore to primary school that was all darns at the back and grey worsted at the front. Darning became a feature of our lives as we had to learn to darn heels and toes in socks, elbows of jumpers and anything else that would keep us clothed.

My summer dress one year was made from two tea-towels sent

from New York by my aunt. She also sent some red striped material which lasted many years as a dress with white sheeting bands inserted in the skirt each year. When I burst out of the top it became a skirt only.

Newspapers took on a new importance as after reading about the war they came in handy for toilet paper, fire lighting, lining shoes with holes in the soles, as long as it wasn't raining, and many other things. One of my jobs was to make squares of paper and thread string through to hang in the toilet. The toilet always had a certain smell because my mother would seek sanctuary there for a quiet smoke, her only luxury.

I had my own methods of making up for the lack of luxuries in our diet. With my friends I used to eat lime leaves and vinegar leaves (sorrel). In the autumn there were plenty of sweet chestnuts, cobnuts and beechmast. I didn't need to go scrumping for fruit as we had six apple trees in the garden.

There were always plenty of vegetables grown on the allotments, along with soft fruit. We picked blackberries from the hedgerows and sometimes rose-hips. Rose hip syrup was free along with cod liver oil and milk, supplied by the Government to keep us all healthy in the absence of fruit like oranges and bananas from abroad.

The meal we had most often we called Irish Stew. It was always neck end of lamb, carrots, onions and potatoes and pearl barley. I don't know who had the rest of the lamb or mutton but we never did. Rabbit stew was another regular. My mother kept rabbits for eating at the bottom of the garden behind the shop and beyond the glass accumulators and bottles containing acid for recharging. Occasionally we had horsemeat from Kingston market. It was always recognisable from its yellow fat.

At the Teddington end of Bushey Park, the American GIs arrived in the middle of the war and we could see them playing baseball and basketball. It must have been those same soldiers that decided to give the local children a party. I was going but I cried for days beforehand because I thought the party was in America and I didn't want to leave home!

We were collected from school in enormous army lorries and taken to their base, where we had marvellous food that we hadn't seen before like doughnuts, hot dogs, ice cream and jelly. My tea at home was usually bread soaked in warm milk or bread and marg with homemade plum jam or toast and welsh rarebit.

On the way home I cried again because I'd left my party shoes behind. The whole convoy turned back to pick up my shoes.'

MICKEY MOUSE AND MUNITIONS

'My earliest memory is of going to a school called Blue Gates opposite The Organ inn at Ewell. The greater part of my first day there, as a six year old, was taken up with gas mask practice. We younger children had Mickey Mouse masks. I can still remember the smell of warm rubber and the strong desire to get it off, as we crouched beneath our desks for the statutory five minutes. The teachers were obviously endeavouring to make it seem like a game but it was never a popular one!

When I went to boarding school and my brother joined the army, my mother was called up and went to make munitions at the Ronson factory at Dorin Court in Leatherhead. When I was home from school I was sometimes allowed to go with her. We were met at Leatherhead station by a lorry with a tarpaulin top and an open back. All the girls – somehow in wartime all working women seemed to be spoken of as "girls" whatever their ages – piled in the back of the lorry and were driven to the factory, which was minute compared with the later factory that Ronson's opened when their cigarette lighters were at the height of their popularity. As a small child I was spoiled disgracefully by the people working there. All the women wore their hair in turbans fashioned from scarves and all seemed to enjoy the time they spent there.'

TAKING IN STRANGERS

'When the Battle of Britain started, we had to double up in order to take in an evacuee family from the East End. They were not actually homeless but thought that they were in danger. There always seemed to be an unpleasant odour about. There were always wet nappies around and they weren't too keen on using soap. They did not stay long but they left their mark in more ways than one. Both of us ended up with lice and also impetigo, Annabel suffering more than I as she had to have her hair completely shaved off.'

THANK YOU, MR HITLER!

'My brother and I went to the village school in the middle of Cranleigh. I hated every moment of this confusing life with much unkindness shown to me and a cruel amount of torment which I shall never forget. John and I had to walk one mile to school, but one day I decided to run away. I asked to go to the toilet for which I was severely reprimanded, but allowed to leave the class. It was then that I saw my chance to go the long way around that we knew, so I would arrive home at the same time as usual. However, some older children were sent to my house to find me and all was discovered. I do not know how I managed to escape real punishment, but the misery continued.

We always watched on a Sunday if we heard a doodlebug. They usually passed over to reach London, but on this day the engine stopped and it landed on the empty school. Next day my brother went our special way to school, of which nothing remained. My brother found a compass from the doodlebug. This of all the happenings of my life will remain as an enormous joy, that never again would I go to that terrible school and I inwardly said "Thank you, Mr Hitler." In my childish mind I thought school was over forever.'

EVACUEES AND EXAMS

'When war broke out in 1939, Headley received its quota of evacuees. We were allocated a girl of about my age. By this time my brother had been given his bed in our sitting room, so Joan not only shared my room but also my bed! It must have been a tremendous cultural shock for those children to leave their families in urban Forest Hill and come to strangers in our quiet little country village where we made our own amusement. The only organised entertainment we had was Children's Hour on the radio from 5–6pm each day! It was something of a "them and us" situation at first, but they very soon became integrated and Joan corresponded with my mother regularly until my mother's death a few years ago. My start at the grammar school was also affected by the evacuee situation. Our school premises had to be shared with Sydenham secondary school so, after a delayed start, we went to school in the mornings and brought home loads of work to do at home in the afternoons and Sydenham went to school in the afternoons. This continued for some months until they organised other premises.

My mother organised the local National Savings group – people would buy National Savings stamps regularly as part of their war-effort. My mother's responsibility was to buy stamps from the post office and supply them to her collectors, who each had a round of customers. They would then pay the money back to her so that she could buy more. It was a successful way of encouraging people to invest money which they would otherwise not have bothered with. My mother also undertook the organisation of our "library". The County Library supplied boxes of books which we set out in the village hall for a couple of hours every Tuesday afternoon. From time to time the County Library exchanged the original boxes for new ones so we always had a supply of reading matter.

We had our share of bombs during the war. We were on the flight path to London, and German bombers often unloaded their "cargo" early rather than face the guns and barrage balloons that surrounded London. Because of the rural area, very little serious damage was done. My uncle was a Special Police constable and one of their responsibilities was to trace where all the bombs in a stick had fallen. He spent several hours one night searching for the last one in vain, only to return home to find the crater in his back garden. Our war stories were often touched with humour, like the old lady found sitting up in bed, surrounded by broken glass from the window and a picture, with the picture frame around her neck. A flying bomb had landed a short distance from her home but luckily she was completely unhurt and more puzzled than shocked!

When the time came to take my School Certificate, we were still having almost perpetual air raids so our exams were taken in a variety of strange venues. I remember taking a French paper in a cellar underneath the electricity show rooms in Dorking. There was a grating from the street in one corner down which a toddler dropped a penny. He stood above it and howled until the invigilator sent a message for someone to sort the problem out for him. Our Art exam was taken in a ground floor classroom (the Art rooms were on the top floor). We had two buckets of water – one clean, one used – and the sash windows were all open at the bottom. A member of staff was posted on the flat roof of the school with a whistle which he blew whenever there was any sign of enemy activity. We then all had to clamber out of the windows and get down the nearest shelter. I remember it happened one time when I was halfway through a sky wash!'

WARTIME SCHOOLDAYS

'Arriving at the railway station on Saturday afternoon, 2nd September 1939, homeward bound after a brief stay with relations, I was astonished to see crowds of children milling about, mostly around my own age – between eight and ten years old, with a few younger ones. They were all wearing labels and had their gas-masks slung across their chests in the familiar square cardboard boxes, and carried carrier bags, parcels or small attaché-cases. "They are evacuees from London", my mother informed me. Secretly the idea of being evacuated appalled me, but they looked cheerful. The teachers, on the other hand, looked harassed! These were the first of many. It was the moment when the possibility of war, that grown-ups had been talking about for so long, suddenly became a certainty. The talking was about to stop.

The next day, Sunday 3rd September, we gathered round the radio at 11am (a Pye radio, the front of which depicted a fretwork rising sun) and heard the solemn voice of Neville Chamberlain saying "I have to tell you now that no such undertaking has been received". We were at war. Within minutes the air raid siren wailed! Incredible – how did Hitler know so soon! It was unreal . . . no-one knew quite what to do. Before we had time to decide – or panic – the All Clear sounded. A false alarm. Phew!

The blackout curtains were already installed – we had had trial blackouts in 1938. We also had trial runs at school wearing our gas masks. They were smelly and uncomfortable, but they were a novelty. The father of one of my friends was a Quaker and a conscientious objector (a brave thing to be at that time, I realise now, as feelings ran quite high). He refused to let any of his family have a gas mask and kept the children away from school on the days when we had gas mask practice. Even at that young age I pondered how he would feel if there was a gas attack. Fortunately it never happened. Brown sticky paper was being criss-crossed over the window panes. We were preparing for war in earnest.

At the start of the new school term we were amazed to be told that another convent school from Willesden was joining us to share our school. The good news was that we were to go to school in the mornings only, from 8am – 1pm, and then the London school took over the premises for the afternoon. Joy at the idea of free afternoons was short lived. We were given a mountain of homework to keep us out of mischief. This proved to be the time of the "phoney war", and gradually most of these evacuees drifted back home to London. The few girls that remained were integrated into our classes, and school life resumed its normal pattern.

Twelve months later things were different. The Battle of Britain was in full swing, and it was decided that it was not safe for us to be roaming the countryside during the long summer holiday. Everyone feared that invasion was imminent. So we had to go to school every day as usual; but rules were relaxed and no work was done. We played board games and cards, sat in the orchard in the sun and read "William" books, and produced concerts – it wasn't all that bad, in fact we quite enjoyed ourselves.

Our headmistress was tiny, determined and dynamic . . . and we were all in awe of her. She was a great believer in the power of prayer, and was determined to beat Hitler single-handed – with a little help from her 400 girls! She divided the school into two at Assembly, and gave each half something different to pray for: the current battle; that a ship should not be sunk; or that one should be sunk (the battle of the river Plate is vivid in my mind); or that planes should return without loss. I always seemed to be on the wrong side of the hall, praying for the impossible to happen – and thus felt personally responsible for some of the disasters of war!

Many nights were spent sleeping in an air-raid shelter – a reinforced cellar shared with our immediate neighbours. We had a succession of evacuees and soldiers billeted on us, some of whom my parents kept in touch with. One of the soldiers, George, a lad of 18 from Eltham, my mother treated like a son. I thought he was marvellous because he did my maths homework for me. My marks plummeted when he moved on! He subsequently went to the Far East and was captured by the Japanese. Years later, after he was repatriated, he invited us to his wedding in London. He met us at the station, and the only way we recognised him was by his Australian-style Army hat. Although still in his early twenties he looked an old man, emaciated and yellow with tropical jaundice. I remember that my mother cried.'

LIFE WITH MY GRANDPARENTS

'My grandfather built our house in 1932. I was three when the war started. My father spent his war as a driving instructor of ten-ton lorries on the mountain roads of North Wales, and unless he was home on leave my mother and I lived with my paternal grandparents.

There was "ration swapping". The lady next door was a great tea drinker, so we exchanged tea for sugar. My grandmother made preserves from hedgerow and garden fruits. The straining and jelly cloth was made from an old nightie or butcher's muslin, tied to the legs of an upturned chair with a bowl to catch the drips, and left for 24 hours. If I could keep my fingers off it for that time, I was allowed to play with it afterwards.

We had an air-raid shelter dug in the garden. It was equipped with two camp beds and a chair. Duck boards were necessary on the floor as it was always covered with water. It smelled dank and clammy and I didn't like it. At first when the air-raid siren sounded we went in. Cooking on a primus stove, with lighting also by paraffin, tainted everything.

We watched "our boys" going over in formation and saw some of them coming back. Looking north and east we could see flashes and hear thumps and felt very sorry for London. The lady next door had a son in the RAF and several times he flew over, leaned out of the plane and waved to us, such excitement!

During the day, mother hung a little bag on a string round my neck. I didn't understand why, but she showed me a picture of a man with a very cross face and a tin hat and said "if a man like this came I was to throw the bag in his face and run away". I never found out where I was supposed to run to, but years later she told me the bag had pepper in it. She must have been so frightened, her husband away, two ailing in-laws and me, and the Germans just a few miles away over the Channel.

I remember seeing pyramids of bombs hidden under the trees at the road side round the lanes of Newdigate and Charlwood. On the back of my mother's bike or beside her on my tricycle, you felt you had to pass by very quietly. Canadian soldiers were living in the wood at Ewood. There were trenches and dug-outs; where the clay had been brought to the surface it gleamed orange, yellow and red when wet. Apparently notices were put on the trees telling the men to watch their language if we children were about.

Grandfather went up to London for two days most weeks to open the family upholstery and soft furnishing business and to check for bomb damage. All materials were rationed, it must have been very difficult. Blackout curtains kept the workrooms busy at the beginning of the war for private customers, the Bank of England building in the City and for their evacuation premises in Wiltshire. As the men in the upholstery workshop were called up that department was "closed for the duration".

Toys were scarce but I had plenty to amuse me. On wet days I was allowed in the garage. With hammer and nails, screws and driver and my own piece of wood, I was very busy making "something". I eagerly awaited grandfather's return from London, he might have taken a rabbit and come back with fish. The rabbit skin would be nailed to the garage door (for gloves and slippers). I had the feet and scud for the cat and I to play with, but fish heads were more fun, only they didn't last as long. On very special occasions we had a chicken. I sometimes got the feet with long tendons to make the claws work, that is if grandmother hadn't put them in the stock pot.

Another treat was to be allowed to help grandfather remove the road chippings from the car tyres. We sat on fishing stools, each wheel removed in turn and we would dig away with penknives, using the "thing that got stones out of horses hooves". We also spent time re-painting the sidelights of the car. Two thirds of the glass had to be blacked out. They looked like half closed sleepy eyes. Only a glimmer of light was allowed. I don't think headlights could be used at all.

In the evening if I stayed very quiet in the corner of the settee, the grown-ups might forget I was there, our neighbours would come in and gossip, and tell snippets from their husband's letters.

Their conversation was accompanied by the rhythmical splosh of the butter ration, the marg ration and the top of three days' milk being gently shaken together in a Kilner Jar – to make it "go a bit further". Sometimes I was sent to bed but mostly remember going to sleep to the splosh-splosh-splosh of the jars.

Double summer time meant it didn't get dark till ten or eleven o'clock at night; this helped the war effort, but everyone got very tired. As a child who had to go to bed early, it was too light even with the blackout curtains to sleep and sometimes very hot, voices from the garden, greetings from callers and people cycling past. "They" sometimes relented and I went to sleep in a deck-chair. In the mornings it was really cold going to school, as the equivalent time was 6 am. One had to wear a cardie or coat, but at 3 pm all these extra clothes had to be carried home.

With most of our food stuffs being rationed and delivered, home grown or picked from fields and hedges, or acquired by "swapsies", a trip into Dorking was quite an outing. We had a two hourly bus service (7am – 11pm). The bus was usually full and children were expected to give up their seats and sit on laps. The conductors were friendly, helping people on and off with children, prams and shopping, and taking messages and parcels between stops.

Sometimes if we had petrol I went with grandfather in his little Austin 7. It seems funny now, but we had no difficulty parking in Dorking. We would stop outside MacFisheries (opposite the post office), drive up to Woodcock's, then on to Kingham's, Sainsbury's and Clear's and on to the Band Stand for my special treat, a visit to the Black & White Milk Bar, then a long look at the tools in Cumming's window and also the fishing tackle shop. On market day it was better to go by bus, as the High Street was busy with cattle, sheep and pigs. The animals were penned on the cobblestones. Benches and trestles were put outside the Three Tuns for the farming folk. There was so much noise from the clatter of the weighing machines as the bulls and cows were weighed.

On VE day we were in the front garden, when Olive from the farm came running down the lane – "The war is over, it's on the wireless". Grandfather went up in the loft and brought out the big Union Jack which he had hidden under the eaves for years, and like many others in the village, it flew proudly from our roof.'

EVACUATION TO AUSTRALIA

'If it wasn't for the war I would never have been to Australia. In August 1940 at the age of eleven I set sail with 480 boys and girls between the ages of five and 15 from all over the country, from every home background, every size and shape. We embarked at Liverpool after four nights in a school, the classrooms being the dormitories and the only experience I had of air raids. We had been gathered together by train, bus and really we could have had no knowledge of the adventure that was about to begin.

Our ship was Polish, with Polish crew and Polish food! Called the *Batory*, she acted as our home for eleven weeks. We had lots of uncles, as aboard were several Air Force members who disembarked at Freetown, West Africa, also hundreds of Army personnel who came all the way to Singapore. They patrolled the ship and were more than kind to us "kids". How many, I wonder, returned from that country? We were in convoy, the largest to leave England to date, I think about twelve ships, some cruise ships, some cargo ships, we saw them about us every day and they kept close guard against German submarines.

So, out into the Atlantic and about five days later I think it hit us what might be happening and emotions ran high; our escorts had a difficult time – as there was this great team of adults to look after us, each had about twelve children under their wing. But time calmed us all, the sea sickness went, the homesickness receded and our confidence returned. We had classes and entertainments, games and talks about Australia. We produced a magazine, had fun, and were spoilt by those "Tommys". We travelled to Capetown, to Bombay, to Colombo and to Singapore. Everywhere we were feted and spoilt and shown the zoos and botanical gardens. And always a reception at Government House and oranges and presents and such hospitality.

Our soldiers left at Singapore, we missed them and the ship was quiet. Then Fremantle, Western Australia, greetings and we had arrived at our home for the next five years.'

EVACUATED TO THE COUNTRY

'My earliest memories go back to when I was evacuated from London to the country on 3rd September, 1939. For about a week before that we had gone to school each day with our gas mask, case and barley sugar. As you can imagine, my mother had to renew the barley sugar every day! Eventually, the day arrived and we were off!

We were vetted, medically inspected and sent to various homes (there were five of us in the first one). Eventually four returned to London: I was the only one of this group to stay. I never did return to London to live again. How I loved the country – woods to walk in, birds and lovely flowers.

The only "near disaster" experience I remember was being in an open-topped car, with other children, driving down a country lane and being machine-gunned by an enemy plane. The driver stopped the car and told us to lie down in the ditch. We did so, and we all survived. We children thought it had all been great fun, needless to say.'

HAPPY MEMORIES

'Although filled with sad memories for so many, the war was for me in New Malden a pleasant time when rigid routines seemed not to matter any more. Gone was bedtime at seven during the Blitz. Instead lovely evenings sitting under the stairs with Grandma doing jigsaw puzzles, while my brother and mother and father, when he was not doing his Red Cross duties, shared more sedate accommodation in the coat lobby. At nine o'clock there always seemed to be a lull in the bombing so we all emerged, drank hot cocoa and then went to bed in the dining room, which had been lined with wooden sheets to stop the flying glass. School during the day was a sketchy affair with many lessons in the cellars and gas masks hanging on our chairs always at the ready.

The garden was given over to digging for victory and fruit and vegetables abounded. One spare bedroom, its bookcases bereft of books, became a storeroom full of Kilner jars, beans in salt and pots of jam. My mother heard from someone that Headley WI were serving egg teas, so she took my brother and me by train to Epsom. We then walked up to the Downs and across them to Headley church, behind which is the WI hall. Here we demolished bread and butter (I expect it was marg) and a boiled egg. Back across the Downs we tramped and down to the station, my mother pleased with her efforts at ekeing out the rations. Alas, Lord Woolton stepped in after a short while and the WI were not allowed to serve eggs any more. So we took to keeping hens, and we collected revolting scraps from the neighbours to be exchanged for eggs when the laying was good. More storage – buckets of eggs in preservative.

Going away for holidays of course was not possible, but my father would take a week off and we went out for days. Blackberrying on Bookham Common and then walking into Leatherhead for tea, gazing up at the brick shell of Guildford cathedral and writing our names on a brick for sixpence, walks along the towpath at Kingston and a rowing boat on the river, and Bentalls of Kingston ran concert parties and acrobatic displays as part of their holidays-at-home policy. The variety was endless and we were never bored for a moment. After the war a fortnight in one place on the coast seemed quite dull by comparison.'

SERVING THEIR COUNTRY

THE WOMEN'S LAND ARMY

'I joined the Women's Land Army in 1941, first at a market garden then I was transferred to the Surrey War Agricultural Committee, which was a depot at Stoke Park. We worked a 48 hour week which included Saturday mornings for just a shilling per hour. We were used as group labour for farms in the area in need of help or on land owned by the County used for growing food such as potatoes and carrots. Plenty of commons had to be cleared and ploughed during the winter months to use for growing food. We were trained in quite a few farming skills such as fruit tree pruning, thrashing on the corn machine, before the use of combine harvesters, and thatching on the stacks to keep them dry. It was an interesting way of life with sowing and hoeing in spring, harvesting in the long summer evenings and then the bitter winter jobs like picking sprouts for several days, which I remember were for use by the Canadian Army stationed on Witley Common and the Hogs Back. We all lived in hostels or billets with families and it was an interesting mixture of people from different walks of life and living out of London.'

'In 1942 my parents bought a house in Farnham and during the latter part of the war I started to work on the land. At first I worked at a nursery garden on the outskirts of Farnham. Some flowers were grown out of doors but the green houses contained tomatoes and cucumbers grown mainly for seed. The cucumbers were allowed to become really ripe and squashy and then our task would be to extract the seed. During that time our hands were as white and soft as a queen's.

After a few months I was able to join the Women's Land Army and was attached to a Surrey War Agricultural Executive Committee (SWAEC) hostel in the Bourne, Farnham. About 50 girls, mostly Londoners lived at the hostel, but I, and four other girls, lived at home. One had been a hairdresser in "civvy street" and she was much in demand for a quick set during the lunch hour, her salon being a barn or even the open field.

On joining the WLA we were issued with a large quantity of warm, practical uniform. Breeches, dungarees, milking jackets (I still have one which comes in useful for messy jobs), shirts, tie, jersey, a

During the Second World War many women 'did their bit' by joining the Land Army. They replaced men on the farms, growing food essential for Britain's survival.

beautifully warm greatcoat and porkpie hat. Leather shoes, leather boots (very comfortable when broken in), rubber boots, oilskins and sou'wester. The WLA office was near Guildford station, there second hand uniform could be bought. It was useful to have extra clothes so that a set of uniform could be kept for best. We made shorts for use in hot weather by cutting the legs off old dungarees or breeches. Most of the girls acquired a battle dress top to wear for working as this was warm and weatherproof and not as cumbersome as a greatcoat. The "in" headgear was a scarf worn "mammy" fashion.

Work started at 7.30 am when we reported to the forewoman at the hostel. We were allocated jobs, and two comfortable coaches were provided by the local garage to take us to the various farms on the day's schedule. A great variety of work was undertaken. Potato picking was back breaking work which needed a large gang of girls, cabbage planting needed two girls to feed seedlings into the ever hungry planting machine. The coldest work was sprout picking on a frosty morning with the sprouts frozen onto the stalks. If the temperature rose and they thawed out then gloves and sleeves became saturated. The most pleasant job was fruit picking on a hot sunny day under the shade of a blackcurrant bush. Harvesting was fun and had the added benefit of extra rations in the form of tinned corned beef or Spam or some other hard to come by food and extra cheese. The normal cheese ration for agricultural workers was eight ounces per week, twelve ounces at harvest. We were also given a permit to buy a thermos flask.

The corn was cut and bound into sheaves by the cutting machine (sometimes horse drawn) while the stooking gang followed propping up the sheaves seed heads upmost, six or eight to a stook. After a few fine days, when the corn was judged to be dry, it was pitchforked on to wagons and carried to the rick. Wagon loading and rick building were skilled jobs usually done by the farm workers. As the rick grew in height an elevator was used to send up the sheaves.

Threshing was carried out by contractors, helped by a gang of about five land girls, visiting various farms in the locality. Usually the threshing machine was pulled and operated by an ancient steam engine which required stoking at regular intervals. The contractor's men would cut the binder twine around the sheaves and feed the corn into the machine (one false move and you could emerge in small pieces), while the land girls pitched sheaves from the rick to the man on the machine, raked away the chaff and changed the bags for grain when necessary. A bailing machine was normally attached to dispose of the straw. As the rick was uncovered nests of mice and rats might be found and towards the end rats would run from the bottom of the rick to be killed by dogs and men.

We rarely had to work with animals though one girl spent several weeks helping at a pig farm.

In wet or snowy weather, unless travelling was impossible we always had to go out to the farms. Sometimes indoor jobs could be found, otherwise we were allowed to shelter in a barn or nearby cafe until it cleared up or the forewoman called out the coach to take us home.

We were allowed to work alongside gangs of conscientious objectors and Irishmen, also employed by the SWAEC, but prisoners of war worked separately. We were paid a shilling per hour for a 48 hour week, overtime during harvest.'

'I was a volunteer in the Women's Land Army at Bell Farm, Felcott Road, Walton-on-Thames. We were out on the market gardens at 7am until 5.30pm in rain, snow and shine. We worked 7am to 12 noon Saturdays, 57½ hours a week for 15 shillings per week! One day as we were packing up on Friday, our boss came along and said "Back on the turnips – the Jam Factory want a ton of turnips," so now you know what plum jam was made from!

The day that is still so vivid is 6th June 1944 – D-Day. We were pulling carrots and the ground was shaking from the vibration of hundreds of four-engined bombers from American bases nearby. We looked up and saw layers of planes with the sides open and guns facing out. They were so low we waved to the airmen and they waved back to us. After several hours of quiet we heard them coming back. One had two engines out, one working and one ticking over in jerks, and the airmen on board were firing Very lights to signify "wounded on board". The other planes were grouped around it like mother hens trying to keep the plane flying. We all stopped work and watched and prayed for that plane. We listened, but it did not crash as we did not hear an explosion. Then that afternoon the white painted Red Cross trains were coming along the Portsmouth – Waterloo line, which went alongside our farm. Some of the soldiers were "walking wounded" and as the train was going so slowly the soldiers were throwing bits of paper to us with addresses on. We picked up every one, and then turned out our pockets to see how much money we had to post them. We got the envelopes from houses along Felcott Road. Then we saw our first Germans – very sullen looking – standing in the corridors.

We had Italian prisoners of war working on the farm, with one English soldier with a gun looking after them. They were like us – always singing. They used to make coffee and put a white enamel pot with a lid on it at the end of a row for us to share. We were not to speak to them, so we used to stick our thumbs up to them to say "thank you". Before we could start work we would pick up all the "silver metal strands" the Germans used to drop to upset the Radar. Still, we loved our life out there.'

THE WOMEN'S VOLUNTARY SERVICE

'Widowed in January 1940, my mother was only too eager to get thoroughly involved in war-time activity, and was glad to be asked to start a WVS branch in Farnham. The work expanded rapidly and one of the first challenges was to deal with evacuees. A train-load arrived at Farnham station, to be met by many women prepared to take a child home with them. Most were sorted out, but at the end there was a mother with two young children. Few people had room for so many, so this was the family that came to stay at Highlands for the next four years.

Being a large house, Highlands became the centre for many activities. It had been a convalescent home in the First World War. Now it had a twice-weekly working party making central hospital supplies. Half a dozen sewing machines fitted on the billiard table for stitching shirts and pyjamas; hand-sewing for "many-tailed" bandages and endless knitting of operation stockings. It was also a potential rest centre, with piles of blankets and emergency food and fuel. The latter were eventually recalled, but not the blankets. These found their way to many different homes as well as chicken houses and dog baskets.

Meals on Wheels and the British Restaurant in Gostrey Meadow, Farnham were run by the WVS. It was a great help to get a meal at a reasonable price that didn't require any food tokens. Villages benefited from the "Pie Scheme" and here the WI were involved. Food rationing was fair and we all survived. How would the modern housewife manage with one egg a week?'

THE ATS

'My first view of Surrey was from the back of an Army lorry! It was a freezing cold day in February 1941 and there had been a heavy fall of snow. It was early morning, and as we reached the top of Reigate Hill, I was spellbound at the view. In the slight glow of sunrise, the whole valley lay in the Christmas card beauty of undisturbed snow, broken only by the houses and dark outlines of the trees; in the distance the hazy South Downs. We could have been in Switzerland. Coming from the flat lands of Essex, I had never seen anything so lovely.

We were in a convoy transporting personnel to the newly formed South Eastern Command, which eventually played a significant part in the organisation of the D-Day landings. Poor Reigate, all the large houses, especially those of the north side of the town, had, a few months before, been requisitioned, the owners given just a short time to vacate and empty their houses, ready for our takeover. I often wonder what happened to all those people. Other families in Reigate and Redhill had been detailed to billet troops and civilian personnel if they had a spare room. We ATS had to live in some of these large empty houses, and there were no home comforts – it was a long hard winter and we were all so cold. There was no heating, unless we gathered wood and lit the old kitchen range, and that was also the only way in which to get hot water to wash (often the pipes froze!). The only way to have a bath was to go home, or to use the old Public Baths in Castlefield Road. And I can assure you that I did just that – sixpence a bath, fourpence to the Forces, twopence if you needed soap and a towel, and a shilling deposit on the towel. But – masses of glorious hot water, how I used to wallow in it, till the attendant shouted out that I had been in long enough.'

'During the war the Army sent me on an ATS Company Commanders' Course to be held in the Royal Holloway College, Egham. Arriving from the depths of West Wales completely unaware of events taking place in the south-east of England, I found a very frightening welcome awaiting me.

Like most people, the first thing I did on entering the large bay windowed room which was to be my quarter for the following five weeks, was to go and look out of the window. Imagine my surprise to see a torpedo like object with stubby wings and blazing tail, streaking across the sky only a few hundred yards away. I had never heard of flying bombs.

Before I could draw my young batwoman's attention to it I found myself grasped around the knees in a superb rugger tackle and thrown under the bed with the full weight of the girl on top of me. The noise of the engine ceased, there was a deadly silence, then a roaring crash and the bay window flew inwards smashing glass all over the bed. What an introduction to Surrey!

The next five weeks were a nightmare, however we got any work done is a mystery. Day lectures were interrupted so often that we automatically dived under the tables when a bomb was heard approaching. With the exception of one night, our beds remained unslept in. Fortunately the Royal Holloway College had large deep cellars where we stretched out on the floors trying hard not to think about the gas and water pipes which lined the walls.

On the night that a flying bomb scored a direct hit on the Bells of Ousley pub in Runnymede, I had crept into my bed determined to have at least a proper mattress on which to rest my weary bones. I was by then so exhausted that I did not hear a sound all night. The next morning I was told that it had been the noisiest and worst night ever! One of my fellow students had to rush back to London as her company headquarters had had a direct hit and 26 of her ATS had been killed. Wales was a haven of peace after all this.'

'At the beginning of 1943 I was one of the first half dozen or so junior ATS officers to find myself on a course at the hitherto all-male Army Radio School in Petersham. It was an extremely intensive and highly top secret course: so much so, in fact, that we weren't allowed to take our notebooks, circuit diagrams or any technical data outside the classroom, so swotting in the evenings was out. Despite this restriction, most of us passed and emerged as Radio Maintenance Officers capable of looking after the RDF (Radio Direction Finding) equipment on AA gun sites. These were the days before the acronym RADAR (Radio Detecting And Ranging) was invented and the transmitters and receivers we were responsible for were each the size of a small room and usually two fields apart. Each sprouted a formidable array of aerials which we had to test at frequent intervals and keep tuned. The RMO lived on one gun site and looked after its RDF equipment and that of another three. Apart from a REME craftsman on each site, the RMO was the first to be called on if the equipment failed in any way. As the gun sites we served were many miles apart, the RMO had to have his/her own transport to answer calls at any time of the day – or more usually, night. This was a rare privilege in those days of stringent petrol rationing and we were careful not to abuse it.

Most of my service in AA Command was on gun sites round Southampton Water and we had our share of excitement. Shortly before D-Day the entire south coast was sealed off, movement was restricted and we were briefed on the coming invasion. The air of tension and expectancy was almost palpable. One of my sites was at Exbury, overlooking the Solent, and on my frequent visits I had watched the build-up of small craft lying off-shore until the sea was covered with them as far as the eye could see. On the morning of D-Day there was not a landing-craft or any other small boat to be seen. Every one of them had gone across the Channel to Normandy during the night and my thoughts and prayers went with them.'

THE ARP

'After my marriage early in 1941 I lived at our little house in Warwick Wold, a hamlet in the parish of Bletchingley, about three miles from Bletchingley and two miles from Merstham. There were two rows of cottages, a corner shop, a few separate cottages, a pub, a farm and four or five larger houses. There was a small chapel and a tin hut, which used to be a Men's Social Club.

The shopkeeper, Mr Tidmarsh, deserved a medal for all the help that he gave his neighbours during the war. Many of the inhabitants of the cottages were elderly and incapable of understanding the rationing regulations. Once a year we were given new ration books, which we had to fill in and then register with a supplier for rationed goods. Mr Tidmarsh used to take the new books from many of his neighbours, fill in their sections as well as his own, keep the books in his shop and regularly supply his customers with the goods to which they were entitled. His shop was tiny, but he sold all the rationed goods except meat – sugar, bacon, fats, cheese, jam, tea, eggs – and he also had a reasonable stock of goods which could be bought on "points", such as tinned fruit and sweets.

Needless to say, Mr Tidmarsh was the Chief ARP Warden for the area and had a team to support him, but gradually the younger people were called up or went away to work in factories, with the result that the remaining wardens were hard-pressed. Accordingly in 1943 a scheme was devised to incorporate other residents, who would get up at night in rotation when the siren sounded, and keep watch, only calling on the wardens if there was an incident in the area.

All men and women between 18 and 60 who had no special responsibilities were liable for this duty; although I had a small baby I also had an elderly family retainer living with me, so she was deemed to be looking after John and I was able to join the scheme.

We had three training sessions, attended by 30 to 40 men and women. The first took place in the tin hut, when we were harangued by an elderly warden, who gave a sketchy demonstration of using a stirrup pump and then rambled on about incidents in his Army career. On the second occasion we were honoured by a trailer pump team from the Fire Service, who demonstrated how the apparatus was fixed to a standpipe and shot out a fierce stream of water.

For the third meeting we were promised a treat – we were going to put out a real fire! The area had previously been divided, on paper, into smaller sections, so that the watchers would only be responsible for their immediate neighbourhood. The leader of our group was a stalwart ex-sergeant from the Irish Guards, who kept the "local" at the bottom of our drive. The rest of the team were his 19 year old daughter, a Land Girl in charge of some pedigree Jersey cows, and myself, and for good measure Barney Reilly had also added a man called Kenward from a nearby cottage, who was deaf and dumb and married to a deaf and nearly dumb wife! When the scheme got under way one member of each group was supposed to be on duty each night in rotation, so every fifth night we could have burned in our beds, as Mr Kenward and his wife slept through any sirens, but it meant that we only had to be on duty one night in five instead of one night in four!

The Fire Service had erected a hut in a field and provided bales of straw and paraffin. They also produced overalls and the idea was that three members of each group would don the overalls, a fire of paraffin-soaked straw would be lit in the hut and we would have to put it out.

Paddy, as the most agile, was given the job of putting the bomb out, while Eileen and I pumped and ran to and fro, keeping the buckets filled. Paddy, as instructed, wriggled forward on her stomach and, holding the nozzle high above her head, directed the water at the fire and it was soon out – to thunderous applause from the audience.

Luckily we never had to go into action, though once a couple of incendiaries fell in a field in a neighbouring area and all our team went to investigate, despite the strict orders which we had been given, that we must remain on our own patch during a raid.

By the middle of 1943 air raids became less frequent and the "watchers" scheme was superseded by a simpler one – a Housewives' Post, to supplement the work of the wardens. Mrs B. was responsible for setting up the Post, which was to function in the Tidmarshes' house, and a team of four women was chosen.'

WORKING ON THE LAND

'"Dig for Victory" was one of the slogans used for the war effort. Everyone was exhorted to grow their own produce and my family certainly did. In a very small garden we grew root crops, greens and fruit and also kept tame rabbits to supplement the meagre meat ration.

Farmers and growers were short of labour and children were a welcome source of labour. From the age of nine to 16 I spent each eight week summer holiday working from 8am until 1pm Monday to Saturday picking peas, beans and sweetcorn for a local horticulturalist. In the early years we sometimes paused to look up at the dog fights of our pilots in the Battle of Britain – we never worried about taking cover when we were working in the fields.

My mother expected me to hand over my earnings each day but she usually allowed me sixpence to spend (if I could find anything unrationed on which to spend it).

On transfer to the grammar school I discovered that every junior girl had to spend one afternoon per week working on the land. By coincidence I was sent to the grower that I already knew – he was delighted to see me in term time and appointed me the chargehand of the field.

I thought my farming days were over when I started work in the Civil Service in January 1949. But soon I discovered that the Ministry of Agriculture ran special farming camps that needed labour during the summer and that if a civil servant spent two weeks at one of these camps it only counted as one week's holiday instead of two.

So the end of June 1949 saw my arrival with a friend at the farming camp at Shepperton. We lived in Nissen huts. We got up early in the morning and were taken by lorry to neighbouring farms where we toiled for eight hours at cutting cabbages, weeding spinach and fruit picking. I was often working in the fields near London Airport. It was hard work but great fun with the company of many other young people.'

THE LOSS OF LOVED ONES

A MOTHER'S ANGUISH

'I remember the expression of anguish on my mother's face as she listened to Neville Chamberlain's broadcast to the nation on 3rd September 1939. She had lost three brothers in the First World War and she now had a twenty year old son who was "itching to have a go at the Jerries".

I well remember that expression again the following year when, outside my school in the pouring rain, she waved me off in a coach (a charabanc we called them then) bound for an unknown destination where she hoped I would be safe from enemy bombing.'

MY BROTHER JOHN

'It was a depressing drive home – death seemed everywhere – squashed frogs, dead birds. On my auto-cycle I was aware of everything on the ground so close to me.

I had been called soon after coming off night duty at Botley's Park (now St Peter's, Chertsey). A message from my mother that brother John was missing. Fighter Pilot, Squadron-Leader, he had failed to return from a mission over France. I was immediately given leave to go to my mother at Farnham. That was on a Friday. Anxious waiting through Saturday. He might have baled out and be a prisoner of war. One brother was already "in the bag", having been taken prisoner at Tobruk.

On Sunday we went, as usual, to morning service at St Thomas on the Bourne. The lesson was that of the Prodigal Son. "This my son was dead and is alive again, was lost and is found". How prophetic! We got back home to hear that there had been a telephone call – John had been picked up from a rubber dinghy in the Channel! After his parachute descent into the water, he managed to inflate his dinghy and climb into it – no mean feat in heavy flying kit. Although quite near the Brittany coast, he chose to paddle north towards England, through two long days and nights. A compass was concealed in a uniform button. He had little food and the only water to drink was the rain collected in the dinghy. One boot had been lost and the exposure of the foot led to subsequent problems.

Still in the dark of the Sunday morning, John awoke to find himself in the middle of a British convoy steaming up the Channel. No one could see him, of course, but he had a whistle, another real blessing, and eventually this attracted the attention of a look-out on a destroyer. Stopping alongside, a rope ladder was lowered, but John found he could hardly stand, much less climb. A seaman came down to help him and the news of his escape quickly spread.

Awarded the DFC, John soon returned to flying. When several months later he was once again reported missing, I felt certain that he would be managing another escape. But, alas, he never came back. With no known grave, he has memorials at Runnymede, his prep school, Winchester College, Christ Church, Oxford, St Thomas-on-the-Bourne and the church where we grew up in Alexandria, Egypt.'

VE DAY

'One of my most vivid and lasting memories is of VE Day. After hearing the momentous news that the horrors of war were over, I was walking to the shops in Sanderstead village. On nearing the church there could be heard all over Sanderstead a recording of Isobel Baillie's beautiful voice singing "I know that my Redeemer liveth".

We had friends living in a cul-de-sac near by, and that evening together with all the neighbours we lit an enormous bonfire in the road to celebrate.'

All over Surrey street parties were arranged to celebrate the end of the Second World War.

THE AFTERMATH OF WAR

The end of the war brought its own problems, in particular a lack of housing. How many golfers on the prestigious Wentworth course know that there was once a squatters' camp near the clubhouse? Rationing continued for some time, and a first confrontation with a real egg could be a daunting experience. Refugees from countries such as Poland were reminders of the dangers still existing in Europe. But there were hopes for the future – and at last women could begin to think about new clothes!

SQUATTERS ON WENTWORTH GOLF COURSE

'When the war finally ended my family were homeless. We were evacuees; in September 1940 my mother, younger sister, five month old baby brother and I had been evacuated to Callow Hill, Virginia Water, Dad remaining in London. He was head porter/caretaker of a block of luxury flats in Drayton Gardens, South Kensington and we lived in a semi-basement service flat. He was called up in 1941, posted to the Far East and subsequently reported "missing", "missing believed killed" and finally in February 1942 "presumed killed in action".

The flat went with his job, and it was impossible for us to remain where we were billeted. We were on the housing lists of both Kensington and Egham but so were hundreds of others. The situation seemed hopeless.

Our problem was solved by an illegal act. Squatters occupied an empty Army camp in Wellington Avenue. To avoid further unauthorised action and to ease their desperate housing situation, Egham Council adopted the squatters camp together with three other unused camps in the area, and that is how, early in 1946 when I was 15, we moved into Hut 4, B Camp, Wentworth Drive, next door to the clubhouse on the famous Wentworth golf course.

B Camp was situated in woodland adjacent to the clubhouse, and consisted of 23 Nissen huts with the rounded corrugated roofs. D Camp was on the opposite side of the road to us (where the car park is now), slightly larger, set in a three-sided square of wooden barrack-type huts with an apex roof. The squatters became A Camp and C Camp was in Portnall Drive.

Electricity was connected to all huts but water had to be carried from half a dozen standpipes dotted around the camps. Toilets were in a block with three or four families sharing. Breeze blocks partially divided each hut into three, but with a large roof gap from front to back. Milk, meat etc were kept fresh in a large biscuit tin buried in the ground. The only means of cooking and heating was a small free standing coal burning kitchen range. These had extremely narrow chimneys and required frequent sweeping, which was achieved by clambering onto the roof and pushing down a large bunch of holly.

Our furniture had survived more or less undamaged in the warehouse where it was stored, but for the majority of our neighbours furniture was rather scarce. Most of them were young couples who had served in the armed forces or worked in munition factories, married during the war and remained living with parents, so had never had a home of their own. A minimum of Utility furniture was obtainable on dockets, but most of it was borrowed. It wasn't just a question of money, more of availability.

No one had a car, everyone walked or cycled. A Green Line service ran every half hour from the Wheatsheaf Hotel on the A30 a mile and a half away, the nearest bus one mile away with a two hour weekday service, not on Sundays. Also over a mile away in the opposite direction were the nearest shops and trains at Virginia Water station.

My mother was school secretary and every day escorted a chattering assortment of children on the long walk to and from Christ Church school, again over a mile away.

1946/47 was one of the most severe winters ever recorded. Every standpipe on both camps froze solid for weeks. Water was at a premium, collected whenever possible in any container available and frequently filmed with ice inside the huts. My mother had to deliver a baby, while the father spent several hours struggling in unbelievable conditions to the nearest telephone, then on to the District Nurse. The baby arrived before the nurse could and the ambulance got through some hours later.

Storm damage uncovered a rotted door and children's tales of caves and dungeons worried parents into investigating. My mother told me it led to a huge self-contained complex which must have spread a considerable distance under the golf course. Endless corridors going in all directions, huge kitchens with steel sinks and cookers, shower and toilet blocks, dozens of empty rooms, rooms with tiered bunks and telephones everywhere. Rumour had it, it was the secret underground HQ of General Eisenhower. Whatever it was or may have been the dangers were all too obvious, so the authorities were informed and the entrance sealed up.

With the easing of wartime restrictions improvements gradually took place. Fibreboard sealed one of the roof gaps, "cooking stoves" with two paraffin burners were issued, more toilets built so only two families shared, a public telephone was installed in D Camp, we became Browning Grove and Dempsey Close, flowers and some vegetables were planted and best of all, water was connected to the bath hut and a copper installed. Before actually having a bath the copper had first to be laid and lit, and filled with buckets of cold water which, when hot, had to be bucketed across the hut into the bath. Previously most families went back to Gran or made the long trip to the Public Baths in Staines. My grandfather had "acquired" a large zinc "bungalow" bath for us which the four of us used in front of the range one after the other. I could never decide if it was better to go first and have two inches of clean water, or be last and have more, but dirty, water.

Shortly before we were allocated a newly built house in Firbank Place, Englefield Green, water was connected to all the huts but without drainage, so waste water still had to be bucketed to the toilets.

Despite the primitive conditions there were only the usual minor illnesses and cuts and bruises, no epidemics or catastrophes. There was never, ever, any trouble. I never worried about the long walk home alone after going to a Staines cinema or dance, indeed, at certain times of the year it was sheer delight with hundreds of glow-worms twinkling along Pinewood Road.

There was an extremely good community feeling, everyone helping everyone else, and a "special relationship" evolved, still discernible to some extent today. The location was and still is supremely beautiful.

As more and more houses were built and people moved out, B Camp was not re-let. The last few tenants moved across into D Camp which was occupied for a couple more years until also becoming empty and deserted. And so at last, Wentworth was once more its normal, exclusive and expensive self.'

EVERYTHING WAS SCARCE

'During the early days after the war everything was scarce. I remember having to get up and be at the butcher's by 7 am on the day our letter (surname initial) came up for offal, and how we enjoyed our liver and onions for dinner that day. Also queuing in Dorking market for at least two, sometimes three, hours for the sweet man to come so that we could spend our sweet coupons. I remember, too, getting extra coupons because my feet were big! We had to have them measured once or twice a year, and mine were well over the line. I also had to walk about a mile to the gas works before going to school, for 28 lbs of coke. I had to push an old cart my father had made – the worst part was pushing it home full and then lugging it up twelve steps to our house.

Dorking, a market town, was always busy. We lived next to the market and used to watch the animals in the pens on market days. I can still hear the squeals of the pigs when they had their ears punctured with a number. During the war years we had some near misses with the bombs and I well remember seeing the red glow in the sky on the nights of the worst of the blitz. Even now I find it hard to believe there was so much fire we could see it in the sky from where we lived.'

'I can remember going on holiday in the late 1940s when little luxuries were beginning to appear again. Choc ices would be delivered to the beach kiosk each afternoon and my Dad and I would be there near the front of the queue. I was on holiday in Shanklin when sweets came off ration and there again my Dad and I were always there each day when new deliveries were made.'

GETTING MARRIED

'We had enough coupons to buy a wedding dress in 1947 but couldn't spare enough for the underslip, so a nightdress had to double for the job. The local restaurant wasn't offering a very good wedding meal, due to restrictions, so we decided on a local hall and self-catering. We started collecting almost a year in advance but spirits were in very short supply. The milkman had a friend in an off-licence so nearly every week he managed to get a bottle of whisky or gin, at a slightly higher than normal price. It was all stacked under my bed and after a year, a veritable collection. Tinned fruit for trifles and dried fruit for the cake came via an Army friend in Jamaica, in little parcels over several months. Two dozen eggs needed for the cake were all provided by relatives who gave up their egg rations.

Four small bridesmaids needed twelve yards of material between them for the dresses. The shop wouldn't let us have that amount as they only had one roll of that material in the required colour, so each bridesmaid's mum bought three yards of material – one after the other – and handed over their coupons.

Embroidery on the dress, to give it a bit of individuality, was done with silken parachute cords which were unpicked and stranded. Silver sandals for the bridesmaids were plain white ones (very utility) painted with silver paint. I regret to admit my going-away outfit was bought with the help of coupons purchased at two shillings each from someone who didn't need their allocation.

It was a day to remember, especially when the vicar asked me if I would "take this man to be my lawful wedded wife"!'

'When I married in 1949, we still had both food and clothing rationing. I managed to come by an old parachute (I forget how) from which I made undies for my trousseau. Family and friends all saved their points for dried fruit and contributed butter, sugar etc for a friend to make a magnificent four tier wedding cake for us. The usual wedding cakes at that time were cardboard mock-ups "iced" with some sort of plaster and concealing a small fruit cake inside which was cut up and distributed. We were very lucky. It was virtually impossible to buy or rent houses for some years after the war so we lived with my parents at first. After a few months, we managed to rent two rooms with a shared kitchen and bathroom and lived there till our first child was 16 months old, when we were allocated a council house. That two bedroomed house felt like a palace!'

THE FIRST BANANA

'When I was a child of about five years old I saw all my school friends looking in the back of a little van with porthole windows, and when I joined them I saw for the very first time beautiful bunches of yellow bananas – the first I had ever seen. Later on, when my mother bought me a banana for my school lunch, my school teacher laughed at me because I didn't know how to eat it. I ate it like a melon (middle first) and my sister being a little older stood up for me, and told the teacher I had never had a banana before.'

THE NEW LOOK

'The war was over, and the second half of the 1940s found my husband (then boyfriend) at the Royal Military College, Sandhurst – later to become the Royal Military Academy – training to be an "officer and a gentleman". Camberley, a small town dominated by the College in those days, had many large houses hiding behind the pines and rhododendron hedges, inhabited mainly by contingents of retired Army officers and ex-colonials. For the Officer Cadet, however, "Camberley" was a railway station and Surrey was seen as an endless trail of roads and lanes to be marched along, carrying a heavy pack – fit but fed up!

The great day came at last. The immaculate passing out parade was performed without a hitch; the Adjutant rode his white charger up the college steps and into the building; and the "passing out dinner" lived up to its name in more ways than one.

My problem was the first "date" with this newly-fledged officer. How to match the sartorial elegance of the brand new uniform with its one shining "pip" (from Camberley's Gieves, just across the road from the college). To the rescue came no less a person than the couturier Christian Dior, who chose that time to unleash The New Look. And there it was in a shop window – a coat with soft lines, nipped-in waist and long full skirt. After years of austerity, school uniform and "make-do-and-mend", the impact of the New Look is hard to appreciate these days. Coupons were scrounged and the coat was mine.

As we left the theatre he suddenly said to me "Why are people looking at you?" The answer – *"Because of the length of my skirt!"'*

POLISH CHILDREN COME TO CHURT

'Situated on a crossroads in the village of Churt stood a small Bargate stone building, with gothic windows and doorways under a steep pitched tiled roof. It was September 1955 and the school was divided into three classrooms; glossy dark green paint halfway up the walls and then cream paint thickly applied straight onto the brickwork for the rest. It was not possible to see out of the high set windows – there could be no distractions – and the heating was supplied by iron stoves protected by high black guards, very useful for drying out wet clothing! There was a cloakroom sporting one cold tap at each end of the school and projecting from the centre of the main part of the school a general, all purpose room where the school helper officiated. A village school of the period you may say; what then makes for the difference?

During the war a camp had been built between Churt and Thursley to accommodate Canadian servicemen and afterwards it became the home of many Polish families. I have no knowledge of the background of this arrangement, or of the political or humanitarian significance. My concern was with the children. They had a very limited knowledge of English and had been distributed amongst the surrounding schools in order not to overwhelm any particular one. The dozen or so who came to us provided a delightful addition to the life of Churt school.

In those days when clothing was not so standardised, they somehow looked different from the local children. They also favoured different haircuts. With an earnest determination to learn they took part in every activity and their parents were most supportive. I particularly recall a Parents Evening when an

Maypole dancing is remembered by all those who had performed it in their schooldays.

extremely large Pole asked me how I found his small, fair-haired son's behaviour. Henryk, for such was his name, was fine, but his father obviously had his doubts. I can hear him, even now, saying "You haf trouble with Henryk . . . I fix Henryk!" and I am sure that he meant it.

Maypole dancing was a feature of the school and its mysteries were rather beyond our Polish friends with attendant language problems. The practices used to take place in the headmaster's garden next door to the school. The day came when bullet-headed Tadeuz couldn't keep up the pace despite much pushing and shoving from the other dancers. They overtook him so many times that he was bound securely to the centre support (pole seems an inappropriate word to use here) and I have a vision of his grinning face protruding from a mass . . . and mess . . . of brightly coloured ribbons. The subsequent unravelling was equally hilarious but after that he was put in charge of the gramophone and lifted and lowered the needle, on the given signal, with great aplomb.

Eventually the Polish children left. Not all at once, fortunately, but as opportunities for re-settlement arose. Some went to the United States, Chicago being particularly favoured, and others to various parts of England. For a while there were letters, the occasional visit and then they drifted away.'

234

HIGH DAYS
&
HOLIDAYS

SPORTS AND ENTERTAINMENT

How to fill leisure time was not a pressing concern for many Surrey folk in the past – no leisure, no problem. Yet there was always someone to organise a social, or a village band or concert, or to start up a cricket team or a stool ball team. The 'big house' might also take an interest in the physical welfare of local youngsters. Thankfully, dancing bears have long disappeared from the scene. The 1930s saw a positive passion for pageants by the middle classes, with normally staid businessmen donning flamboyant costumes with enormous enthusiasm. In the late 1940s and 1950s the young generation discovered Youth Club dances and milk bars – as seen on American films. And there was always the simple pleasure of sitting outside a country pub watching the world go by, searching for that little blue bag in the packet of crisps!

DANCING BEARS

'A 96 year old friend can remember that when she was a child, men used to come round Betchworth village with dancing bears.'

VILLAGE ACTIVITIES

'At Lingfield in the 1920s and 1930s, there was a village cricket and football team, a choral society, concerts with visiting London artists, and a WI Drama Group. The silver band (originally the brass band) played at the pond on Saturday evenings and a special Band Weekend was held every summer when a visiting band would join with Lingfield in a concert held at the pond on the Saturday evening. A church service accompanied by the two bands would be well attended on Sunday morning and a Grand Concert in the racecourse bandstand on Sunday afternoon was always well supported by the local people. The visiting bandsmen and their families were entertained by the Lingfield bandsmen in their homes for the weekend. The Horticultural Society was in existence, started at the beginning of the century. At one time there were races for penny farthing bicycles in the village too, and a bicycle could be seen for many years in the Cage, which was once a small museum, by the pond. The Cage (once a lock-up) still stands but the museum had gone and the penny farthing rusted away.'

'We always had good cricket and football teams at Capel. Cricket was played on Misbrooks Green, half a mile from the village, until Mr Mortimer from Wigmore presented the village with a large field to be used as a recreation ground. This was a great asset as it was situated adjoining the Church Room, as it was then known. That has since been extended and modernised and is now known as the Memorial Hall and is used by everyone.

At one time we had a village band. This was started, and conducted, by a local builder, Mr G Mitchell, who taught and encouraged boys to play various instruments. They won many prizes at contests at home and away.

Capel Flower Show has been held every August since 1892. I can well remember these as red letter days. Gardeners from the big houses all around would come through the village at about 6 am and erect a marvellous display of their choicest flowers in the centre of the marquee, then they would put out their various items of garden produce for judging. There was great competition in those days, particularly with vegetables. We even had to have a special onion tent. There was the usual fair, which was well patronised, with steam roundabout, dodgem cars, swing boats, coconut shies, shooting gallery etc.

I remember another event that took place about 1913 when the village school entered a dancing contest. I was with the younger children dancing the maypole; we wore smocks in red, white and blue. The contest was held at Pippbrook in Dorking. We travelled there by horse and wagon; it took quite two hours each way. We won the contest and came proudly home with the banner.

We had (and still have) a good Choral Society and entered in the Leith Hill Festival which was founded in 1905 by Lady Farrer and Miss Margaret Vaughan Williams, with Dr Ralph Vaughan Williams as its permanent conductor. Capel was one of only five choirs taking part in that first festival, and is the only one to have competed in every festival since then, winning many banners in all classes through the years.

The WI in Capel was started in 1921. There was an excellent response and at one time we had over 100 members. The Wesley Guild, connected with the Wesleyan church (as it was then known), was started in 1919, always presenting a varied programme for young and old. We also had an excellent drama group giving performances every year, with the assistance of a string orchestra, largely made up of the Myall family from Pleystowe Farm.'

'We had our own dance band in Badshot Lea – violin, piano and saxophone. The chaps playing these instruments all lived in the

237

village, and the saxophone player's young lady did the singing. We danced to such tunes as *Margie*, and *Who's taking you home tonight?* before the last waltz. Happy days! There were church fetes and village fetes. Usually in the winter a group of people that could sing or recite would get up a concert.'

'Living in a village, Shalford entertainments in the 1920s were largely of the villagers' own production. My mother and father were very musical, mother playing the piano and father singing. Together they would organise concerts in the village hall, composed of schoolchildren in the first half and adults in the second. My mother was responsible for the children's section. The boys were dressed up to look like pirates and were called the Bold Brigand's Band. The girls were dressed as gipsies. We all had a turn, those who could play the piano, sing or dance. In the second half the adults came into their own with ballad singing and acting little sketches.'

CHILDREN'S SOCIALS

'During the 1920s the Burgh Heath Memorial Hall featured in the life of the local community. The headmaster and his wife ran children's socials on Friday nights in the winter. They started at 6pm and finished at 9pm. There was just time to walk home (leaving school at 4pm), have tea, wash and change from school uniforms to a best dress, then walk back to Burgh Heath with brother and sister and friends for the fun at 6pm. There were games and dances – Sir Roger de Coverley, barn dance, one-step and in later years the Charleston. For younger children there was musical bumps. My pet horror in games was musical chairs. I always endeavoured to get out of this fairly quickly. The entertainment usually included Mrs Read, the baker's wife, singing *Moonlight and Roses*. The boys sat on one side of the hall and the girls sat opposite. This meant that the boys had to pluck up courage to cross the floor to ask a girl for a dance. I always had a partner. I always hoped he wouldn't have warts on his hands. There were refreshments halfway through the evening. I expect it was all home-made – lemonade and buns. It was exciting going home. Our fathers would be waiting outside with oil lamps and candle lights. It was really dark – no street lights at all until 1938. So our little group would walk along laughing and joking and whooping just to hear our own voices in all the vast dark. We also could see the stars. When we reached home our eyes – used to the dark – would hurt as we came in at the back door into the gas-lit kitchen.'

THE LADIES CRICKET TEAM

'After the First World War a ladies cricket team was started in Chobham. The venue was in a small field where the Arthur Lord's music shop is now. The annual subscription was two shillings and sixpence. Eventually the field proved too small and the one at Flexlands Farm was hired. Once a year a match was held against the men on their ground and tea was provided by the ladies.'

STOOL BALL

'My mother was captain of the Bookham stool ball team, which met at Mrs Willoch Pollen's field at Manor Farm before the First World War. Stool ball was a game that originated in Sussex. Milkmaids played it using their milking stools as bats. Rules were similar to cricket and it was mostly played by women with a slightly softer ball, and eight balls to the over.'

SUMMER ON MERROW DOWNS

'There was a Merrow Downs Cricket Club which was carried on for

The Bookham stool ball team relaxing after a match. Stool ball was a popular game for women in Surrey before the First World War.

many years on the Downs, also football pitches. We also had swings and we still have a golf course. We had the Merrow Flower Show in the cricket field, with tents, and always had a fair. The village fete was held in Levylsdene field – we did country dancing, the WI did teas and had stalls and we always had pony or horse rides.'

THE BISLEY SHOOT

'Bisley is known the world over for rifle shooting, promoted by the National Rifle Association, and the chief event each year is the shooting for the Queen's Prize. Some local men have always obtained work on the Ranges, and in my young days they walked across the common to work there from the surrounding villages. When we were young in the 1920s the Queen's shoot was a grand fortnight for local people. There was no shooting allowed on the middle Sunday (and no shooting after 6pm on any day). All the villagers used to go to the Ranges on the middle Sunday for a big service, and afterwards to view all the wonderful silver trophies. There were concerts every night the first week, and bands the second week. The competitors used to be boarded out with local families, and it was not unusual to be knocked up at nearly midnight and asked if you had rooms to let. One of the winners of the Queen's prize in Queen Victoria's time lodged every year with our Aunt Charlotte. The "shooters"" used to travel by train to Brookwood station, and then change to the Bisley Bullet, a special train on a loop line from Brookwood station to the camp on the Ranges. This line is no longer there, but the Bisley Bullet remains up on the Ranges.'

VILLAGE SHAKESPEARE

'The Merstham Women's Institute was founded in 1919 and in 1921 an elocution class was started, which led to a most outstanding achievement – the performance of three Shakespeare plays in their entirety: in 1922 *Twelfth Night*, in 1923 *The Merchant of Venice* and in 1924 *As You Like It*. Two performances of each were given, in the afternoon and evening of the same day, in the open air in the grounds of Merstham House.

The inspiration was their producer, Miss Gwen Lally. She used to say that Merstham was a milestone for her, as it gave her her first chance to direct a complete Shakespeare play, but it was also a milestone for the WI. The performers were varied in age, experience and background, but the feat of learning long parts was an enormous task, let alone the acting. The daughter of a member who played Sir Toby Belch remembers how she and her sister used to read their mother's part to her while she was doing her chores and so help her to learn her lines.

The productions were so unusual that they were reported in the national press. The *Daily Express* reported "Those who undertook the male roles were particularly convincing, although most of them had never in their lives worn tights. They stalked across the stage with complete self-possession". A final comment asserted that "The husbands of the actresses turned out in large numbers at the evening performance. They came to scoff, but remained to cheer vociferously".'

MY FIRST VISIT TO THE THEATRE

'At our girls only school in Cobham in 1929 we had a new headmistress. She was like a real breath of fresh air throughout the school. We started to have swimming lessons, sports teams and above all, visits to the Old Vic in London. Twelve of us were going on our first trip. We met at Cobham station, one and a half miles walk from the village, to catch the train for Waterloo. The fare was one shilling and sixpence return, the ticket for the Old Vic was a shilling. We walked to the theatre from Waterloo, our eyes looking everywhere; it was the first time most of us had been to London. *The Merchant of Venice* was the play we saw, performed beautifully by John Gielgud and Laurence Olivier, who were then in their early twenties. The headmistress treated us all to tea and buns before we caught the train back to Cobham. It was a day we will always remember.'

OUR FIRST GRAMOPHONE

'One Christmas after the First World War my father bought a gramophone. It was very up to date, as it was in an oak case and did not have a horn, like the one in the advertisement for His Master's Voice. The first record which we played was an orchestral piece called "El Relicario"; this was played almost non-stop over the whole Christmas period! Later we had some Gilbert and Sullivan operas and my father was fond of Wagner.'

A PASSION FOR PAGEANTS

'Runnymede Pageant, in about July 1936, was held in an arena near the present day Royal Air Force Memorial, opposite the river Thames. My father was asked to produce and direct the Chertsey Abbey episode, which depicted life when Chertsey and its abbey was all-powerful over large areas of Surrey. The pageant was supported by many towns and villages, and each one depicted a different historical event.

Many adults and children attended the preliminary meetings, and came from all walks of life. They performed as peasants, monks, farmers and church workers, thanes, lords and ladies, pages and warriors. My father took part as a thane chieftain and looked quite fierce in his helmet and beard! We also "borrowed" horses and Irish wolf-hounds. Rehearsals started in local school halls, later transferring to Runnymede to get used to the setting. The period costumes, many of them velvets, satins and brocades and some trimmed with ermine, were hired in London, and I well remember visiting Nathans with my father to choose from an amazing wardrobe.

Some of us used to go along to the make-shift stables at Runnymede to watch the Household Cavalry cleaning and sprucing up their horses and equipment for the twice daily performances.

The sun seemed always kind to us, but some participants became rather hot, with their wigs and beards to contend with, as well as the heavy clothes. When we were able we popped over to the river for a quick dip!

This magnificent pageant, supported by so many willing people, was a huge success both for those who took part and the audience too. Later that year we attended a dinner, when my father was presented with a fine silver replica of a "thane's" axe.

The next year my father arranged a Tableau of Saint George and the Dragon, which was mounted on a float. This was held in Windsor during celebrations for the Royal Family. The Princesses, Elizabeth and Margaret Rose, were watch watching at the roadside, and my brother made the dragon look as if it was expiring as we passed them. Another memorable and lovely day to remember.

Chertsey held a Water-Pageant on the river Thames one summer, so father decided that our theme would be "King Neptune". Our boat was decorated with cardboard shells and nets, and a sail was made of muslin dyed pink. There was a mermaid figurehead too. Mr Combes was an admirable Neptune, but his crown blew overboard, much to the delight of the onlookers. Young girls were mermaids carrying shells in baskets. Older ones were a little uncomfortable coping with their fish-tails, but managed to smile! It was a lovely sight to see all the different floats sail by, and fireworks concluded this event.'

DANCES, MILK BARS AND YOUTH CLUBS

'In the late 1940s, when I was about 14, dancing lessons became necessary and we all went off one evening a week to the local evening class at the school in Sparrow Farm Road, Stoneleigh. It was no good in those days to contemplate going to a dance without knowing the necessary steps of the waltz, the quickstep, the foxtrot and the samba. Later we all went to the local dances held regularly at the Stoneleigh Hotel. There was great excitement when a Milk Bar was opened by the local dairy. It was for some time a regular meeting place after school and reminded us deliciously of the ubiquitous milk bars in the many American films we queued up to see every week at the Rembrandt cinema.'

'In the early 1950s when my friends and I were in our early teens, we used to go to the Saturday night dances in Horley that were held in the Constitutional Hall, in Albert Road. My father would come to meet me, to walk me home, as we lived in a small row of houses between the Chequers and the Wagon Shed, quite a way from the town centre and in the opposite direction from my friends' homes. He would wait opposite the Hall by the windows of Stapleys, the ladies outfitters, as these were in an unusual triangular formation and gave him shelter if it was raining. I never asked if he enjoyed the walk but I'm sure he was glad, when I acquired a boyfriend, to be relieved of the task, although that must have given rise to other parental misgivings.'

'I met my future husband at a Youth Club in Cranleigh in the early 1950s, organised by the curate. There were games, talks, quizzes, rambles, cycle rides, amateur dramatics and the new American square dancing, which drew over-17 year olds from the neighbouring villages too. There was no drinking – pubs were places that only old men attended, and drugs had never been heard of. We queued for the cinema on Saturdays at a shilling and ninepence and usually watched the main film, or a "B" film, newsreel and adverts. We also joined local choirs and earned tenpence for singing at weddings.'

LEMONADE AND A PACKET OF CRISPS

'When we were about nine years old, on a Sunday evening in the summer we would walk to Burpham, about two miles, and sit in the garden of the Green Man public house with our father and have a lemonade and a packet of crisps with the salt in the blue bag. Sometimes one of us would get two twists of salt. We would watch the traffic going home from a day at the sea travelling along the old A3.'

THE CINEMA, THE WIRELESS AND TELEVISION

The magic of hearing the radio for the first time, or seeing television in your own home, can never be recaptured by a generation who have grown up with instant communication on tap.

THE 'CAT'S WHISKER'

'I clearly remember our first little cat's whisker set, which my father had built himself. The aerial was to be in our big loft and he had bought a length of suitable cable to instal it but discovered it was only long enough to reach halfway down the loft ladder. However, it worked, much to his delight, so we took it in turns to sit up on the ladder, earphones clamped to our ears, and listened to some very crackly music – Mozart I was told. It seemed to me like magic.'

AMATEUR BROADCASTING

'My husband's grandfather was a signalman for the London, Brighton and South Coast Railway that, before nationalisation, became the Southern Railway. On arriving in Epsom in the 1890s, he took over the manual signal box at the Epsom railway station which then was located in Upper High Street, Epsom.

The family lived on high ground half a mile from Epsom Downs where in the 1920s, my husband's uncle had one of the first amateur broadcasting stations in the South East – his call sign was G5VP. From here he transmitted music, speech and morse and received numerous responses, known as QL cards, from all around the world including far distant and mysterious places such as Australia, Canada, and Africa – quite an adventure in those days. Twin pivoted masts, giving 100 ft of aerial, were a distinctive landmark for many years, but for security reasons had to be dismantled at the onset of war.'

UNCLE MAC

'I can still see the large radiogram in the drawing room at which I listened avidly to "Uncle Mac" and "Toytown", and Henry Hall's signing off signature tune at six o'clock indicated my bedtime (would that my grandchildren disappeared at that hour too!).'

THE BAKELITE BOX

'During the week teatime was the highlight of the day, because it built up to a climax with listening to Children's Hour on the wireless. It's strange, but looking back now I can't remember anyone else in the room while I was listening, and yet there must have been. I was lost in a world that was entirely my own imagination as I listened to all the familiar and loved programmes – Toytown, Cowleaze Farm, the quizzes and nature programmes and, my undisputed hero, Jennings. How I looked forward to each episode with eager anticipation; what scrape would he get into – and out of – this week? When dear old Uncle Mac signed off with the words "Goodnight children, everywhere", I knew without a shadow of a doubt that he was speaking to me. He was the unseen friend of thousands of children who, like myself, were gathered around their firesides at teatime.

When I was about nine years old our lives changed. One Saturday afternoon my father came home with a strange, heavy box made of bakelite with a screen of greenish coloured glass at the front. My sister and I had never seen television before – we were the first people in the road to have one. Just on Sundays and Wednesdays there were children's programmes. I now had new friends I could actually see, and no longer had to rely on the pictures in my mind. How I loved the antics of Mr Pastry, Billy Bunter and Muffin the Mule; I remember Humphrey Lestocq with a programme called *Whirligig*, and serials of my life-long companions, *The Railway Children* and *Little Women*. Often the room would be full of my friends sitting on the floor enjoying the programmes with me. How did my mother always manage to find something for tea for all these hungry children in the days when there were still shortages after the war?

This was a new world which gradually, almost imperceptibly, shifted the focal point of the room from the fireplace to the recess on its left-hand side. But my love of the wireless as a small child has not faded. No-one can take away my treasured and happy memories of listening to Children's Hour, curled up in an armchair, in a child's world of peace and contentment.'

THE MOBILE CINEMA

'There was a cinema in Bagshot, but we younger ones used to see our films in the Men's Club where a mobile unit used to visit West End weekly every Thursday. It visited other areas around on their special nights. The whirr of the thing was nearly as loud as the dialogue!'

PLAYING FOR THE SILENT FILMS

'My mother was, when young, known in Dorking for her piano playing and singing. When still in her teens she played the piano for the silent cinema in the old Electric Cinema in South Street. She was involved in the 1930s and 1940s with the local operatic societies, and gave piano lessons to local children at one shilling an hour. I can remember family entertainment in those days as a "sing-song" round the piano. During the interval of the children's matinees at the Embassy in the 1940s my mother played the piano and my sister sang and played the piano accordion. On VJ night celebrations in South Street, my sister sang with the band and we danced in the street.'

SATURDAY AFTERNOON AT THE PICTURES

'How well behaved my sister and I were on Saturday mornings – whether or not we received our Saturday twopences depended on it. We cheerfully fed the chickens, tidied our bedroom and dusted the stairs. After dinner, our twopences tucked in our pockets, we joyously set out with our friends to the pictures.

On our way, one precious halfpenny was spent at the sweetshop. The lady in the shop waited patiently whilst we made important decisions . . . should it be the sherbet dabs – a thin pipe of liquorice inserted into a paper bag of sherbet . . . or humbugs – they lasted a long time . . . or dolly mixture?

The momentous decision made, off we sped to the pictures – a two mile journey, mostly uphill. What did we care? We soon reached the cinema, a converted chapel, small, cramped and draughty.

After passing our sticky three-halfpences to the bored young woman in the paydesk, we streamed – an excited bunch – into the auditorium. We were shepherded by Mr Bennett, a blue and gold uniformed commissionaire. He was a tall ex-guardsman with a large elaborate moustache, small darting blue eyes and a stentorian voice. We treated him with great respect.

Beside keeping an eye on us, Mr Bennett had another duty. During the interval, he sprayed a foul-smelling disinfectant in the air – concentrating on where we sat, crammed en masse in the first six rows – which was reasonable enough as we were the only audience there . . . all except my brother who sat in solitary state in the tuppenny-ha'pennies well behind as befitted a pupil of a minor public school. He completely ignored us. How proudly I pointed him out to my cronies.

The first film was usually a cowboy picture. Egged on by us, the enthusiastic pianist zealously supported the action. The house echoed with the groans and shouts from the audience. Nobility triumphed in the end.

Next we watched Charlie Chaplin. He was more to the boys' taste than the girls'.

Then came the great moment for me. Mary Pickford appeared on the screen. My cup of happiness overflowed. With her fat curls and graceful, petite figure, she was lovely. During that short time I identified myself with her, my long gangling figure, my fine straight hair forgotten. When, accompanied by a passionate rendering of *Hearts and Flowers*, she lifted glowing eyes and chaste lips to the hero, I wept.

Next came the newsreel and at long last the serial. An anguished Pearl White, horror in her eyes, strapped on the railway line with an approaching express train in the distance or the sight of the sinuous, uncurling tentacles approaching nearer and nearer was too much to bear.

Suddenly the film ended with a jerk and the titles of next week's pictures were flashed on the screen.

The pianist played *God Save the King*. We all obediently stood patiently until she had finished. Dazed with emotion, we then lurched into the fresh air. Hot sunshine in the summer and the cold wind whipping our bare legs in the winter.

My brother, still aware of his superior status, hurried on ahead, travelling by a different route from my friends and me. We hurtled down the hill, past the huge blue reservoirs, the bakery with its lingering smell of warm new bread, the milkyard echoing with its clanging iron cans, the church, the shops . . . then home.

Then our Saturday teas. Big brown boiled eggs, crusty bread and my favourite strawberry jam.

My brother dropped his superiority and we eagerly discussed the films, particularly the serial. We felt sure that Pearl would escape death. Wasn't she appearing in next week's programme? We exchanged clues. Wide-eyed, we were always deluded by the red herrings strewn across the films.

Lovely, lovely days.'

FILMS IN THE MAKING

'In the 1940s at Chobham, a film crew shot the scenes for a St Trinians's film, and managed to do it on a Wednesday afternoon as that was half-day closing! They also shot the film *Danger Within* at Chobham Clump with several very famous names. When we eventually saw it in a Woking cinema (there were three then, the Ritz, the Odeon and the Plaza) the film opened with several of the stars lying in the sun, and the caption underneath stated "Italy 1944" – which caused much laughter and cheering from the locals. The film *A Kid for Two Farthings* starring Diana Dors was shot at Twelve Oaks Farm in Windlesham.'

EVENTS TO REMEMBER

Sometimes moments of history are brought alive by the memories of those who actually participated in them. One of the momentous events which has particularly stayed with those in Surrey, who held the building in great affection, is the burning of the Crystal Palace in 1936, the glow in the sky being seen for miles around.

THE PUBLIC HANGING

'My great-uncle, Thomas Catling, was editor of *Lloyds News*, and related his experience of seeing a public hanging in January 1855. The victim was a murderer named Barthelemy. People had gathered overnight so as to get a good view. My Uncle Tom managed, however, to find a space by arriving early morning. Stout barriers had to be put up to avert a dangerous situation as the crowds were so dense. The silence was intense as the time grew nearer. When the bell of St Sepulchre's church sounded the knell a few minutes to eight, murmurs arose as a relief for the long night's vigil. Every eye was fixed on the fatal doorway. The murderer's last words were "Now I shall know the secret".'

Facing the great gates at Wandsworth Prison was a beautiful avenue of trees. This led on to the Common. On Sunday mornings the town brass band would arrive and play for one hour.

As a child, and lover of band music, I used to stand fascinated by watching the conductor's baton. It was no more than six inches long and the arm movements were a jerky "up and down". It never looked to me as if the players ever took any guidance from this. I often wondered if the prisoners ever got some comfort or uplift from listening to the music.'

THE TURN OF THE CENTURY

'By the later 19th century the Wesleyan Methodist Church was very active in the growing community of Knaphill, and as the century drew to an end a letter was delivered to every house in the village inviting the occupiers to spend the last moments of the 19th century and the first moments of the 20th century at a service. This did in fact draw a large congregation.'

THE BOER WAR

'My mother worked at the village post office in West Clandon during the Boer War. She had to go in on Christmas Day to receive a phonogram from Guildford of the war news, which had to be displayed in the shop window for people to read.'

'I was born in January 1895 – the year the river Thames was frozen over. The joy of the Relief of Mafeking in 1900 I can well remember. I went round Tadworth with my father and most houses and cottages had flags flying.'

THE R101 OVERHEAD

'The church school I went to in Shottermill was a lovely warm red brick building, gabled at each end and set back from the road behind a big lawn and a row of lime trees which scented the air in summer. I was playing in the sandpit in the infants school playground one day in 1930 and saw a big airship glide slowly by. It had R101 on its side; a few days later, there was its picture on the front page of the newspaper as it crashed coming in to land, all a mass of flames.'

LINDBERGH AT CROYDON AIRPORT

'One day in May 1927 my father told me that Charles Lindbergh had flown non-stop, single-handed, from New York to Paris. Not long after this we heard that Lindbergh was flying from Paris to Croydon Airport – so off we went on our bicycles! He landed in his plane "The Spirit of St Louis", fought his way through a great crush of people into the main building and out onto a balcony, where he made a speech. He thanked everyone for their welcome and said "I thought Le Bourget was some 'burg', but this beats that". I remember his exact words as I had never before heard a place referred to as a "burg"!'

THE 1936 AIR CRASH

'On 9th December 1936 a KLM Douglas DC-2 took off from Croydon Airport for Amsterdam in thick fog. The only help available for the pilot at that time was a whitewashed line across the grass. Sadly, the pilot must have lost sight of the line and instead of aborting and trying again he continued his take-off. This took him off course and the plane caught the roofs of numbers 12 and 14 Hillcrest Road in Purley and then crashed into the front of number 25 where it caught fire and caused extensive damage to that house and number 23 next door (our old house). Fortunately number 25 was empty at the time and was "To Let" and the only occupant of number 23 was a Russian governess who only suffered shock. Fourteen people died in the crash, one of them being Don Juan de la Cievra, the inventor of the Autogiro. Another passeger died later in hospital and the only survivors were the stewardess and one passenger.

In spite of this tragedy (at the time the worst aircrash in this country) we found no strange vibrations in the house and indeed spent almost 22 very happy years there.'

THE CRYSTAL PALACE

'Every summer a Choral Festival was held at the Crystal Palace – also on the following Saturday an Orchestral one – from all the schools in Surrey. I believe I am right in saying a thousand or more voices took part. The choirs from these schools were tested and numbers were selected to perform on the day. I was fortunate to be among the chosen. I was twelve years old at the time.

It was a warm glorious day, and the journey by train was in itself very exciting. All the morning was taken up by sightseeing or enjoying the fun fair. Then a picnic lunch. How we ever managed to sing after such a hectic morning, goodness knows!

Finally, tidied up and calmed down, we entered the beautiful hall and took our places. Our music books had coloured backs for each different school, so that under instructions from the conductor during the concert, arm movements were made forming various designs. It must have been a colourful performance. I think we were all very tired at the end of a long and exciting day. But what an experience for a young child.'

'As a special treat in the 1930s we were taken to the Crystal Palace on

Bank Holidays to watch the motorbike racing and we used to visit the prehistoric stone animal area and feed ducks on a pond. Our school put a choir in for the annual schools competition at the Palace and I managed to be picked one year. We had to be in school uniform for this and wear our navy velour hats with school badge on the front, long black stockings, navy drill gymslip and white blouse with school tie. No running allowed and keep in twos in a long "crocodile" when moving from place to place! The Palace we thought was beautiful, with the glass walls and ceiling so high above. The beautiful plants grew up to terrific heights, it seemed, and the floor was all tiles, I think, creamy fawn in colour. How sad we were when it burned down in 1936. An aunt of ours lived in the shadow of the North Tower and brought her two boys, in their pyjamas with an overcoat on top, to our house in Croydon, as she was sure the tower would fall on her house. However, that one was left standing, untouched by the fire.'

'Before the fateful fire in 1936, a visit to the Crystal Palace made a great impression on me. The vastness of the glass building with its tall plants and ferns made the place immense. The red glow the night it was burned down filled the sky, in spite of Carshalton being some miles away.'

'I remember the night the Crystal Palace burned down. My parents used to live near there, and when they heard about it on the nine o'clock news, I was woken up and walked to the top of the hill nearby to see the sight. I can see the glow in the sky to this day, an awesome sight.'

THE OLYMPIC FLAG 1948

'In 1948, when the Olympic Games were held in England, the Olympic Flag was carried through Bletchingley, and it seemed as though the world and his wife had turned out to watch. One family got up at 2 am to go to Godstone to watch. I watched from opposite the cemetery at White Post and remember the torch-bearer having a very sunburnt back and someone slapping him on it to urge him on his way to the stadium in London.'

ROYAL OCCASIONS

GOD IN AN AEROPLANE?

'I think I must have been about four years old, when I was taken to London for the Coronation of George V in 1911. Unfortunately I lost my parents for a few terrible minutes, which I shall always remember. Soon afterwards my mother took me into the garden and I saw for the first time an aeroplane up in the sky. As she had previously told me that God was up there, I became a little worried and confused.'

JUBILEE 1935 AND CORONATION 1937

'I was a very keen Guide and later a Sea Ranger and in due course had my own Guide company. We used to enjoy weekend camps on the lovely commons and farmland of Kent which are now largely built over and unrecognisable. These outings and weekends were a new experience for the girls from families which had recently been moved out from the slum areas of Deptford and dockland to a new, well designed council estate on the border with Kent. They were super children to work with. We also took part in the 1935 George V Jubilee celebrations in Wembley Stadium in the presence of Princess Mary and I had helped to train some of the Guides who signalled (in semaphore) the good wishes of the Guide movement. Quite an experience! On the actual Jubilee Day I was able to watch the Royal procession in the Mall.'

'The village of Old Carshalton was the main setting for Carshalton's Jubilee celebrations in May 1935 for George V and Queen Mary. The Grove and surrounding area was lit by red, white and blue bulbs, and a small boat was decorated likewise on the east pond. It was an extremely pretty sight. For the Coronation of George VI the same area was illuminated. This time the gala celebrations lasted for four days.'

'On royal occasions, such as the Jubilee of George V, and the Coronation of George VI, we were marched up to the south side of Clapham Common in order to line the route of the royal visitors when they made their traditional "progress" to the four compass points of London. We waved our Union Jacks and cheered everything, especially the Council dustcarts which cleared the roads in front of the Royal party!'

'I remember the great to-do over the Abdication. There was nothing about it in the English papers but one girl in our class had an aunt in Canada and she sent the Canadian papers over to her sister. Jean brought them to school and we all poured over them in our lunch hour. When I got home and told my parents about it my father was very angry about the papers printing such gossip as he didn't believe it. Soon afterwards the story broke in our papers.

The Coronation of George VI came during my last summer at school. We had a sports day and party in the school field and were each given a Coronation mug. A big pageant of English history was put on in the Borough. Local organisations were asked to stage a scene and Battlebridge WI did Queen Elizabeth. My mother belonged to Battlebridge and we were all roped in. A plump little member was the Queen and the tall thin ones were courtiers. The scene was staged on a coal lorry but there was only room for the main characters and the rest walked at the sides and behind. The members' children were cast as peasants and my mother made our costumes out of sacks dyed a dirty green shade. I was a boy with a tunic over a pair of baggy bloomers. I had long lisle stockings sewn to the bottom of the bloomers and had to stop frequently to hitch them up. It was a very not day and we walked from the Memorial Sports Ground in Redhill to Reigate Heath where we were given lemonade and then had to walk all the way home again – about six miles altogether.

Sir Jeremiah Colman lived at Gatton Hall then and he had a passion for fireworks. There were big displays to celebrate his son's 21st birthday and his own Silver Wedding and the Park was opened to the public. The best one was for the Coronation when everyone for miles around went to the park to watch. The fireworks were set off by the lake and the centrepiece was a portrait of the King and Queen. One of the gamekeepers had to go across the lake in a rowing boat to set it off.'

THE FUNERAL OF GEORGE VI

'Back in London after the war, I was working in Berkeley Square when the funeral procession of George VI passed along Piccadilly in February 1952 on the way to Windsor. I went to stand at the end of Berkeley Street to watch it go by. To me, the most impressive and unforgettable aspect was the utter silence of the hundreds of people in the crowds along the route. It seemed as though no one breathed. All we could hear was the muffled regular beat of the drums in the distance and slowly coming nearer. Then, like a whisper superimposed on this, was the soft shuffle of marching feet. And that was it. Just drums and feet. The sound came nearer, was upon us, and faded into the distance. It was some time before anyone moved. Without a word we went away.'

THE CORONATION OF ELIZABETH II 1953

'At the approach of the Coronation, when I was seven, we decorated our schools and houses. On the 2nd June we all went to my aunt's house to watch this square box with moving pictures – it was the first television programme I had seen. We had a party on our village green at Send Marsh, when we all dressed in fancy dress. I was a fairy and my friend was covered in sweets as they were now off the ration.'

'In 1953, I was 18. My sister and I and several of my special friends travelled up on the District line the evening before the Coronation and camped on the Mall pavement. It rained and a clergyman father of one friend bought up all the *Evening Standard* newspapers he could carry to help keep us dry as well as to soak up the water. We took it in turns to go off for walks to keep the circulation going. Finally, we

Special events were held throughout the county to mark the Coronation of Queen Elizabeth II in 1953, like this fancy dress party. For many people the Coronation holds memories of their first television set, purchased for the occasion.

were all huddled together for warmth trying to doze off. We saved a little of our drink and food for the next morning. Unfortunately the police made us stand at 6 am, at which time the gate opened into St James's Park where the toilets were situated. We went off in pairs so we could still keep our place on the pavement. I certainly didn't sleep a wink. With banana oozing out of my overnight bag (satchel), my head was throbbing and I was feeling decidedly nauseous. I bid the hardier ones farewell and made my way back home. I missed the entire procession. I finished up in bed with a hot water bottle.'

'On 2nd June 1953 my sister and I were invited to a friend's house to watch the big event, the Coronation of Elizabeth II. There were about 20 adults and us two; we had to sit on the floor in the front not daring to move or speak, we could only move if there was an interval. The lady I remember most was a large dark lady from the far east in an open carriage enjoying the rain. I think she was the Queen of Tonga.'

'One of my first recollections is the Coronation of Elizabeth II. I was only three at the time, but I do remember we had a street party for all the children, which included a fancy dress competition. My mother made me a Little Red Riding Hood outfit. For our tea we had fish paste sandwiches, tinned peaches and evaporated milk, followed by some very weak orange squash. We had a new television for the Coronation and I sat and watched it on my grandmother's lap, after I had managed to pull the teapot off the dining room table and burn myself!'

SPECIAL DAYS IN THE YEAR

Every year brought its familiar round of celebrations and events. Some were universal, others were special to Surrey. Boat Race Day was eagerly contested by favour-wearing supporters, and Derby Day was a great occasion, even if you were only watching the racegoers pass by in their charabancs. Yet others have disappeared from the calendar for ever – Empire Day, 24th May, was once an event in every schoolchild's life, but it has passed away along with the British Empire it celebrated.

THE BOAT RACE

'At Badshot Lea we always made our own favours for Boat Race Day – light blue ribbon for Cambridge and dark blue for Oxford.'

'We had no radio at home in Great Bookham, but I remember hearing the Oxford and Cambridge Boat Race on the set in the shoe repair shop and wearing a Cambridge badge which cost half of my Saturday penny, which was the usual pocket money.'

'On Boat Race Day, we showed a great interest and always wore favours in the shape of gollywogs, boats etc.'

MAY DAY

'On 1st May before the First World War there was a parade round Tadworth by a string of dancers following a man dressed in a wire cage which was covered in greenery – hence the name "Jack o' Green". All the children following carried posies of flowers tied to the ends of 18 inch sticks, and when it was time to disperse the children would knock on doors and sing appropriate songs for the spring in the hope of pennies.'

'My mother told me that when she was young in Limpsfield, on May Day all the children were dressed in their best and decorated with wild flowers, which their mothers sat up all the previous night arranging. They would parade through the village singing and dancing. In those times the parents had to pay twopence a week for each child to go to school.'

'Marchants Hill Camp, built in 1938, was taken over by the London County Council in 1939 and used as an evacuation centre for school children from Camberwell. Obviously the staff thought it right and proper to celebrate May Day now that they were in the country. Their plans were made well in advance but just a week before the event it was thought fitting to invite the village school children to take part.

A vote was taken among the Infants and I was chosen to be May Queen. At the end of school I rushed out to my waiting mother to tell her that Miss Middleton wanted to see her. Their discussion was about my dress and it was agreed that Miss Middleton's tennis dress could be adapted while one of my grandmother's lace curtains would be the train. There were to be three boys in the procession, the crown-bearer and two pages and about a dozen girls as ladies-in-waiting who had to have white or pastel coloured dresses.

The celebrations were held in the Hindhead playing fields. The big procession was that of the camp children, their throne was the centre one and was a considerable structure. To the left was the throne of the Portsmouth Queen – many Portsmouth children attended school in various buildings in the village – the village throne was to the right. After the crowning ceremonies there was maypole dancing and tea provided by the camp cooks.

The following year it was decided to have similar celebrations but instead of May Queens there were June princesses. This meant that everyone was dressed in sweet pea colours and there was the band of an American airforce battalion – or were they Canadians? It seemed an altogether grander affair.'

EMPIRE DAY

'In the morning we all turned up at school in Merrow in our Sunday best. The Boy Scouts, Girl Guides, Cubs and Brownies all wore their uniforms. After Assembly and when our hands had all been inspected by the teachers for cleanliness, we all trooped out into the playground and formed a semi-circle around the flagstaff. The senior Boy Scout then ran the Union Jack up and we all sang *God Save the King*. One of the school managers would then give a short talk on our wonderful Empire. I particularly remember the late General Sir

Empire Day, 24th May, was one of the special days in the school calendar when pupils sang patriotic songs round the flagstaff such as 'Rose of England' and 'Land of Hope and Glory'.

257

Edmund Ellis telling us the Empire was like a Christmas pudding – the various ingredients being parts of our great Empire.

After this we all sang *Land of Hope and Glory*. I'm afraid there was also a school version of this which was sometimes sung under our breath! I remember singing *Jerusalem* as well. Then we would all be given an orange or a few sweets and home we went for the rest of the day.'

'On Empire Day we all wore white dresses with a sash across our chests of red, white and blue ribbon. We sang *Rose of England, Rule Britannia* and *Jerusalem*, and then had a half day holiday. We loved it. We were so proud to be British. I remember the first poem I learned at school:

> See my bunch of daisies
> Little English Flowers.
> Picked from grassy meadows
> In this land of ours.
>
> See this flag I'm waving
> Tis Red, White and Blue –
> The Union Jack is British
> and . . . I AM BRITISH TOO.'

'The day I always enjoyed as a child was Empire Day, when we marched from our school at Clapham, dressed in white, with our little Union Jacks to the rectory gardens belonging to the vicar of our parish church, where we sang patriotic songs.'

'On Empire Day all the schools in Reigate would meet on the top of the castle grounds. We had little Union Jacks and sang the appropriate songs for the day. We children had to write an essay about the Commonwealth and we would get a medal for the best ones.'

'On Empire Day in the 1930s we had School Sports, when schools from all over the area would meet at Kingfield Sports Ground, now Woking Football Ground. It was quite an adventure for us to go down to Kingfield from Horsell.'

'On Empire Days at Headley before the First World War, the pupils would walk in twos (often in costume) and carrying flags, to the rectory garden. There would be singing and entertainment followed by tea and games. There would also be a "hurdy-gurdy" with a live monkey, which provided much amusement.'

DERBY DAY

'We lived on the top of the hill at Wandsworth, and at the bottom was "The Lane", where there were shops, and where the "poor children" lived. It was only after the First World War that these children were allowed to attend our school, during which time they were given during the day a helping of cod liver oil and a lunch to build up their "constitution". We were never allowed to visit this area or mix with the children.

On Derby Day, full of daring, my brother and I would go "down the lane" and watch the carts and carriages on their way to the Derby on Epsom Downs, especially the "Costers" with their feather boas and gaudy hats.

The children, mostly shoeless, would dart out into the road and yell out "Throw out your mouldy coppers", and the good-hearted crowd would throw out their loose change. There was a scramble, and sometimes a fight to pick up the coins.

There was no doubt that my brother and I were very envious, but whether a sense of honour or fear of the consequences prevented us from joining in, I am not certain.'

'Traditionally, there was always a large fair on Epsom Downs the weekend before the Derby and we all went there for the day. We walked to the Downs from Coulsdon and took a picnic with us. Of course, the sun shone and after eating and playing a few games we were taken across to the fair, having first been told to stay together and not wander. We could hear the jolly music long before we reached the fair but what a riot of colour, noise and smells hit us as we strolled with the crowds amongst the stalls, rides and sideshows. Many colourful gipsies were there with their baskets full of clothes pegs and other wares begging the pretty lady or the handsome gent to buy! Such excitement! I don't think much money was spent – certainly not by our party, there wasn't very much to spare in the 1930s but everything was such fun then and life seemed full of adventure.'

'Epsom being within easy reach, we saw much activity during the racing week in the 1920s. Clapham was one of the main exit routes from Epsom to London and beyond, resulting in crowds lining the main road along Clapham Common and the High Street to watch the racing fraternity return home in vehicles of all shapes and sizes. Children from poorer homes would shout "Throw out yer old mouldies" – and depending on how well the racegoers had done, the coppers would be thrown out.'

259

'I lived in Epsom during my childhood in the 1930s and my most vivid memories centre around Derby Week.

On the Sunday preceding the Derby my father would take my elder sister and I up to the Downs where tents, marquees and stalls of all shapes and sizes were springing up covering the normally green wide-open spaces. There was an air of excitement all around and the traders, gipsies and other colourful characters made a spectacular show.

We always had Derby Week as our half-term at school (whether or not it coincided with Whitsun which most schools had off) so we had time to savour the full atmosphere. On Derby Day we would stand on the corner of one of the main streets in the town where we knew the Royalty would pass by – we tended to think of them as "our" Royalty as they came every year.

I remember cheering and waving to George V and Queen Mary (looking very regal) followed by the Prince of Wales and the Duke and Duchess of York. There was special excitement in 1936 when the new king, Edward VIII drove by and we all cheered very loudly – little did we realise that it was the last year that we would see him. However, we cheered just as loudly the next year when the new king George VI and Queen Elizabeth passed by and there seemed to be special affection for them.

On Derby night we came with our parents into the town where there was a festive air – I remember particularly one pub, the Marquis of Granby, which had a large forecourt where the gipsies and others danced and sang and created a wonderful atmosphere.

The Oaks was held on a Friday in those days and again many Royalty came and drove through the streets on the way to the racecourse and we waited for them and cheered again, although there was not quite the excitement of Derby Day itself.'

'Mother told my brother and I that as we were going to live on top of a hill, the nursery table would go round and we'd have to eat quickly, snatching our food as it came past each round. We were bitterly disappointed – it was no hill either, but in the direct route to Epsom and the Derby. This was a great day – the schools closed and we were all on holiday. Hundreds of children lined the road, watching the traffic go by – governess carts, pony carts, coaches and four, all sorts and all walks of life, laughing and joking, full of anticipation. Coming back after the first race until late afternoon, all the children would yell "Chuck out yer mouldies, chuck out yer mouldy coppers!" If they were smiling, luck was in and the air rained pennies and ha'pennies. If not, they scowled and brandished their whips. We had a grandstand view from the bedroom windows, but one day mother coming home from a tea party caught my brother among the other children. My word, he copped it, but not coppers!'

'From 1950–1957 we lived on Epsom Downs right near the racecourse. On Derby Day all my friends and I walked up to the Downs and stood by the Derby start watching the starter trying to get the horses in line, as in those days there were no stalls. We would walk over to the fun fair and saw the colourful gipsies and Prince Monalulu, that great character who had a vivid head-dress made of feathers and shouted "I've got a horse". Among all the fun, noise and crowds of people the sky larks used to flutter into the sky uttering their trilling song.'

'As a child in the 1950s I always had a special treat of being taken by my mother on the day of the Derby (always Wednesday) to watch the Queen and other members of the Royal Family returning from the racing down the Hook Road, which was situated near our home at Plough Road, West Ewell. Most people in Epsom (I generally found) never went to the races and if they did, they only managed to see the heads of the jockeys, since the Downs were packed with people from miles around.'

TO THE SEASIDE

'Every year my parents used to take me to the seaside for two weeks holiday. Instead of taking one or more suitcases, we had a large trunk. I remember it well! It was light brown in colour and although it was sturdy, it had a basket-like weave appearance and was reinforced with three wooden ribs.

Our trunk had three deep drawers, one for each of us. My mother would pack our summer clothes with much care, and she never forgot to squeeze in my rain-cape, sou'wester and wellies. At the seaside my father would enjoy long walks whatever the weather, often taking me with him. The smell of the sea was wonderful then – it's not the same now.

Long after the holidays were over, I would open the trunk which was always kept in my attic playroom. It smelled of seaweed, sand and sea-shells from one year to the next, and I was transported back to the sea-shore again . . . sheer magic!'

ON THE RIVER

'Nearly 50 years ago we thought to take a week cruising on the River Wey Navigation in a camping boat. We took a punt rather than a skiff, and for sleeping one could take the back rests out and lie at full length on the cushions in a sleeping bag. Very comfortable!

Propulsion was by punt pole (tricky!), by paddle from the back, or by towing with a line from the towing path with a steerer on the back to counteract the pull towards the bank . . . In this case, with the nose of the boat slanted outwards. If it rained the steerer could pull the canvas half over and still be able to see ahead. I might then be seen striding along the towing path in the rain, pulling, while the steerer sat under cover.

Cooking was by a Primus stove and a Woolworth's methylated spirit stove costing sixpence. We lived very well and regarded the whole enterprise as most enjoyable, not to say luxurious. It was also astonishingly cheap, even by the standards of the time. Boat hire for one week was 30 shillings, passage through the lock sixpence.'

FAIRS AND CARNIVALS

'Until the Second World War there was always a fair on Thorpe Green on 29th May, Oak Apple Day. The showmen didn't put up a stall on the green during the war, so that was the end of the fair, which was a highlight of the year.

In what is now King George Playing Field, village sports were held in the 1920s. These were preceded by a procession through the village led by two clowns and Egham Band. A lady in a farm cart portrayed Britannia and there were four other ladies as England, Scotland, Ireland and Wales.'

'There was always an annual fete and flower show at Millbridge. My father remembered a fair coming in his youth and an old lady remembered the mummers, dressed with strips of wallpaper and ribbon pinned to their clothes. They played pipes and beat drums, then performed their play when enough people gathered.'

'The highlight of the year in Reigate in the 1920s and 1930s was the carnival, always held in September. All the shops would dress a vehicle up and also we had the fair in Park Lane, where the allotments are now. In the evening on the Saturday, the traffic would be diverted and we would have dancing in the square. Mr Beacher, our then Chief Constable, would ride about on his white horse, very impressive. The first time we had a Carnival Queen I was chosen and we had the Canadian Mounted Police as an escort throughout the week. The carnival was held on a Wednesday because that was the half day closing for all the shops.'

'The 12th to 14th August each year was a red letter time for all in Mitcham. The fair was opened by the mayor with a golden key, proudly displayed on the roundabout he had used. Little boys who helped behind the scenes were given a book of tickets to use on the rides in lieu of payment. Pulled toffee made in front of our eyes was one of the delicious memories of childhood. Naptha flares, boxing booths, dancing girls and rows of coconut shies were all magic for the unsophisticated prewar child of the 1930s.'

'The first really wet day after Merstham Fair on 17th September was the first day of winter, so my grandfather told me.'

'In the early days Quality Street Fair was really a fair in the true sense of the word. In fact it was not known as Quality Street Fair. Edward III had granted a charter for a fair to be held each year, when the street was the main road through Merstham. I am told that it was really the gipsies who had the fair and camped the night before, putting up their stalls for the following day when the fair was held. I can remember when I was young how noisy it was, especially in the evening. It was no wonder that many of the houses were boarded up in case of damage. There were coconut shies, a helter skelter, swings, a roundabout, shove-ha'penny – the heaviest man, the fattest woman, a fortune teller and many other forms of entertainment. You could buy lovely hot potatoes and big humbugs, having seen them made. You could buy water pistols and use them, to many people's annoyance. It must have been very annoying for those residents living nearby and perhaps it is just as well that there have been many changes over the years.

The Second World War ended the fair for some years and it was the rector, the Rev Philip Duval who brought it to life again. Many of the stallholders are the residents themselves and there is not nearly so much noise these days. In fact in comparison it is quite a "refined affair".'

THE FLOWER SHOW

'A highlight of the village year at Headley in the 1930s was the annual flower show. One of the "gentry" would allow a field to be used and two huge marquees would be set up. Everyone grew vegetables in those days so there was no shortage of entries. My father was a gardener and always won lots of prizes. For the women of the village there were cooking and craft competitions and the children arranged wild flowers. There always seemed to be a challenge to get as many different kinds as possible into our jamjars!'

THE RICHMOND HORSE SHOW

'A special day was the Richmond Royal Horse Show, where the beautifully groomed horses and splendid polished carts would pass the top of our road on their way to the show. They were all there – the milk and the coal carts, greengrocery and rag-and-bone carts, ironmongers and brewers' drays, and the lovely carriages and horses. A wonderful sight.'

POUND DAY

'The local charity I best remember in Egham in the 1920s is Pound Day. We took a pound of some sort of food – flour, sugar, dried fruit etc to school for the local cottage hospital. There was also a table outside the church and the hospital for donations.'

BONFIRE NIGHT

'My father, born in 1868, used to tell us as children that when he was a young boy, he and a group of boys, needing help to buy fireworks, as was the practice, would visit the inns and coffee houses of Wandsworth and recite this poem.

Please to remember the 5th of November
Kind Masters and Mistresses all
When we are sure to prepare
With Guy Fawkes in a chair
To pay you an annual call.

Fawkes you all know did try to o'erthrow
All whom did his religion not share
To establish his hope by the rule of the Pope
To blow King and Commons in air.

But he failed in his plan for King James was the man
On discovery bent – for Suffolk he sent
To search beneath Parliament House
There Gunpowder found hid snug under ground
And Guy Fawkes creeping out like a mouse.

Fawkes by the Jury was tried and all did decide
That his body should take
And tie up to a stake
And his ashes let with the wind fly.

So Hollah Boys, Hollah Boys
Shout and Hooray,
Hollah Boys, Hollah Boys
Keep up the day
Let the bells ring
Down with the Browns* and GOD SAVE THE KING.

(* "Browns" were copper coins.)

It was a history lesson in itself. Boys had to earn their reward!'

'The whole of Headley would turn out for weeks beforehand to build the fire in the 1930s, and we all pooled our few fireworks for a display on the night. One year some boys from a neighbouring village set fire to it a couple of days before 5th November and all work stopped in the village for us all to build another in time. Another year, I remember, a baby cousin of mine died at the beginning of November and the village decided unanimously to postpone the fire for a week so that it took place after his funeral.'

'There was an institution in Albury before the First World War known as "The Bonfire Boys". Near to 5th November, a huge bonfire was built on Shere Heath and the young men of the village dressed in an odd collection of fancy dress and, accompanied by the village brass band, processed through the parish rattling collection boxes, and letting off fearsome home-made fireworks. They finished up at the bonfire, and it was the event of the year. The money collected went to the Guildford Hospital.'

REMEMBRANCE DAY

'On 11th November at Wood Street, guns were fired and all traffic and work stopped to observe the two minutes silence. The pupils at Bellfields school were all marched to Stoughton cemetery to stand and observe the silence.'

'On the 11th November, between the First and Second World Wars, being Remembrance Day, irrespective of the day, we all marched down to Shalford church, gathering round the war memorial, whilst the Headmaster, Mr Carley and later Mr Barringer, read out the names of the village boys who had fallen in the First World War. When the last names were read, they were Frank Worsfold and Percy William Worsfold, my two uncles and brothers of my father. They had both been killed at the Somme. The two minute silence was respected as there was no sound of traffic or voices; then we all marched back to school.'

CHRISTMAS

'Once or twice when I was very small in the 1920s, I was woken early on Christmas morning by carols being sung outside our house at Kenley by the choir of the Salvation Army. It was very dark as it was only about two o'clock. I can still hear the magical sounds of "Hark the Herald Angels Sing" come floating through the still night air and of course I crept out of bed to feel the bulging stocking hanging on the bedpost. Father Christmas and the beautiful singing – my heart was just bursting.'

'Once a year before Christmas in the 1920s, the Rev Grundy arranged a Parochial Tea in Chobham village hall. This cost sixpence and there would be readings from Dickens. Just before Christmas a pig would be killed and hung up outside the shop of Lascelles, opposite the church. On the appointed evening, flares lit up the scene and folk paid sixpence to guess the pig's weight. The winners had vouchers to be cashed in the shop; needless to say the local farmers were often the lucky ones.'

'A truly exciting memory is of the lighting of the Christmas tree with candles, which burned with a flickering light in the metal holders clipped on to the branches.'

'At Christmas in the 1930s the grocer's window was transformed into an Aladdin's cave. The shop window was beautifully set out, not *months* ahead but early in December, with boxes of crackers edged with glitter and some of them with little celluloid dolls on the front. Baskets of crystallised fruits, jars of stem ginger and round boxes of Chinese figs. Marzipan fruits, glistening piles of shiny unstoned raisins and tall glass jars of sugared almonds. Large York hams, jars of game in aspic and Gentleman's Relish with hunting scenes painted on the pottery lids. Families had fairly plain and wholesome food most of the time. The Christmas feast, therefore, was very special – and not surprisingly often ended in tears, or worse, for the younger members of the family . . . and some of the older ones too!

Christmas Day was magical. The tree was always dressed on Christmas Eve after the children had been put to bed. We went downstairs on Christmas morning to see the lighted tree for the first time. My mother always expected to have at least a dozen people round the table at lunchtime, to be joined by another dozen or so assorted aunts, uncles, cousins and friends for tea and the rest of the day. The preparation involved must have been awesome, despite the many pairs of willing hands. We always played party games between tea-time and supper – Chinese Whispers, Postman's Knock,

Charades, Pass the Parcel and Consequences etc. Two things made Christmas Day complete. First, when supper was cleared away (how did we tuck away yet another meal!), we played hilarious card games when everybody cheated – "Chase the Ace" and "Newmarket". A halfpenny on the cards and a penny in the kitty! The thrill if you won at the end when all the money was piled on to one card. The other was the whole family round the piano singing carols and favourite songs. My father and his elder brother led the singing, with another brother playing the piano; their "pièce de resistance" was "Just a Song at Twilight". It brings a lump to my throat to hear it now, and memories of many happy Christmases – and a very happy and secure childhood – come flooding back.'

'Grandmama was less than five feet tall but she ruled her twelve children and 16 grandchildren with a rod of iron.

It was she who organised the family preparations for Christmas and as we children became old enough to "help", the weeks before 25th December became filled with excitement.

Pudding making was an activity which involved every available member of the family. Raisins, sultanas, prunes, cherries and lumps of sticky dates had to be washed and then laid out on large meat dishes to dry. They took days to reach the stage at which they could be handled.

Armed with a sharp knife and a basin of hot water, Grandmama sat in her wing chair before a roaring fire and expertly removed the pips from every single fruit.

We children were allowed to grate the suet which came from the butcher in huge lumps. Horrid stuff, suet – so much skin on it – but not on our fingers by the time we had finished. The more responsible of us were given the task of beating the dozens of fresh farm eggs into a foaming yellow mass.

Eventually the day dawned for the mixing of all the ingredients. This was done in an earthenware crock normally used for the preserving of eggs. A whole bottle of brandy was added and all the family came together at a set time to stir the mixture and make a wish. If you could get the wooden spoon to stand up in the middle of the glorious-smelling mess then your wish was supposed to come true. I never did get the pony which I wished for every time for years. Fourteen greased pudding basins, 14 cloths and a ball of string were used to make neat little parcels which were then placed in a scullery copper filled with hot water and kept boiling by means of a roaring fire underneath. The puddings were simmered for three days and nights, filling the house with a mouthwatering aroma and clouds of steam which floated about like a fog.

In the days when families made up their own entertainment, Christmas was a time for dressing up and performing the traditional Mummers play.

I use my Grandmama's recipe today but my fruit and suet comes from packets and I only use a small bottle of brandy. Somehow, my puddings do not taste like Grandmama's.'

'Although our family were quite poor, Christmas was always reserved as a very special occasion, small sums of money being regularly set aside throughout the year and paid into what was known then as a "farthing club"; the name presumably deriving from the share disposal at the termination of the year, when the cash was paid out to subscribers. This regular saving enabled my parents to buy fruit, nuts, additional vegetables, joints of pork or beef, and generally a chicken as well – a rare and welcome treat during my childhood. Expensive gifts were beyond reach, but inevitably, come Christmas morning, there would be a special something you had been hoping for, in the shape of a coveted book or a doll or, in my brother's case, some additional pieces for his Meccano collection. And, of course, our stockings would be bulging with inexpensive items such as fruit and sweets. A child's thrill on waking up on that special morning is not diluted nor marred by the absence of wealth or sophistication, and my memories remain vivid and warm.'

Index

270